Wittgenstein

on the Arbitrariness

of Grammar

WITTGENSTEIN

ON THE ARBITRARINESS

OF GRAMMAR

Michael N. Forster

PRINCETON UNIVERSITY PRESS

PRINCETON AND OXFORD

Second printing, and first paperback printing, 2005
Paperback ISBN-13: 978-0-691-12391-2
Paperback ISBN-10: 0-691-12391-8

The Library of Congress has cataloged the cloth edition of this
book as follows
Forster, Michael N.
Wittgenstein on the arbitrariness of grammar / Michael N. Forster.
p. cm.
Includes bibliographical references and index.
ISBN 0-691-11366-1 (cl. : alk. paper)
1. Wittgenstein, Ludwig, 1889–1951. 2. Grammar,
Comparative and general. I. Title.
B3376.W564F67 2004
121′.68—dc22   2003055536

British Library Cataloging-in-Publication Data is available

This book has been composed in Dante Typeface
Printed on acid-free paper. ∞
pup.princeton.edu

Printed in the United States of America

3 5 7 9 10 8 6 4 2

For my daughter, Alya

Contents

Acknowledgments   ix

Abbreviations   xi

INTRODUCTION   1

PART ONE

GRAMMAR, ARBITRARINESS, NON-ARBITRARINESS

1. Wittgenstein's Conception of Grammar   7
2. The Sense in Which Grammar Is Arbitrary   21
3. The Sense in Which Grammar Is Non-Arbitrary   66
4. Some Modest Criticisms   82

PART TWO

THE DIVERSITY THESIS

5. Alternative Grammars? The Case of Formal Logic   107
6. Alternative Grammars? The Limits of Language   129
7. Alternative Grammars? The Problem of Access   153

APPENDIX. The *Philosophical Investigations*   189

Notes   193

Index   241

Acknowledgments

My INTEREST in Wittgenstein goes back many years, to the late 1970s when I was an undergraduate at Oxford University and the early 1980s when I was a graduate student at Princeton University. I have accordingly accumulated many intellectual debts in this area, only a few of which I can gratefully record here.

At Oxford I was especially fortunate to learn about Wittgenstein from two people: Peter Hacker, whose writings on this subject have also been invaluable to me, and Ralph Walker.

At Princeton I benefited from the teaching of Saul Kripke, whose written work on Wittgenstein has again been invaluable to me.

I have also benefited greatly from discussions of Wittgenstein, begun when we were graduate students at Princeton and continued on and off since then, with Paul Boghossian, whose written work on this subject has also been a model for me, and Mark Johnston.

I would also like to thank my many colleagues at the University of Chicago, who have provided such an intellectually stimulating, supportive, and friendly environment over the years.

I also owe thanks to audiences at several institutions who heard parts of this work delivered as talks and offered helpful feedback, including, in the United States, the University of Chicago, New York University, and Northwestern University, and overseas, the University of Athens, the Friedrich Schiller University in Jena, and Peking University.

I am also heavily indebted to several people who were of crucial help in the late stages of this project. I was extraordinarily fortunate to have Paul Horwich and Gideon Rosen as readers of the manuscript for Princeton University Press. Both provided many acute criticisms and suggestions which have made it possible to improve the work in important ways.

Warm thanks are also due to Ian Malcolm and Harry Frankfurt for their great care and good judgment in shepherding the project through to publication, and to Jodi Beder and Debbie Tegarden for excellent editorial work.

Whatever faults may remain are of course entirely my own responsibility.

Abbreviations

This essay uses the following abbreviations for editions of Wittgenstein's texts (I have occasionally amended the English translations in these editions without specific notice, though conservatively).

BB   "Blue Book," in *The Blue and Brown Books*,
          Oxford: Basil Blackwell, 1975.
BrB   "Brown Book," in *The Blue and Brown Books*.
BT   "The Big Typescript," in *Ludwig Wittgenstein:
          Wiener Ausgabe*, vol. 11, ed. M. Nedo, Vienna and
          New York: Springer, 2000.
CV   *Culture and Value*, tr. P. Winch, Chicago:
          University of Chicago Press, 1980.
LC   *Wittgenstein's Lectures: Cambridge 1930–1932*, ed.
          D. Lee, Chicago: University of Chicago Press,
          1982.
LCAPRB   *Lectures and Conversations on Aesthetics,
          Psychology, and Religious Belief*, ed. C. Barrett,
          Oxford: Basil Blackwell, 1966.
LFM   *Wittgenstein's Lectures on the Foundations of Math-
          ematics, Cambridge 1939*, ed. C. Diamond,
          Chicago: University of Chicago Press, 1989.
LSD   "The Language of Sense Data and Private Expe-
          rience," in *Ludwig Wittgenstein: Philosophical
          Occasions 1912–1951*, ed. J. Klagge and A.
          Nordmann, Indianapolis: Hackett, 1999.
LWPP1/2   *Last Writings on the Philosophy of Psychology*, vols.
          1–2, ed. G. H. von Wright and H. Nyman, (vol.
          1) Chicago: University of Chicago Press, 1990,
          (vol. 2) Oxford: Basil Blackwell, 1994.

N	*Notebooks 1914–1916*, ed. G. H. von Wright and G.E.M. Anscombe, Oxford: Basil Blackwell, 1979.
NFL	"Notes for Lectures on 'Private Experience' and 'Sense Data,'" in *Ludwig Wittgenstein: Philosophical Occasions 1912–1951*.
NPL	"Notes for the 'Philosophical Lecture,'" in *Ludwig Wittgenstein: Philosophical Occasions 1912–1951*.
OC	*On Certainty*, tr. D. Paul and G.E.M. Anscombe, Oxford: Basil Blackwell, 1977.
P	"Philosophy," in *Ludwig Wittgenstein: Philosophical Occasions 1912–1951*.
PG	*Philosophical Grammar*, tr. A. Kenny, Berkeley and Los Angeles: University of California Press, 1979.
PI	*Philosophical Investigations*, tr. G.E.M. Anscombe, Oxford: Basil Blackwell, 1976.
PR	*Philosophical Remarks*, tr. R. Hargreaves and R. White, Oxford: Basil Blackwell, 1975.
RC	*Remarks on Color*, ed. G.E.M. Anscombe, Berkeley and Los Angeles: University of California Press, 1978.
RFGB	"Remarks on Frazer's *Golden Bough*," tr. J. Beversluis, in *Wittgenstein: Sources and Perspectives*, ed. C. G. Luckhardt, Ithaca, NY: Cornell University Press, 1979.
RFM	*Remarks on the Foundations of Mathematics*, tr. G.E.M. Anscombe, Oxford: Basil Blackwell, 1978.
RPPI/2	*Remarks on the Philosophy of Psychology*, vols. 1–2, tr. G.E.M. Anscombe, C. G. Luckhardt, and M.A.E. Aue, Chicago: University of Chicago Press, 1980.
SRLF	"Some Remarks on Logical Form," in *Ludwig Wittgenstein: Philosophical Occasions 1912–1951*.
T	*Tractatus Logico-Philosophicus*, tr. D. F. Pears and B. F. McGuinness, London and Henley: Routledge and Kegan Paul, 1974.

WL   "Wittgenstein's Lectures in 1930–33," by G. E. Moore, in *Ludwig Wittgenstein: Philosophical Occasions 1912–1951*.

WLC   *Wittgenstein's Lectures: Cambridge 1932–1935*, ed. A. Ambrose, Chicago: University of Chicago Press, 1982.

WLPP   *Wittgenstein's Lectures on Philosophical Psychology 1946–47*, ed. P. T. Geach, Chicago: University of Chicago Press, 1989.

WWK   *Wittgenstein und der Wiener Kreis*, ed. B. F. McGuinness, Frankfurt am Main: Suhrkamp, 1984.

Z   *Zettel*, tr. G.E.M. Anscombe, Oxford: Basil Blackwell, 1987.

Wittgenstein

on the Arbitrariness

of Grammar

Introduction

RECENT PHILOSOPHERS—Donald Davidson, for example—have been much concerned with the topic of "conceptual schemes" and the question of whether or not there are radically different and incommensurable "conceptual schemes."[1] Roughly the same themes already appear in the later Wittgenstein's work under the rubric of "grammar" and the question of the "arbitrariness of grammar."

Wittgenstein's views on these matters indeed occupy a central place in his later philosophy. One could, I think, make a good case that they are at least as important for the understanding of his later thought, and at least as philosophically interesting, as his views on such other central topics as the nature of rule-following, the impossibility of a private language, and the character of psychological states and processes. And yet, in comparison with such topics, they have been relatively neglected by the secondary literature.[2]

The reasons for this neglect are doubtless multiple, but neither severally nor collectively do they constitute anything like a justification of it: Wittgenstein's views on grammar and the question of its arbitrariness are not set out in any detail in the only late work polished for publication by Wittgenstein himself, the *Philosophical Investigations*.[3] Their fullest statement is instead found in such works as *The Big Typescript*, the *Philosophical Grammar*, the *Remarks on the Foundations of Mathematics*, *Zettel*, and *On Certainty*, which are commonly thought to have a less official status and are less often read. Also, Wittgenstein's views on the question of the arbitrariness of grammar entail, or at least seem to entail, positions which contemporary philosophers are often prone to regard as anathema (though usually due more to questionable philosophical instincts than to good reasons): in particular, deep mental pluralism and a sort of relativism.[4] Also, Wittgenstein's views on the question of the arbitrariness of grammar tend to give an even stronger impression of unclarity and ambiguity than other areas of his later thought—an appearance which this essay will be concerned to minimize in certain ways, but will by no means entirely dispel. (This essay is not intended as an exercise in the—rather intellectually unhealthy—activity of Wittgenstein-interpretation as bible-study.[5])

This essay is devoted, then, to an examination of the later Wittgenstein's views concerning grammar and the question of its arbitrariness.[6] The essay is divided into two parts. Part 1 begins by providing a brief introductory characterization of Wittgenstein's concept(ion) of "grammar" (chapter 1), and then goes on to pursue the first of the essay's two main goals: to explain Wittgenstein's general position on the question of the arbitrariness of grammar. One's initial impression on reading the texts is likely to be that he is unclear and inconsistent on this subject, since some passages seem to say that grammar is arbitrary (for example, PG, I, #68, #133; Z, #320, #331; PI, #497) whereas others seem to say that it is not (for example, Z, #358; PI, #520, p. 230; WL, p. 70; LC, p. 49).[7] This impression is a superficial one, however. For his considered position is one which he sums up succinctly in the following remark from *Zettel* concerning a specific area of our grammar (our color system): "It is akin both to what is arbitrary and to what is non-arbitrary" (Z, #358; cf. WL, p. 70; LC, p. 49). Accordingly, my main exegetical task in this part of the essay will be to distinguish and explain in turn a sense in which he supposes grammar to be arbitrary (chapter 2) and another sense in which he supposes it to be non-arbitrary (chapter 3). Doing this should considerably reduce the appearance of unclarity and ambiguity in his views on the question of the arbitrariness of grammar. I then conclude that exegetical exercise by arguing that the position which emerges from it stands in need of certain modest revisions, however (chapter 4).

Part 2 pursues the second main goal of the essay. This is to focus on an especially fundamental, dramatic, and—both exegetically and philosophically—controversial component of

Wittgenstein's claim that grammar is in a sense arbitrary, namely a thesis to the effect that for all grammatical principles in all areas of our grammar, alternatives are either actual or at least possible and conceivable (for short, "the diversity thesis"), and to consider three aspects of his later thought which seem to stand in rather sharp tension with this thesis (chapters 5, 6, and 7). The tendency of these chapters will thus initially be to accentuate rather than reduce the appearance of ambiguity and tension in his position. However, their end result will be a certain sort of dissolution of the ambiguity and tension in question, leaving a position that is both unified and philosophically compelling.

PART ONE

Grammar, Arbitrariness,

Non-Arbitrariness

1

Wittgenstein's Conception of Grammar

WE SHOULD BEGIN by considering what Wittgenstein means by "grammar." For, although, as we shall see later, he himself sometimes in fact implies otherwise, he at least seems to employ this word as a term of art with a meaning which bears only a rather remote resemblance to that which it has in everyday usage.

Wittgenstein's most basic conception of grammar is that it consists in rules which govern the use of words and which thereby constitute meanings or concepts.[1] Thus, he identifies grammar in general with the "rules for use of a word" (PG, I, #133; cf. BT, p. 136); or to cite a more specific example, he says of mathematics, which he understands to be an important part of grammar, that "in mathematics we are convinced of *grammatical* propositions; so the expression, the result, of our being convinced is that we *accept a rule*" (RFM, III, #26). And since, famously, he believes that a word's use may (generally) be equated with its meaning, he holds that the rules for use of words which make up grammar "determine meaning (constitute it)" (PG, I, #133), that "the meaning of a sign lies . . . in the rules in accordance with which it is used/in the rules which prescribe its use" (BT, p. 84); or to cite a more specific example, the mathematical part of grammar again, he says that "mathematics forms concepts" (RFM, VII, #67).[2]

Wittgenstein maintains, in an important and persistent analogy, that "grammar . . . has somewhat the same relation

to the language as . . . the rules of a game have to the game"
(PG, I, #23; cf. WWK, pp. 103–5; LC, pp. 48 ff.; BT, pp. 138–39,
168; WLC, pp. 3–4; OC, #95). Hence in his notorious characterization of linguistic practices as "language-games," grammar plays the role of the rules which govern these "games" in
contrast to the moves that are made within them.[3] To pursue
some of the more central implications of this analogy:

(1) Just as the rules of a game constitute the game and first
make possible the moves which occur within it, likewise
grammar constitutes an area of language and first makes possible the linguistic moves which occur within it.[4]

(2) More specifically, just as in a game such as chess the
rules prescribe or permit certain moves and proscribe others
for the pieces (for example, the bishop may move diagonally
but not orthogonally), and thereby also constitute the identity
of the pieces required for making particular moves within the
game (for example, the bishop in essential part simply *is* the
piece subject to the rule just mentioned), likewise grammar
prescribes or permits certain linguistic moves and proscribes
others (for example, it prescribes or permits that in a context
where one has counted 2 items and another 2 items one judge
there to be a total of 4 items, and it proscribes that one judge
there to be a total of 5 items), and thereby also constitutes the
identity of the concepts required for making particular linguistic moves (for example, the concept "2" in essential part
simply *is* the concept subject to the mathematical rule just
mentioned).[5]

(3) Just as the rules of games not only govern and essentially constitute the particular moves made within games but
also provide a standard for adjudicating these moves' success
or failure, so the rules of grammar in addition to governing
and essentially constituting particular linguistic moves also
provide a standard for adjudicating their success or failure.[6]

(4) Just as the rules of a game are not assertions but instead
more like commands or imperatives, similarly grammatical
rules are not assertions but more like commands, commandments, or categorical imperatives (RFM, V, #13, #17; VI, #30;
VII, #72).

(5) Like the rules of games, grammatical rules are in some sense *conventions*: "Grammar consists of conventions" (PG, I, #138; cf. BT, p. 167; PI, #354–55).[7]

(6) Just as the rules of games may be either explicitly formulated in language (as in most commercial board games, for example) or else implicit (as in some young children's games, for instance), and in the latter case they may subsequently achieve explicit formulation (see PI, #54), likewise the rules of grammar may either be explicitly formulated in language (as they are in the case of the principles of mathematics, for example) or else implicit, and if they are implicit they may subsequently achieve explicit formulation.[8]

(7) Again, just as the rules of games may in some cases be definite but in others vague or fluctuating, so the rules of grammar may in some cases be definite but in others vague or fluctuating (PI, #79–83; Z, #438–41).

The above gives what one might perhaps call Wittgenstein's *generic* conception of "grammar." However, he usually employs this term in more specific applications, and it is especially important to focus on one of these in particular. Not every actual or conceivable "language-game" need include propositions, candidates for truth and falsehood. For example, the primitive language-game played by the builder and his assistant which Wittgenstein describes near the start of the *Philosophical Investigations* does not (PI, #2; cf. WLC, pp. 11–12). However, many of *our* language-games do, of course, include them, and Wittgenstein's interest in grammar is above all an interest in the grammar which constitutes such "true-false games" (PG, I, #68).[9]

The role of the grammar of "true-false games" is a special case of the role of the grammar of a language-game in general, as this was described above. Here the main linguistic moves which are regulated by the grammar and made possible by its constitution of their concepts, and whose success or failure is adjudicated by means of a standard set by the grammar, are what Wittgenstein describes as "empirical" or "factual" assertions. Their success is truth and their failure falsehood.

Wittgenstein's basic two-component model of "true-false games"—one component consisting of empirical or factual claims which are true or false, the other of the grammatical rules which regulate them, constitute their concepts, and set a standard for adjudicating their truth or falsehood—is reflected not only in his metaphor of "move within a game" and "rule of a game" but also in various other metaphors which he uses. For example, he writes that "the *limit* of the empirical—is concept-formation" (RFM, IV, #29; emphasis added), where "concept-formation" is identical with grammar (cf. PI, p. 230). Or again, he likens empirical propositions to the waters of a river and grammar to the channel or bed of the river (OC, #96–99).

Wittgenstein is happy to allow that the line between empirical or factual propositions, on the one hand, and grammatical rules, on the other, is not a sharp one, and also that it may shift with time so that principles on one side of the line cross over to the other; but he nonetheless insists that there is such a line to be drawn (OC, #96–97; cf. RC, I, #32; WLC, pp. 90–91).

What sorts of principles does Wittgenstein recognize as rules of grammar governing our "true-false games"? He believes, first and foremost, that all principles which have the character of *necessity*—or, more precisely, of a necessity that is more than mere causal necessity (more than "the causal *must*" [RFM, I, #121])—are grammatical rules. Thus the *Philosophical Grammar* and the *Philosophical Investigations* both suggest the following slogan in the context of discussing grammatical rules: "The only correlate in language to an intrinsic necessity is an arbitrary rule" (PG, I, #133; PI, #372; cf. PI, #371; RFM, I, #73–74, #128; LC, p. 55; WLC, pp. 16, 18; BT, pp. 24, 166). One striking feature of Wittgenstein's later philosophy is indeed his practice of using the presence of (non-causal) necessity as a sort of heuristic litmus test for detecting the grammatical status of a principle ("This *must* shows . . ." [RFM, VI, #8]).

Accordingly, all principles of formal logic and pure mathematics belong to grammar (hence, for example, the remark quoted earlier that "in mathematics we are convinced of *grammatical* propositions" [RFM, III, #26]). Likewise, necessities which have traditionally been classified as analytic, such as "Every rod has a length" (PI, #251). Likewise, various other necessities which the philosophical tradition has been reluctant to classify as analytic, such as "There must be a cause" (WLC, p. 16), "Green and blue cannot be in the same place simultaneously" (BB, p. 65; cf. LC, p. 94), and "There is no such thing as a reddish green" (Z, #346).

The grammar governing our "true-false games" also for Wittgenstein includes certain sorts of principles which we do not usually think of as exhibiting necessity—though I think that Wittgenstein would say that on closer inspection they really do; in other words, I think that for him (non-causal) necessity is not only a sufficient condition of grammaticality, as explicit remarks such as the ones recently quoted imply, but also in some sense a *necessary* condition of grammaticality.[10] Thus ostensive definitions such as "This color is called 'red'" or "This color is red" also belong to grammar for Wittgenstein: "The interpretation of written and spoken signs by ostensive definitions is not an *application* of language, but part of the grammar" (PG, I, #45; cf. #46). So too do criteria, such as the behavioral criteria which warrant ascribing mental states to another person: "To explain my criterion for another person's having toothache is to give a grammatical explanation about the word 'toothache' and, in this sense, an explanation concerning the meaning of the word 'toothache'" (BB, p. 24). And, especially according to Wittgenstein's last work, *On Certainty*, so too do a variety of fundamental propositions which *appear* to be empirical in character, such as those which G. E. Moore claimed to know—for example, "Here is a hand" and "There are physical objects" (OC, #51–53, #57). For, Wittgenstein argues in *On Certainty*, "not everything which has the form of an empirical proposition *is* one" (OC, #308), and "propositions of the form of empirical propositions, and not only propositions of logic [i.e., formal logic],[11] form the foundation of all operating with thoughts (with language)" (OC, #401).[12]

On closer scrutiny, it is easy enough to see that these further parts of grammar can plausibly be considered to possess
(non-causal) necessity along with the more paradigmatic
cases: If "This color is red" really serves as an ostensive definition, then what it expresses is in a certain sense necessary
rather than contingent; if the criteria of a psychological state
are realized (at least in an appropriate context), then this in a
sense necessitates the presence of the state in question (or at
least the appropriateness of a judgment that it is present);[13]
and Wittgenstein clearly thinks that the apparently-empirical
propositions of grammar in a sense *cannot* but hold.

The connection which I have just stressed between Wittgenstein's conception of the grammar of "true-false" language-
games and *necessity* is crucially important. For it reveals one of
the fundamental motives behind his—prima facie, rather surprising—conception that the sorts of principles which have
just been listed are all grammatical in the sense of being not
assertions of facts but something more like commands or imperatives with which we regulate our factual assertions, chan-
neling them in certain directions and away from others.

Essentially, Wittgenstein is here adopting, but radically ex-
tending, and otherwise modifying, a position of Kant's.[14] Kant
had believed that there were several quite sharply different
types of necessity: *logical* necessity; *analytic* necessity, which in
Kant's view was either reducible to logical necessity (Kant
usually says more specifically: to that of the law of contradiction) or a matter of truth-in-virtue-of-meaning (Kant says
more specifically, but too restrictively: the containment of a
predicate-concept in a subject-concept); and the necessity of
synthetic a priori propositions (which for Kant saliently include, for example, the proposition that every event has a
cause, and the propositions of pure mathematics). Kant's position on the nature of necessity rested on an important (and
usually overlooked) assumption which he took over from earlier tradition: namely that modal facts (i.e., facts involving
necessity or possibility) cannot simply be primitive but must

instead in some way or other be constituted by and explicable in terms of *non*-modal ones, in terms of *actualities*.[15] He was not puzzled by the necessity of logical or analytic principles, because he thought that in these cases it was easy enough to identify the non-modal facts, the actualities, which constituted the necessity in question: the necessity of logic consisted in the fact that logic was *constitutive of the very nature of thought*,[16] and the necessity of analytic propositions consisted either in such logical necessity once again or in truth-in-virtue-of-meaning (the containment of a predicate-concept in a subject-concept). However, he was deeply puzzled about the necessity of *synthetic a priori* propositions. For in this case (and this much follows simply from the definition of "synthetic" as "non-analytic") the necessity resisted the foregoing, seemingly easy, explanations. Consequently, he found himself driven to offer an alternative, and very surprising, explanation for this case: the non-modal fact, the actuality, which constituted synthetic a priori necessity was that *our (human) minds impose the principles in question, constituting and structuring all of our experience and its objects in accordance with them*, and that *our (human) minds are somehow constrained to do so by their very (noumenal) nature*. In other words, his explanation was a "transcendental idealist" one.[17]

Wittgenstein is essentially offering the same sort of solution to the same sort of puzzle. However, he is also generalizing both to cover not only what Kant would have classified as synthetic a priori necessities but also what Kant would have classified as logical and analytic necessities (as well as making some further modifications). This generalization is due to the fact that Wittgenstein does not believe that logical and so-called analytic necessities are susceptible to the sorts of easy alternative explanations that Kant thought he had for them. Roughly, he believes that Kant's explanation of logical necessities as consisting in logic's constitutiveness of the very nature of thought is at best inadequate, and that truth-in-virtue-of-meaning is a philosophical illusion (we will see why he believes these things in chapters 2 and 5). Consequently, for

Wittgenstein these necessities are no less puzzling than the so-called synthetic a priori ones. And he therefore extends Kant's solution for the latter to cover the former as well.[18]

In the process, Wittgenstein also makes several further significant modifications, including the following (most of which will be discussed in more detail later in this essay). First, and perhaps obviously, unlike Kant, who was still wedded to a common Enlightenment assumption—which was already beginning to be challenged in his day by philosophers such as Herder—that thought and conceptualization are in principle autonomous of language, Wittgenstein accords *language* a fundamental role in his account.[19] Second, Wittgenstein's notion that grammatical principles not only channel empirical ones but also *constitute concepts* is foreign to Kant's way of understanding the role of synthetic a priori principles. Kant, lacking the conception, which is (at least relatively) new with Wittgenstein, of a type of principle that is internal to concepts not in the sense of being derivable from them by analysis but in the sense of constituting them,[20] would have tended to see any such notion as making the principles in question *analytic*, and hence susceptible to an entirely different sort of explanation. Third, Wittgenstein accommodates a plurality of alternative principles in each area of grammar, in a way that is quite alien to Kant's conception of synthetic a priori principles or necessary principles in general (see chapter 2). Fourth, Wittgenstein modifies the second limb of Kant's explanation of synthetic a priori necessities—Kant's claim that our human minds are somehow constrained by their noumenal nature to impose the principles in question—in a more naturalistic and complex direction: He argues that we are indeed in a way constrained towards imposing the necessary principles that we do by our nature, but by our *empirical* (not noumenal) nature; and he argues that we are also constrained in imposing them by our social practices and traditions, and by the principles' usefulness and empirical applicability. (These are the several aspects of grammar's non-arbitrariness which will be explored in chapter 3.)[21] Fifth, because of the preceding modifications, Wittgenstein's full account of the nature of necessity is in certain ways both different and richer than Kant's explanation of the nature of synthetic a priori necessity: Whereas Kant makes no essential reference to language, Wittgenstein does. Whereas Kant appeals only to the human mind's imposition of certain principles in making empirical judgments and to human nature's constraint of the human mind to this imposition, Wittgenstein in addition appeals to the internality of the principles in question to the concepts which they involve (i.e., to the impossibility of rejecting the principles without thereby changing the concepts).[22] Whereas Kant appeals simply to *the human mind's* imposition of certain principles, Wittgenstein appeals to *diverse* human minds imposing *diverse* principles. Whereas Kant appeals to *noumenal* human nature constraining the human mind to this, Wittgenstein appeals to *empirical* human nature as one of the things that does so. Whereas Kant *only* appeals to human nature as such a constraint, Wittgenstein also appeals to social practices and traditions, as well as the usefulness and empirical applicability of the principles in question.

Does this make Wittgenstein's position, like Kant's, a form of idealism, then? The answer, I think, is that it *does*.[23] This is so for two reasons.

First, like Kant's position, Wittgenstein's entails that many fundamental, necessary features of our experience which we are prephilosophically inclined to ascribe to a world independent of our minds—namely, grammatical features, such as the impossibility of two colors being in the same place simultaneously, or the "fact" that $2 + 2 = 4$—turn out instead to have their source in our minds. Hence, for example, Wittgenstein writes in *Zettel*, "Do the [color/number] systems reside in our nature or in the nature of things? How are we to put it? *Not* in the nature of things" (Z, #357).

Second, it seems that, again like Kant's position, Wittgenstein's also entails that all *other* features of our experience, because they essentially depend on grammar for their essential form—specifically, in the sense that grammar both constitutes all of the concepts which articulate our factual judgments and regulates which (combinations of) factual judgments it is appropriate for us to make and which not—in essential part have their source in our minds as well. Hence he suggests that (mathematical) grammar "create[s] the form of what we call facts" (RFM, VII, #18).[24]

Wittgenstein's Lectures on Philosophical Psychology 1946–47 contains an (admittedly, not fully dependable or easily interpretable) passage which is intriguing in this connection, both for an apparent implication of the two types of idealism just mentioned and for a nod towards Kant in connection with them. In the course of discussing the grammatical principle of an asymmetry in the use of psychological terms in the first and third persons, Wittgenstein says: "*Objection*: This is not characteristic of psychological concepts but of psychological phenomena. *Answer*: . . . When we try to describe phenomena which we think are mirrored in our concepts, we go wrong over and over again; therefore we describe concepts . . . Remember Kant. (1) shows us how we look at the phenomena and (2)—someone might say—shows us what phenomena are like" (WLPP, p. 154). The last part of this seems to be an allusion to Kant's famous slogan that "the a priori conditions of a possible experience in general are at the same time conditions of the possibility of objects of experience" (*Critique of Pure Reason*, A111).

Attributing the former of these two types of idealism to Wittgenstein is less controversial than attributing the latter. For example, Anscombe and Bloor have both argued for his commitment to an idealism of the former type (albeit without noticing its Kantian background), but not for his commitment to an idealism of the latter type.[25]

Wittgenstein certainly himself seems much more confidently committed to the former than to the latter. But, besides the sort of textual evidence for his commitment to the latter that has just been cited, there is also a deep reason of principle why he cannot easily avoid it. Philosophers who stress the human mind's activity in constituting concepts and who then go on to infer that reality itself is (in essential part) mind-dependent sometimes encounter a protest that this inference is a non sequitur, that one can quite well affirm the mind's activity in constituting concepts without incurring any such counterintuitive idealist consequence: we may indeed create the concepts, but the reality which we cognitively grasp with them is nonetheless independent of our minds. Such a protest is often reasonable, but not against the particular form of such an account that Wittgenstein has developed. For his account says not *only* that it is our imposition of grammatical principles that constitutes the concepts in terms of which we articulate any factual judgments, but also that this imposition of grammatical principles *regulates which (combinations of) factual judgments it is appropriate for us to make and which not*. And indeed, it is essential to his account's fundamental goal of explaining necessity that it include this feature.

In sum, it seems to me that, for the two reasons mentioned, Wittgenstein's position can quite properly be described as idealist, in a sense closely analogous to that in which Kant's was.[26]

Finally, two further aspects of Wittgenstein's conception of grammar should be discussed briefly. First, as I hinted earlier, Wittgenstein sometimes implies, contrary to a strong initial impression which one receives from his treatment of the subject, that he is not using the word "grammar" as a term of art with an unusual sense but in the same sense that it usually bears (and that only the examples on which he focuses, the nature of the problems to which they give rise, and his purposes in focusing on them differ from those involved in standard grammar).[27]

It is somewhat tempting to dismiss this as merely a case (among several others which we shall encounter) of Wittgenstein's dubious conceptual quietist, or "ordinary language is all right as it is," side getting the better of him. Further encouraging such a diagnosis, there are in fact other passages in which he seems more inclined to concede that his "grammar" is importantly different in nature from ordinary grammar.[28]

However, it is, I think, possible to make better sense of his tendency to say that he is using the word in its usual meaning,

namely by focusing on what I above called his *generic* conception of grammar, defined by the idea of rules for the use of
words which constitute meaning, and by the analogy with the
rules of games. For if one goes through the several components of that generic conception, a claim that it defines not
only Wittgensteinian grammar but also the usual concept of
grammar looks at least somewhat plausible.

This suggestion helps, not only because it leaves many of
Wittgenstein's most distinctive views about grammar, such as
his whole quasi-Kantian account of the grammar of "true-
false games" described above, out of the very *concept* and so
prevents these from constituting a semantic difference between his term "grammar" and the ordinary one, but also
because, conversely, it in a plausible way leaves many of traditional grammar's more distinctive features out of the very
concept, such as an emphasis on morphology as a principle of
classification (in contrast to Wittgenstein's own emphasis on
use in context regardless of morphology), and so prevents
these from constituting a semantic difference as well.[29]

The second aspect of Wittgenstein's conception of grammar which calls for some explanation is the following. Wittgenstein sometimes seems to use the term "grammar," not in
the primary sense that has been explained above, but in a
secondary sense in which it refers to the *description* of grammar in the primary sense, or the *discipline which describes* it.
For example, he writes that grammar "describes . . . the use
of signs" (PI, #496), and he characterizes it as "the account
books of language" which "must show the actual transactions
of language" (PG, I, #44; cf. WLC, p. 31; BT, pp. 50, 351).[30]
Such a secondary sense also seems natural given Wittgenstein's just discussed assimilation of his grammar to ordinary
grammar (since in ordinary usage the word "grammar" can
similarly refer *either* to aspects of languages *or* to the description thereof, or the discipline which describes them). Not surprisingly, therefore, much of the secondary literature explicitly distinguishes such a secondary sense from the primary
sense in Wittgenstein.[31]

However, Wittgenstein was himself at least not clear that

there was such a distinction between two different senses of the word. This can be seen from the following passage, for example: "Grammar describes the use of words in the language. So it has somewhat the same relation to the language as *the description of a game, the rules of a game, have to the game*" (PG, I, #23, emphasis added; cf. BT, pp. 171–72; also Moore's report at WL, p. 62 that Wittgenstein himself failed to draw any such distinction). And I would suggest that this apparent conflation is in fact quite deliberate on Wittgenstein's part. Thus at one point in the *Lectures on the Foundations of Mathematics, Cambridge 1939* he explicitly rejects the idea that whereas the rules of chess are arbitrary, there are by contrast descriptions of those rules which are true, and that an analogous distinction holds for mathematics (LFM, pp. 142–43).

Why does Wittgenstein thus deliberately conflate what look like two quite different senses? The explanation is, I think, twofold. First, this conflation has a strong *attraction* for him because it appeals to his theoretical quietist side, the side of him that wants to deny that in doing philosophy he is in any sense developing a theory, a set of novel claims (PI, #128: "If one tried to advance *theses* in philosophy, it would never be possible to debate them, because everyone would agree to them"; LFM, p. 95: "*Turing*: I see your point. *Wittgenstein*: I have no point"; WLC, p. 97: "On all questions we discuss I have no opinion . . . I cannot teach you any new truths"). Thus he says at one point, in this spirit: "When we discover rules for the use of a known term we do not thereby complete our knowledge of its use, and we do not tell people how to use the term. Logical analysis is an antidote. Its importance is to stop the muddle someone makes on reflecting on words" (WLC, p. 21; cf. WWK, pp. 183–86).

Second, the conflation also has a *justification* of sorts, albeit one which ultimately does not really work. This justification lies in a thesis of Wittgenstein's (which we shall consider in more detail later) to the effect that in order to understand a grammatical principle, one must be *committed* to it as a regulating imperative, in particular to the exclusion of alternative grammatical principles which would regulate in incompatible ways (see, for example, WL, p. 52; LC, pp. 36–37). For such a thesis entails that in order really to describe a piece of grammar, one must simultaneously have this sort of commitment to it (given that really describing it presumably requires understanding it). This seems to be part of the force of the following remark, for example: "You cannot describe a calculus without using it, you cannot describe language without giving its meaning" (LC, p. 61).[32]

However, this justification does not really warrant effacing the distinction, as Wittgenstein supposes it to. For one thing, even if one concedes the thesis in question, all that it shows is that "grammar" qua the description of "grammar" qua the commitment to imperatives must itself *include* the latter, not that it must be *exhausted* thereby or *identical* therewith. For another thing, as we shall see later (chapter 7), there are compelling reasons why Wittgenstein ought to abandon the thesis in question anyway. It therefore remains appropriate and important to distinguish between the two different senses of "grammar," despite Wittgenstein's own contrary inclination.

In what follows, this essay will be concerned mainly with "grammar" in its primary sense, and insofar as it governs our "true-false games."

2

The Sense in Which Grammar Is Arbitrary

WITTGENSTEIN, in a number of later works, says that grammar is in a sense arbitrary (see, for example, PG, I, #68, #133; Z, #320, #331; PI, #497; cf. WWK, pp. 103–5). This thesis of the arbitrariness of grammar consists of several component ideas.

First, and fundamentally, Wittgenstein believes that for all grammatical principles in all areas of the grammar which governs our "true-false games," alternative but in some degree similar grammatical principles—and hence alternative but in some degree similar concepts—either have actually been used or are at least possible and conceivable.[1] (Let us call this his *diversity thesis*).

It is *actual* cases that he has in mind when he says such things as that "a language-game does change with time" (OC, #256; cf. #65, #96), and that "if I have made the transition from one concept-formation to another, the old concept is still there in the background" (RFM, IV, #30). It is primarily *possibility and conceivability* that he has in mind when he writes, "I want to say: an education quite different from ours might also be the foundation of quite different concepts. For here life would run on differently.—What interests us would no longer interest *them* [i.e., the other people involved]. Here different concepts would no longer be unimaginable. In fact, this is the only way in which *essentially* different concepts are imaginable" (Z, #387–88); and when he urges us to imagine certain very general facts of nature different from what we are used to, "and the formation of concepts different from the usual ones will become intelligible" (PI, p. 230); and when he says that "concepts other than though akin to ours might seem very queer to us" (Z, #373).

Let us briefly consider each of the six areas of the grammar of our "true-false games" which were distinguished in chapter 1—formal logic, mathematics, other openly necessary principles, ostensive definitions, criteria, and apparently-empirical principles—in order to illustrate this position of Wittgenstein's by reference to some of his own examples.[2]

In connection with *formal logic*, he envisages the (perhaps real) case of a people for whom a double negation would count either as meaningless or else as a repetition of the simple negation (PI, #554; cf. RFM, I, appendix I, #8; LFM, p. 179), so that their logic would, for example, not recognize the law of double-negation elimination (PI, p. 147, note (a); cf. RFM, I, appendix I, #8; LFM, p. 179). And he even imagines a formal logic which ceased to acknowledge the law of contradiction: "Might we not even begin logic with [Russell's contradiction]? And as it were descend from it to the propositions?" (RFM, IV, #59).

In connection with *mathematics*, he offers both real and imaginary examples—for instance, the real example of our mathematics versus that of people who can only count to five (RPP2, #295; cf. RC, III, #155; PI, #555; RFM, III, #84); and imaginary examples in which people had a practice of "calculation" in which "everybody believed that twice two was five" (PI, p. 226), or in which they did not recognize some fundamental grammatical and conceptual features of our system of measurement, for instance employing elastic rulers (RFM, I, #5) or using as the criterion for setting the price of a quantity of wood not its volume or weight but only the area of the surface which it happens to cover (RFM, I, #150). More generally, he says that "there is something like another arithmetic" (OC, #375), and that we can "imagine a human society in which calculating quite in our sense does not exist, any more than measuring quite in our sense" (RFM, VII, #19).

In connection with *other openly necessary propositions*, he argues that someone might be able to dispense with our prohibition against speaking of a reddish green and instead recognize something of the kind: "These people are acquainted with reddish green.—'But there *is* no such thing!'—What an extraordinary sentence.—(How do you know?)" (Z, #362).

In connection with *ostensive definitions*, he contrasts with the grammatical procedure of picking out and classifying as similar the four primary colors a possible alternative classification: "Think of a group containing the four primary colors [blue, red, green, and yellow] plus black and white" (PG, I, #134; cf. Z, #331; BT, p. 167). And more generally, he notes in a lecture, "[Norman] Malcolm felt: 'There is such a thing as the right or proper ostensive definition.' What did his remark reveal? That we are inclined to use the word W in a certain way: we are inclined to think our concepts are the ones, the civilized ones. 'A civilized man won't say X.' But you might" (WLPP, p. 239).

In connection with *criteria*, he points out that there exists (or at least may exist) a difference between a concept of "love" for which a feeling alone is the criterion and a concept of "love" which also incorporates concerned behavior towards the beloved as a criterion (WLC, pp. 90–91). And he imagines a people who in place of our concept of "pain" with its criteria have two quite distinct concepts, one tied to the criterion of visible bodily damage (and associated with sympathy towards the sufferer), the other to the criterion of sensations like stomachache (and associated with lack of sympathy) (Z, #380).

Finally, in connection with the *apparently-empirical propositions* which *On Certainty* identifies as grammatical, he offers several examples of competing alternatives drawn both from the real world and from his imagination. For instance, from real life comes the example of people who believe in the biblical story of creation versus those who do not (OC, #336), and perhaps also the example of people who use our physics versus oracle-users (OC, #608–12). And from his imagination comes the example of an opposition between our commit-

ment to the principle that the Earth existed long before our
birth and the fictional case of a king brought up committed to
the principle that the world began with him (OC, #84, #92).

It is important to keep this sort of textual evidence clearly in
view, among other reasons, in order to discourage hasty acceptance of a certain currently popular but rather extreme
misreading of the later Wittgenstein's position.

According to Bernard Williams, in his seminal essay "Wittgenstein and Idealism," and, following him, Jonathan Lear, in
"Leaving the World Alone" and "The Disappearing 'We,'" the
later Wittgenstein's position is roughly as follows. Just as for
the solipsistic early Wittgenstein of the *Tractatus* the "I" is not
an item within the world but rather a transcendental limit of
language, thought, and world, and the proper philosophical
project is not one of exploring this limit from two sides but
instead of charting it from within by determining at what
point, and how, sense turns into nonsense,[3] likewise for the
socially oriented later Wittgenstein "we" are not some particular empirical group contrasted with other actual or possible
empirical groups but are instead a sort of collective transcendental limit of language, thought, and world, and the purpose
of providing various strange examples from logic, mathematics, and so forth is not to explore the limit of an empirical
"we's" worldview from two sides but instead to show that our
so-called "worldview" is the only one that there is or could be
by revealing the points at which, and how, deviation from it
becomes unintelligible.

However, textual evidence such as that adumbrated above
surely shows that this sort of position would be not only different from but *diametrically opposed to* the later Wittgenstein's
intentions. For such evidence shows that the purpose of (at
least the great bulk of) his examples of alternatives in logic,
mathematics, and so forth is not the negative one of revealing
the alternatives in question to be unintelligible and therefore
illusory but instead the positive one of showing them to be
either actual or possible.

To be a little more precise about this, in developing such

examples Wittgenstein in fact has several distinct sorts of purposes in view. First, as Stroud has pointed out, his purpose is often to discredit a form of Platonism—specifically, a form of Platonism which holds that concepts are *sparse*, as it were.[4] This is at least part of his purpose with all of the examples cited above. But note that this anti-Platonist purpose would only be served if the alternatives exhibited were actual or possible ones.

Second, in another large and important class of cases, especially those involving primitive-looking alternative grammars like the ones sketched in the *Brown Book* and the opening paragraphs of the *Philosophical Investigations*, the purpose is to depict a possible alternative in order thereby to make clearer by specific contrasts or similarities some feature of our own grammar. (Wittgenstein explains this strategy explicitly at PI, #5, #122, #130; WLC, pp. 93–94; WLPP, p. 43.) If considered in sufficient haste, this strategy might look a *little* more compatible with the Williams-Lear reading (because of its ultimately domestic focus). However, on closer reflection, it too is quite inconsistent with their reading, for it essentially depends on the alternatives used for the purpose of comparison being (actual or) possible ones.

Third, and finally, there is in fact a small class of examples which are designed to work in more or less the way that the Williams-Lear reading would lead one to expect, namely a class of examples whose purpose is to unmask seemingly coherent philosophical conceptions as in fact implicitly incoherent. That is to say, Wittgenstein *sometimes does* construct apparent alternatives in order ultimately to reveal some sort of implicit incoherence in them and thereby demonstrate that they were not genuine alternatives after all, as the Williams-Lear reading in effect says that he *always* does. (Oddly enough, though, neither Williams nor Lear does anything to show this, because they do not focus on the examples in question or on Wittgenstein's methodological remarks about them.) Wittgenstein's following methodological remark demonstrates this point: "In these considerations we often draw what can be called 'auxiliary lines.' We construct things like the 'soulless tribe' [at RPP1, #96 ff.; cf. WLPP, pp. 160 ff., 280 ff.]—which drop out of consideration in the end. That they dropped out had to be shown" (RPP2, #47). To illustrate the point in terms of the example which Wittgenstein mentions, the "soulless tribe": In this example he initially posits a tribe which behaves just like us but which lacks a soul, or feelings; but as he develops the example it is gradually revealed that positing that they behave just like us really *was* positing their possession of a soul, or feelings, in whatever sense *we* can be said to possess these things.[5] However, the number of examples in the texts which work in this way is in fact very small.[6] And their presence in the texts does nothing at all to justify the overall Williams-Lear reading. To think that it did would be to commit either the exegetical mistake of assimilating all of Wittgenstein's examples to the model of these few (overlooking the fact that many instead pursue the other purposes mentioned above) or else the fallacy of supposing that in order for a philosopher to hold that all areas of grammar have actual or possible alternatives he would also have to hold that any old thing that had the superficial appearance of being an actual or possible alternative grammar really was one.

In addition (though for our purposes here less importantly), textual evidence such as that adumbrated above also helps to show that, contra the Williams-Lear reading, the later Wittgenstein's "we" is in fact an empirical "we" (albeit a vaguely specified one). Norman Malcolm pointed out in objection to Williams's interpretation of the "we" as non-empirical that Wittgenstein regularly uses "we" to pick out one group from among others.[7] This response to Williams's reading was correct, apt, and important. But it was not by itself quite sufficient to dispose of it, for, as Lear in effect replied on Williams's behalf, the reading could still survive this fact if the contrasting "they's" or their alternative perspectives were always implicitly incoherent ones.[8] However, textual evidence such as that adumbrated above shows that for Wittgenstein they normally are *not*.

Wittgenstein's relevant uses of the term "we" in fact sometimes occur in explicit contrast to an *actual* "they" with a coherent perspective—for example, in the *Remarks on the Philosophy of Psychology* he writes, "Others have concepts that cut across ours. And why should their concept 'pain' not split ours up?" (RPP2, #681)—which shows rather vividly that the "we" in question is an empirical "we" contrasted with (in such cases, not merely possible but actual) empirical others. More commonly, the implied contrast is with an *imaginary* "they" (to focus on a single work, see, for example, RPP1, #98–99, #101–2, #168, #259, #587, #603, #662–63, #957, #1019; RPP2, #398, #640, #660–61). However, these cases too show that the "we" in question is an empirical "we" contrasted with (in such cases, merely possible) empirical others, for Wittgenstein almost always intends the imaginary "they's" and their alternative perspectives involved to be coherently conceivable, possible ones, not incoherent, illusory ones.

In short, there is strong prima facie evidence against the Williams-Lear reading as an account of the later Wittgenstein's official intentions. As far as I can see, neither Williams nor Lear has much to say in answer to such really rather serious objections to their interpretation.[9]

Nonetheless, I do not want to dismiss their reading altogether. Rather, I want to suggest that there is in fact *something* to it, in the sense that, despite Wittgenstein's strong official commitment to the diversity thesis, as revealed by the above evidence, he also advances certain views which at least appear to threaten that thesis and to entail something more like the incompatible position which Williams and Lear ascribe to him. This will be the subject of chapters 5, 6, and 7. Accordingly, these chapters will in effect undertake to make a better case for the Williams-Lear reading than Williams and Lear themselves make for it—albeit while also arguing that ultimately it is instead Wittgenstein's more official contrary commitment to the diversity thesis which carries the day both exegetically and philosophically. The ultimate purpose of this exercise will not, though, be to establish a rather boring moral about the Williams-Lear reading (namely, that it can nearly be made to work but not quite). Instead, it will be to arrive at some (I hope) more interesting morals about Wittgenstein's position and about philosophical matters. The Williams-Lear reading will serve as a sort of stalking-horse for pursuit of this more interesting game—a stalking-horse which, once it has fulfilled this purpose, I shall gratefully euthanize.

Before leaving the diversity thesis and the Williams-Lear reading for a while, though, there is one further question bearing on them that deserves brief consideration: Why does Wittgenstein put so much more emphasis on imaginary alternatives than on actual ones? At first sight, this might *itself* seem to encourage a reading in the manner of Willams and Lear.

Wittgenstein's reason for proceeding in this way is in fact entirely different, however. It is that the question of whether or not alternatives have actually occurred is a matter of philosophical indifference to him because what really interests him is the grammatical or conceptual question of their possibility, and he believes that this question can be answered independently of the question of whether or not they have actually occurred (so that his occasional references to actually occurring alternatives are inessential, merely convenient but dispensable illustrations). Hence, for example, he writes that "[scientific questions] never really grip me. Only *conceptual* . . . questions do that" (CV, p. 79); that "the realities that are discovered lighten the philosopher's task, imagining possibilities . . . Realities are so many possibilities for the philosopher" (LWPPi, #807); and that "we are not doing natural science; nor yet natural history—since we can also invent fictitious natural history for our purposes" (PI, p. 230).

I do not believe that these two questions *are* in fact sharply separable in the way that Wittgenstein takes them to be. They are not sharply separable for roughly the following reason (which will be discussed in more detail later): As we shall see, it is a fundamental insight of Wittgenstein's own, not only that there are alternative concepts of "language," "concept," and so forth (this is in fact already implied by the diversity thesis), but also that our existing versions of these concepts are in crucial respects *vague* or *fluid*, in a sense which involves both indeterminacy and inconsistency in many of our intuitive judgments concerning these subjects, including our judgments concerning whether or not such and such an alternative way of proceeding would really constitute an example of language-use, an example of concept-use. We are therefore bound—on pain of either being inconsistent or else making a merely random choice between inconsistent alternatives—to have recourse to considerations beyond the sheer nature of our existing concepts of "language" and "concept" in order to decide what to say about such matters. And a prime candidate here is a confrontation of the concepts in question with the interpretation of actual aliens in order to see whether such interpretation pushes us, through our inclinations to make certain interpretive judgments about the actual cases in question rather than others, to prefer one consistent refinement of the concepts at issue over another. For example, if our existing concept of "language" turns out to be torn between requiring and not requiring that anything properly called a language must be equivalent in conceptual content to (part of) our own language, then interpreting some actual alien languages and seeing whether or not in particular cases we are inclined to attribute to them concepts which we are unable to express in our own language would be a sensible way of resolving this inconsistency in our existing concept of "language" in one direction rather than the other. It is therefore, I would suggest, in large and important part the discoveries made by such empirically informed disciplines devoted to the interpretation of actual cases of alien verbal practices as classics, anthropology, the history of ideas, and comparative linguistics which should determine the character of the concepts of "language," "concept," and so forth that we as philosophers use, and hence what is and what is not to count for us as a possible grammatical or conceptual alternative.

It is perhaps obvious enough that the persuasiveness of Wittgenstein's imaginary examples of alternative grammars is parasitic on the actual cases familiar from such human sciences as anthropology which they approximately resemble and reflect (and with which he was himself familiar, for example from his reading of Frazer's *The Golden Bough*) in a *psychological* sense—that both he and his readers find his imaginary examples convincing in important part because they have actual anthropological counterparts in the backs of their minds. But the point just made suggests that the same is also true in a deeper, *normative* sense—that the *justification* of any conviction that his imaginary examples show what they purport to show depends in essential part on the existence of the actual counterparts discovered by such disciplines as anthropology as well.

However, this criticism of Wittgenstein's position does not seriously undercut his diversity thesis, or even his way of arguing for it. For it would, I think, be feasible (albeit a large and difficult task) to establish this thesis of the actuality or possibility of alternative grammars across the full range of our language and thought in the sort of empirical, or at least partly empirical, way that concession of this criticism would require.[10] Nor is the criticism even inconsistent with his practice of leaving much in the establishment of the thesis up to the imagination rather than up to empirical investigation, for the criticism by no means entails that *every* putative example of a possible alternative grammar must be empirically discovered as actual in order for the claim of its possibility to be justified. So, having touched on this issue, let us set it aside for now. What matters most for immediate purposes is that the diversity thesis may well be true, and moreover may well be justifiable by using the sort of mixture of actual and merely imaginary examples that Wittgenstein uses (even if he is wrong in thinking that its justification could dispense with recourse to actual examples altogether).

A second component of Wittgenstein's thesis that grammar is in a sense arbitrary holds that there can be no question of *justifying* a given grammar (over against its alternatives). Grammar is also arbitrary in *this* sense. This is the point of the following passages, for example: "Is grammar arbitrary? Yes, in the sense . . . that it cannot be justified" (LC, p. 47; cf. pp. 44, 111; WL, p. 70); "'Surely the rules of grammar by which we act and operate are not arbitrary!' Very well; why then does a man think in the way he does, why does he go through these activities of thought? (This question of course asks for reasons, not for causes.) Well, reasons can be given within the calculus, and at the very end one is tempted to say 'it is just very probable, that things will behave in this way as they always have'—or something similar. A turn of phrase which masks the beginning of the chain of reasons" (PG, I, #68); once one has reached grammar, "justification comes to an end" (OC, #192).

Wittgenstein's case for this position is quite complex. One way in which someone might suppose that particular grammatical principles could be justified (over against alternatives) would be in terms of their being *true in virtue of meaning*, true in virtue of the meanings of the terms which articulate them.

Wittgenstein rejects this notion, however. He does so on two main grounds. First, he thinks that this notion rests on a false picture of the nature of meaning and of its relation to the principles in question. That picture depicts meaning as a sort of prior or independent mechanism which has the power to make certain principles, so-called analytic ones, such as "All bachelors are unmarried," true (and to make other ones, what might be called analytic falsehoods, such as "Some bachelors are married," false).[11] But according to Wittgenstein, meaning and its relation to such principles are not like this at all. Rather, *it is our holding such principles firm* (or in the case of analytic falsehoods, holding them firmly excluded) *that first constitutes the meanings*.[12] In the relationship between meanings and the grammatical principles in which they appear, it is the other party that wears the trousers, so to speak.[13]

Wittgenstein often makes this point in criticism of attempts to justify or explain formal logical principles in such terms, though his point applies equally against such putative justifications or explanations of other necessary principles as well. Thus he says: "The rules constitute the meaning and we are not responsible to it . . . How is the meaning of 'negation' defined, if not by the rules? $\sim\sim p = p$ does not follow from the meaning of 'not' but constitutes it"; "The rules do not *follow from* the idea . . . ; *they constitute it*" (WLC, pp. 4, 86); "(a) 'The fact that three negatives yield a negative again must already be contained in the single negative that I am using now.' (The temptation to invent a myth of 'meaning.') It looks as if it followed from the nature of negation that a double negative is an affirmative. (And there is something right about this. What? *Our* nature is connected with both.) (b) There cannot be a question of whether these or other rules are the correct ones for the use of 'not.' (I mean whether they accord with its meaning.) For without these rules the word has as yet no meaning; and if we change the rules, it now has another meaning (or none), and in that case we may just as well change the word too" (PI, p. 147; cf. PG, I, #133; BT, p. 166; LFM, pp. 184, 190 ff., 282); "Of course, we say: 'all this is involved in the concept itself' . . .—but what that means is that we incline to *these* determinations of the concept" (RFM, VII, #42; cf. I, #2, #10).

Second, as the allusion to "another meaning" just quoted from note (b) in the *Philosophical Investigations* implies, because the diversity thesis is true there will always be alternative concepts available in a given area of discourse, for example alternative concepts of "not." This blocks any attempt to rescue the idea of a justification of grammatical principles as true in virtue of meaning along the lines of conceding that it is the grammatical principles rather than the meanings that wear the trousers, but then arguing that their being required in order to constitute the only possible meanings in a given area of discourse itself justifies them. It blocks such an argument by pointing out that the meanings in question are *not* in fact the only ones possible in that area.

Wittgenstein already makes these points a central part of his case for grammar's arbitrariness in *The Big Typescript* (1932–33), where he concludes an early version of note (b) with the following additional sentence: *"Therefore these rules are arbitrary, because it is the rules that first constitute the sign"* (BT, p. 166, emphasis added; cf. p. 205).

Another part of Wittgenstein's case against the notion that a given grammar can ever be justified (over against its alternatives) consists in an argument that one can never in any manner or degree justify a principle of grammar by appeal to particular facts about the world which make it correct (or more correct than an alternative). As Wittgenstein puts it: "No description of the world can justify the rules of grammar" (LC, p. 44; cf. BT, p. 165; PI, #497). For instance, one cannot justify the grammatical principle that $2 + 2 = 4$ by appealing to the fact that whenever two pairs of things are put together they really do yield four things. Or to quote Wittgenstein on an example from the domain of color: "One is tempted to justify rules of grammar by sentences like 'But there really are four primary colors.' And the saying that the rules of grammar are arbitrary is directed against the possibility of this justification" (PG, I, #134; Z, #331; cf. BT, p. 167).

Complementing this position, Wittgenstein also implies that one can never *refute* grammatical principles by appeal to facts about the world which make them *incorrect* (or less correct than alternatives): "Grammar is not accountable to any reality" (PG, I, #133).

Why, though, should such a justification (or refutation) of grammar by appeal to facts be impossible? Wittgenstein's arguments for this position are rather more complex and diverse than has usually been realized. The following four seem to me the most important:

(1) Wittgenstein holds that attempts to justify grammar by appeal to supporting facts will typically be viciously circular, since the factual claims appealed to in the justification will already presuppose the grammatical principles which they are supposed to justify (and he holds that attempts to refute grammatical principles by appeal to facts will typically be self-defeating for the same reason). This line of thought is summed up in the following observation from the *Philosophical Remarks*: "Grammatical conventions cannot be justified by describing what is represented. Any such description already presupposes the grammatical rules" (PR, I, #7; BT, p. 168; cf. LC, pp. 86, 95). Thus in opposition to the temptation to justify our color grammar by appeal to the fact that "there really are four primary colors," or that we put "the primary colors together because there is a similarity among them," he objects

that "when I set this up as the right way of dividing up the world," I have "a preconceived idea [i.e., of the four primary colors] in my head as a paradigm" (Z, #331; cf. #357; LC, p. 86). And of a somewhat similar attempt to justify mathematical grammar by appeal to facts he says, "That would be a vicious circle" (PI, p. 226).

In what way, though, does Wittgenstein suppose that the factual claims to which one might appeal in justification (or refutation) of grammatical principles typically already presuppose the latter, thereby thwarting the justification (or refutation)? He has at least two distinguishable ways in mind. First, as we have seen, he regards grammatical principles as constitutive of all meanings or concepts, *including those which are used to articulate empirical or factual claims.* It is a special case of this idea in relation to the grammatical principles of mathematics that he has in mind when he writes, "But why should not mathematics, instead of 'teaching us facts,' create the forms of what we call facts?" (RFM, VII, #18), and then illustrates this point with an example intended to show that the grammatical principles of mathematics are constitutive of such concepts as "number" which get used in the articulation of empirical or factual claims (and questions, etc.): "'It is interesting to know *how many* vibrations this note has!' But it took arithmetic to teach you this question. It taught you to see this kind of fact" (RFM, VII, #18; cf. #44–45). To illustrate the bearing of this sort of point on the issue of justifying grammatical principles by appeal to facts, consider again an example that I used earlier: If one were to attempt to justify the principle of mathematical grammar that $2 + 2 = 4$ by appealing to the fact that whenever two pairs of things are put together they really do yield four things, then such a justification would be viciously circular because in articulating the latter fact one necessarily presupposes the mathematical principle in question (along with a host of others), since it is constitutive of the very meanings of the terms used in the articulation of the fact: "two," "pair," "put together," "yield," "four" (and perhaps even "thing" and "really" as well). It is this sort of situation that Wittgenstein has in mind when he writes,

"One wants to say 'All my experiences show that it is so.' But how do they do that? For that proposition to which they point itself belongs to a particular interpretation of them" (OC, #145); and when he writes, "Grammar is not accountable to any reality. It is grammatical rules that determine meaning (constitute it) and so they themselves are not answerable to any meaning and to that extent are arbitrary" (PG, I, #133; cf. II, p. 246).

Second, the acceptance of a grammatical principle that is a precondition of the very meaning of a particular empirical or factual claim adduced in an attempt to justify it (in the way just described) also essentially involves a refusal to accept combinations of empirical or factual claims that the principle proscribes. A grammatical principle is essentially "fixed, like a machine part, made immovable so that now the whole representation turns around it" (RFM, VII, #74); or, to call on another of Wittgenstein's metaphors, it is hardened and functions as a channel for fluid empirical propositions (OC, #96; RFM, IV, #31, #33). To illustrate this point by means of one of Wittgenstein's examples: If the principle that $25 \times 25 = 625$ is part of my mathematical grammar, and by counting a collection of objects in one way (say, by arranging them in 25 rows of 25) I reach the empirical conclusion that there are 25×25 of them but by counting them another way (say, one by one) I reach the empirical conclusion that there are not 625 of them (but, say, only 624), then I *cannot* judge that there are 25×25 of them but not 625 of them (only 624): "To doubt the one means to doubt the other: that is the grammar given to these signs by our arithmetic . . . For arithmetic to equate the two expressions is, one might say, a grammatical trick. In this way arithmetic bars a particular kind of description and conducts description into other channels" (RFM, VII, #3). Thus, returning to the doomed attempt to justify the grammatical principle that $2 + 2 = 4$ by reference to corresponding facts: In judging that whenever two pairs of things are put together they yield four things, not only do we presuppose the arithmetical principle which we wish to support by this factual judgment in the sense that our possession of the conceptual wherewithal to articulate the factual judgment requires that we already accept the arithmetical principle; but in addition, the *strict generality* of the empirical judgment, the "whenever . . . ," is simply an expression of the fact that we have *already* accepted the arithmetical principle, which acceptance essentially involves ordering all of our empirical or factual judgments in conformity with it (looking for ways to explain away apparent counterinstances in which we seem to put two things together with two more things and end up with either less or more than four things by appealing to errors in counting, the intervention of thieves, anonymous benefactors, chemical fusion, breeding, hallucinations, and the like; confirming such explanations by independent means of verification when we can; but continuing to assume their disjunctive truth even when we cannot).

(2) Wittgenstein relies very heavily on the argument just explained, but there is an obvious objection that might be raised against it: Could not the appeal to facts which we use in order to justify (or refute) a particular grammatical principle be an appeal to facts whose articulation does *not* presuppose that grammatical principle itself in either of the two ways just described? Wittgenstein does not devote enough attention to this question. But insofar as he does address it, his answer seems to be that in such a case there would inevitably be a conceptual incommensurability between the factual claim doing the justifying (or refuting) and the grammatical principle to be justified (or refuted), so that the former would simply talk past the latter, neither agreeing with it (this ruling out the possibility of justification) nor conflicting with it (this ruling out the possibility of refutation). This seems to be the implication of the following passage: "The rules of grammar cannot be justified by showing that their application makes a representation agree with reality. For this justification would itself have to describe what is represented. And if something can be said in the justification and is permitted by its grammar why shouldn't it also be permitted by the grammar that I am trying to justify? Why shouldn't both forms of expression

have the same freedom? And how could what the one says restrict what the other can say?" (PG, I, #134).[14]

(3) Someone who still wanted to defend the idea that grammar can be justified (or refuted) by reference to the facts in the face of considerations (1) and (2) might at this juncture be tempted to suggest that the justification (or refutation) should simply take the form of *pointing* at the relevant facts. Wittgenstein considers this suggestion, but rejects it with a string of rhetorical questions: "But can't the justification simply *point* to reality? How far is such pointing a justification? Does it have the multiplicity of a justification? Of course it may be the cause of our saying one sentence rather than another. But does it give a reason for it? Is *that* what we call a justification?" (PG, I, #134). The main thrust of these rhetorical questions can perhaps be put in the form of the following dilemma: On the one hand, to the extent that pointing has that "multiplicity," or, in other words, definiteness of reference (is what is being pointed to an object, a part of an object, a time-slice of an object, the color of an object, the texture of an object, etc.?) and hence conceptual articulatedness, which it would need to have in order to count as a justification, it must be performed within a linguistic-conceptual system of some kind (cf. Wittgenstein's remarks on ostensive definition at PI, #28–30), but in that case it presupposes a grammar and arguments (1) and (2) will again apply. On the other hand, to the extent that pointing lacks such "multiplicity," or definiteness of reference and hence conceptual articulatedness, it can only properly be called a cause, not a justification, of the adoption of a particular grammar.

(4) Finally, Wittgenstein also has a very general argument against the possibility of justifying (or refuting) a particular grammar by reference to facts, one that might carry weight even for someone who was unconvinced by the preceding arguments. This general argument is found in *On Certainty* and rests on two premises. The first is that in order for one proposition to prove, ground, or constitute evidence for another, the former must be firmer, more certain than the lat-

ter: "When one says that such and such a proposition can't be proved, of course that does not mean that it can't be derived from other propositions; any proposition can be derived from other ones. But they may be no more certain than itself" (OC, #1; for corresponding points concerning grounding and constituting evidence, see #429 and #250 respectively). The second premise is that grammatical principles possess a firmness or certainty which no empirical or factual claim can ever have. These two premises immediately yield a general argument against the possibility of ever justifying grammatical principles by reference to facts. The following is a specific application of the argument in question to the case of one of those apparently-empirical principles which *On Certainty* assigns to grammar, the principle that all human beings have parents: "What is the belief that all human beings have parents based on? On experience. And how can I base this sure belief on my own experience? Well, I base it not only on the fact that I have known the parents of certain people but on everything that I have learnt about the life of human beings and their anatomy and physiology; also on what I have heard and seen of animals. But then is that really a proof?" (OC, #240; cf. #250, #429).

It might be objected to this argument that the person doing the justifying need not (yet) accept the grammatical principle undergoing justification, so that the problem in question need not arise for him. However, Wittgenstein can at least mount a prima facie defense against such an objection: For one thing, the objection overlooks his thesis (mentioned in chapter 1, and prominent in *On Certainty*) that in order for a person even to *understand* a grammatical principle, he must be firmly *committed* to it. Also, even if Wittgenstein were to retreat from that thesis to the more modest claim that any *acceptance* of a grammatical principle must take the form of firm commitment to it, he could still respond to the objection that a proof whose acceptance necessarily subverted its status as a proof would be a very strange sort of proof.

In short, according to Wittgenstein grammatical principles

can never be justified (over against alternatives) by appeal to supporting facts.[15]

Nor, according to Wittgenstein, can one justify a particular principle of grammar (over against possible alternatives) by appeal to its *success* in realizing *purposes*. Thus he denies not only that "experience" but also that "its outstanding success" is "the ground of our game of judging" (OC, #131; cf. #474).

Wittgenstein accepts that grammatical principles and the concepts which they constitute often serve ulterior purposes (see, for example, RFM, I, #4, #9; VII, #3, #12), and even that some are embraced because they do so (Z, #700). He also insists that even in such cases they often constitute ends in themselves for those who employ them as well: "What I have to do is something like describe the office of a king;—in doing which I must never fall into the error of explaining the kingly dignity by the king's usefulness, but I must leave neither his usefulness nor his dignity out of account" (RFM, VII, #3). And he sometimes implies that their constituting ends in themselves may in certain cases be the *only* sense in which they realize purposes. Thus, commenting on an imaginary example of people who give and accept money in arbitrary amounts, he says, "It is perfectly possible that we should be inclined to call people who behaved like this insane. And yet we don't call everyone insane who acts similarly within the forms of our culture, who uses words 'without purpose.' (Think of the coronation of a king.)" (RFM, I, #153; cf. LFM, pp. 203–4).

Why, then, is he skeptical about the possibility of justifying grammatical principles (over against alternatives) in terms of their success in realizing purposes? He has several reasons in mind.

One of his most salient reasons is a variant of argument (1) above: The purposes in terms of which such a supposed justification of a grammatical principle might be framed will turn out to presuppose the principle in question implicitly, so that the supposed justification will be viciously circular. This seems to be one implication of a claim he makes in *The Big Typescript*, the *Philosophical Grammar*, and *Zettel* that, unlike cookery's rules, which are non-arbitrary, grammatical rules are arbitrary, because whereas "'cookery' is defined by its end . . . 'speaking' is not" (PG, I, #133; Z, #320; cf. BT, pp. 135–36, 160). For part of his point here seems to be that, unlike cookery's purpose (the production of good food), which is in a sense independent of it, the purposes served by grammar are not independent of it, but dependent on it. Thus in a related remark in the *Philosophical Investigations* he says that "the rules of grammar may be called 'arbitrary,' if that is to mean that the *purpose* [*Zweck*] of the grammar is nothing but that of the language" (PI, #497; cf. BT, p. 137). Accordingly, he argues elsewhere that because the purposes in question will be dependent on the grammar, justification of the latter in terms of the former will involve a kind of circularity: "Why we use certain sorts of concepts is a very queer sort of question. Why do we count? Without it life would be impossible? No, dogs cannot count. We just do it. Once we have counting, we will have a use for it. A bank clerk uses counting and there are reasons. But the reasons are within the institution" (WLPP, p. 226; cf. BT, p. 161). For example, someone might attempt to justify the use of arithmetical grammar by pointing out that it makes business more profitable; but then, if one unpacks the purpose of "greater profitability" a little, one will soon find that it implicitly presupposes our arithmetical grammar.

This argument seems vulnerable to an objection, however. Granted, the purpose appealed to by such a justification might *sometimes* implicitly presuppose the particular piece of grammar in question, and thus involve vicious circularity. But it is difficult to see why it must *always* do so. For example, suppose that instead of attempting to justify our arithmetical grammar in terms of its promotion of greater profitability, we attempted to do so in terms of its contribution to human happiness.

It is tempting to suspect that Wittgenstein is caught between a fallacy and an implausibility here. The fallacy would be an inference from the plausible point that any possession or specification of a purpose must presuppose *some* grammar, to the conclusion that it must therefore presuppose the particular piece of grammar which one wants to justify in terms of it.[16] The implausibility would lie in an attempt to plug this gap by invoking a strong form of linguistic holism, such as Wittgenstein sometimes advocates (for example, at PI, #199). This move would be implausible because any form of linguistic holism strong enough to do the job here—that is, any form of it which implies that every bit of grammar in a language essentially depends on every other bit—will be intrinsically implausible. For instance, is it plausible to say that by adding the new word and concept "camcorder," with its new grammar, to our language we thereby changed the grammar of all other words in our language as well, so that, for example, such sentences as "My cat is a tom" and "2 + 2 = 4" no longer mean what they used to?

In short, it looks as though this first argument of Wittgenstein's can only legitimately rule out *certain* attempts to justify grammar by reference to its successful realization of purposes, not *all* of them.

However, Wittgenstein also has at least two additional arguments in mind which might exclude other attempts as well. First, he insists that there is no *single* purpose served by linguistic practices, only a *variety* of purposes. This is another part of the force of his remark that "the rules of grammar may be called 'arbitrary,' if that is to mean that the *purpose* of the grammar is nothing but that of the language" (PI, #497; cf. BT, p. 137; Z, #320–22). Thus in the *Philosophical Investigations* he follows this remark with an explicit rejection of one likely candidate: "'The purpose of language is to express thoughts.'—So presumably the purpose of every sentence is to express a thought. Then what thought is expressed, for example, by the sentence 'It's raining'?" (PI, #501).[17] And in *The Big Typescript* he follows an early version of the same remark with an explicit rejection of another likely candidate—"Can one say, then: Without language we couldn't reach understanding [*uns verständigen*]. No . . ."—and then goes on to add: "But we can say: Without language we could not influence people. Or, not console them. Or, we could not build houses and machines without language" (BT, p. 137). (His occasional suggestion that in certain cases the only purpose served by a particular grammar may be *itself* constitutes one obvious way in which such a diversity of relevant purposes might occur.)

For Wittgenstein, this diversity of purposes importantly includes differences between our purposes with our grammatical principles and concepts and the purposes that other people who use alternative grammatical principles and concepts have with theirs. Thus he writes: "I want to say: an education quite different from ours might also be the foundation of quite different concepts . . . *What interests us would not interest them*" (Z, #388; emphasis added). And note in this connection, also, his remark concerning an analogy between allowing a contradiction in mathematics and measuring with elastic rulers: "Couldn't reasons be easily imagined, on account of which a certain elasticity in rulers might be desirable?" (RFM, VII, #15). For in the *Lectures on the Foundations of Mathematics, Cambridge 1939* he makes it clear that the reasons in question here could include differences in people's practical purposes, such as their not being concerned with cheating as we are, or their, unlike us, positively approving the consequence that the strongest grocers do the best business (LFM, p. 83).[18]

Such a diversity of purposes obviously poses a serious threat to the idea that one will be able to justify certain grammatical principles and concepts over against their competitors in terms of their superior realization of purposes.

Another argument which Wittgenstein seems to have in mind is a specific application or variant of argument (4) above. Any attempt to justify a grammatical principle by reference to its successful realization of purposes would, it seems, have to rest on a *factual* claim concerning such success. But, according to argument (4), factual claims always lack the certainty or firmness of grammatical principles, so that any attempt to justify the latter on the basis of the former will involve the wrong sort of asymmetry in epistemic status between the two for the attempt to succeed (there will be greater epistemic firmness in the conclusion than in the premise, instead of conversely, which is what a genuine justification would require). An argument of this sort seems to be the force of the following rather enigmatic remark in *On Certainty* (where, as we saw earlier, argument (4) is prominent): "This game proves its worth. That may be the cause of its being played, but it is not the ground" (OC, #474; cf. #429).

Finally, another type of justification of grammatical principles (over against alternatives) which might seem to be available would be a justification of less fundamental ones in terms of more fundamental ones—as might be thought to occur in axiomatizations of logic, geometry, and arithmetic, for example.[19]

Obviously, this could only be a *partially* successful strategy of justification at best. For it would at least leave whichever grammatical principles played the role of the fundamental ones in the purported justifications themselves unjustified (over against competing alternatives).

But Wittgenstein would, I think, in addition argue that the situation is even worse than that, that problems analogous to those which thwart any attempt to justify grammatical principles in terms of facts also thwart any attempt to justify them in terms of other, more fundamental grammatical principles.

Where contingent propositions are concerned, we can often not only deduce them as conclusions from other premises but also thereby justify them. Wittgenstein naturally concedes that we can often *deduce* necessary principles from other necessary principles as well, for example in logic and mathematics. But he is skeptical that we can ever *justify* them in this way.

Already in his early period he had held that it was a mistake to assimilate deductions of necessary principles from necessary principles to deductions of contingent propositions, that there were crucial differences between the two cases.[20] In particular, he had held that where deductions of necessary principles from necessary principles were concerned, there was always a certain equality of status between premises and conclusions.[21] This had promised to preclude any possibility of really justifying necessary principles by deducing them from other necessary principles, in the way that *was* sometimes possible when a conclusion was merely contingent.

He continues to hold a version of such a position in his later period as well. The key doctrine here is one which says that in the case of deductions of necessary principles from other necessary principles, proof and conclusion are in a sense equivalent: "I once wrote [i.e., at *Tractatus*, 6.1261]: 'In mathematics process and result are equivalent'" (RFM, I, #82). Part of what Wittgenstein now means by this—the more textually salient, but here less relevant, part—is that in mathematics the proof is internal to the meaning of the conclusion (see, for example, RFM, I, appendix III, #15–16; II, #7; III, #25, #58). But the other, and here most relevant, part of what he now means is that, conversely, the conclusion, once reached, is in a way internal to the proof as well: "'It is a property of this number that this process leads to it.' But, mathematically speaking, a process does not lead to it; it is the end of a process (is itself part of the process)" (RFM, I, #84).

His point in this converse thesis is twofold, and is analogous to his conception of the implicit twofold internality of a grammatical principle to any factual claims which might be called on in an attempt to justify it, as that conception was explained earlier. First (in analogy to the internality of a grammatical principle to the concepts which articulate those factual claims), when a necessary principle is accepted as the conclusion of a proof, it thereby becomes internal to the concepts involved, not only in its own articulation, but also in the articulation of the steps of the proof: "A mathematical proposition is the determination of a concept following upon a discovery . . . The concept is altered so that this *had* to be the result" (RFM, IV, #47); "'It must be so' means that this outcome has been defined to be essential to this process. This *must* shows that he has adopted a concept . . . He has read off from the process, not a proposition of natural science but, instead of that, the determination of a concept" (RFM, VI, #7–8); "There is something in saying that a mathematical proof creates a new concept . . . The idea that proof creates a new concept might . . . be roughly put as follows: a proof is not its foundations plus the rules of inference, but a *new* building" (RFM, III, #41; cf. #31; V, #45). Second (this time in analogy to the internality of a grammatical principle to relevant factual claims through its having regulated them), reaching the conclusion in question now becomes a criterion of the correctness of the steps of the proof: "See whether [the *kind of way* it is produced from them] does not perhaps itself presuppose the result. For suppose that in *that way* you got one time this and another time a different result; would you accept this? Would you not say: 'I must have made a mistake; the *same* kind of way would always have to produce the same result.' This shows that you are incorporating the result of the transformation into the kind of way the transforming is done" (RFM, I, #86; cf. IV, #35; VI, #15–16).

This conception of the nature of proofs of necessary principles defeats the possibility of their constituting genuine justifications.[22] It does so in several ways, analogous to those which defeated attempts to justify grammatical principles in terms of facts. First, it entails a dilemma for any such putative justifications analogous to that constituted by (1) and (2) in the factual case: *either* there will be conceptual commensurability between the premises and the conclusion, but in order for that to happen the premises will have to presuppose the conclusion implicitly in the twofold way just described, so that the putative justification will be viciously circular (this is analogous to problem (1)); *or* there will (as yet) be no such implicit presupposition, but in that case there will be conceptual incommensurability between the premises and the conclusion, so that the putative justification will fail for this, different reason (this is analogous to problem (2)). The former scenario is the one that Wittgenstein has in mind when he suggests that a proof and its necessary conclusion are "equivalent" (see above), and when he writes that if someone gives a proof, " 'It must be so' means that this outcome has been defined to be essential to this process. This *must* shows that he has adopted a concept. This *must* signifies that he has gone in a circle" (RFM, VI, #7; cf. #8). The latter scenario is the one that he has in mind when he instead writes, "Why should I not say: in the proof I have won through to a *decision*?" (RFM, III, #27; cf. VI, #7, #24).[23]

Wittgenstein also extends the analogy with his argument for the factual case further. In analogy to step (3) of that argument, he considers an attempt to avoid the two horns of this dilemma facing putative justifications of necessary principles by *pointing* to the premises and steps of a proof in order thereby to remain grammatically-conceptually neutral and thus escape the dilemma (such a move might seem especially tempting in the case of geometrical proofs), but he rejects any such attempt on the ground that in order to achieve the determinacy required of a justification, such pointing would need to rely implicitly on grammar and concepts (RFM, I, #88–90).

Finally, the above situation also entails a failure of proofs of necessary principles to constitute genuine justifications that is analogous to failure (4) in the factual case: Since, in order for the premises to be conceptually commensurable with the conclusion, and therefore in order for the proof to have even a prospect of serving as a genuine justification, the premises must presuppose the conclusion in the twofold way described above, there will never be the sort of epistemic asymmetry in favor of the premises that is required for a genuine justification: if the premises essentially presuppose the conclusion in that twofold way, then they can hardly be more epistemically certain than it is. This is another part of the force of Wittgenstein's suggestion that "in mathematics process and result are equivalent."

In sum, it seems that none of the available strategies for justifying grammatical principles (over against alternatives) can work—not justification in terms of truth-in-virtue-of-meaning, nor justification by the facts, nor justification in terms of success in realizing purposes, nor justification by deduction from more fundamental grammatical principles.

The third and fourth components of Wittgenstein's thesis that grammar is in a sense arbitrary consist in his answers to certain questions which naturally arise when one reflects on the two previous components. If, for each grammatical principle in each area of the grammar which governs our "true-false games," alternative but in some degree similar grammatical principles are possible and conceivable, and in some cases indeed actual, and if there can never be any question of justifying a grammatical principle (over against its alternatives), then what are we to say about the correctness or incorrectness, the truth or falsehood, of such principles? And what are we to say about the correctness or incorrectness, the truth or falsehood, of the empirical or factual claims made within alternative language-games constituted by alternative grammatical principles?

Let us begin with the former question (that concerning the grammatical principles themselves). Wittgenstein's position in this area is fraught with ambiguity. But his considered view seems to be that grammatical principles are *neither correct nor incorrect, neither true nor false.*

Thus, regarding correctness and incorrectness generally, the *Philosophical Grammar* and the *Philosophical Investigations* say: "Grammar is not accountable to reality. It is grammatical rules that determine meaning (constitute it) and so they themselves are not answerable to any meaning and to that extent are arbitrary. There cannot be a question whether these or other rules are the correct ones for the use of 'not'" (PG, I, #133; cf. BT, p. 166); "There cannot be any question of whether these or other rules are the correct ones for the use of 'not.' (I mean whether they accord with its meaning.) For without these rules the word has as yet no meaning; and if we change the rules, it now has another meaning (or none)" (PI, p. 147).[24] Again, in a passage from *The Big Typescript*, the *Philosophical Grammar*, and *Zettel* on which I recently drew, he indicates that part of what he means by saying that the rules of grammar are arbitrary is that, unlike the rules of an activity such as cookery which are subject to evaluation as correct or incorrect by reference to a single independent standard (the production of good food), the rules of grammar are subject to no such single independent standard against which they could be evaluated as correct or incorrect: "Why don't I call cookery rules arbitrary, and why am I tempted to call the rules of grammar arbitrary? Because 'cookery' is defined by its end, whereas 'speaking' is not . . . You cook badly if you are guided in your cooking by rules other than the right ones; but if you follow other rules than those of chess you are *playing another game*; and if you follow grammatical rules other than such-and-such ones, that does not mean you say something wrong, no, you are speaking of something else" (PG, I, #133; Z, #320; BT, p. 167; cf. PI, #497).

That these remarks concerning correctness and incorrectness imply, more specifically, that grammatical principles are neither true nor false can be seen from such passages as the following: "The rules of grammar are similarly (i.e. in the same sense) arbitrary as the choice of a unit of measurement. But that can only mean that it is independent of the length of what is to be measured. And that it is not the case that the choice of the one unit is 'true' and of the other 'false,' as the statement of the length is true or false" (BT, p. 166);[25] "I did not get my picture of the world by satisfying myself of its correctness; nor do I have it because I am satisfied of its correctness. No: it is the inherited background against which I distinguish between true and false" (OC, #94); "If the true is what is grounded, then the ground is not *true*, nor yet false" (OC, #205). Or, to focus on particular areas of grammar, formal logic and mathematics, Wittgenstein writes in dismissal of the idea that logical inferences "certainly correspond to the truth" that "there is not any question at all here of some correspondence between what is said and reality; rather logic is *antecedent* to any such correspondence; in the same sense, that is, as that in which the establishment of a method of measurement is *antecedent* to the correctness or incorrectness of a statement of length" (RFM, I, #156);[26] he argues that "because we see the similarity of ~(p & ~p) and p v ~p to true propositions we make the mistake of saying they are true" (WLC, pp. 139–40; cf. p. 156); and he says that "there must be something wrong in our idea of the truth and falsity of arithmetical propositions" (RFM, I, #135).[27]

In short, grammar is neither correct nor incorrect, neither true nor false, but is instead *antecedent* to correctness and incorrectness, truth and falsehood.

Why, though, does Wittgenstein hold this view? I would suggest that his most fundamental reason for denying that grammatical principles are true or false lies in his conception, motivated above all by the need to explain their necessity, that they are *rules* or *conventions*, like those which govern games, that they have somewhat the character of *commands, commandments*, or *categorical imperatives* with which we enjoin ourselves to order our empirical or factual claims in specific ways (see chapter 1). This status precludes their possession of truth-values in two intimately connected ways: First, rules, conventions, commands, commandments, and categorical imperatives have the wrong sort of *force* to be true or false. (Can "Go to your bedroom immediately!" be true or false?) Second, this distinctive force which grammatical principles have precludes their having the force of assertions or statements, that is, the sort of force that *does* involve truth or falsehood. ("Go to your bedroom immediately!" uttered in the usual way as a command cannot also be an assertion or statement.) In somewhat this spirit, Wittgenstein notes that grammatical "rules play a different role than statements" and that "it is confusing to regard [grammatical] rules as statements because this draws our attention to a different kind of question: Are they true or false?" (WLC, pp. 153–54).[28]

Wittgenstein's case against even ascribing grammatical principles any *broader* sort of correctness or incorrectness consists mainly in the two parts of his doctrine of the arbitrariness of grammar which have already been explained in this chapter: his diversity thesis and his argument that it is never possible to justify or refute a grammatical principle (over against its alternatives), in particular by appeal to truth-in-virtue-of-meaning, relevant facts, success, or more fundamental grammatical principles. That this is the nature of his case can be seen from the passages that were adduced above to illustrate his denial that grammars are correct or incorrect (the "not" passages and the cookery passage).

This position and its attribution to Wittgenstein might seem vulnerable to a number of philosophical and exegetical objections, so it may be worth mentioning and addressing some of them here.[29]

First of all, it is natural to retort that grammatical principles at least *seem* to be assertions or statements rather than imperatives, and that they at least *seem* to be true or false (in many cases anyway, for example the mathematical ones).

As we shall see a little later, Wittgenstein is sometimes moved by such intuitions himself. But in his more considered moments he would, I think, resist them on the grounds that deeper reflection on the role that these principles play in our linguistic practices shows the situation to be in fact otherwise, and more specifically that the striking phenomenon of the *necessity* of these principles shows it to be otherwise. In this more considered mode he concedes the data in question as a sort of appearance, but implies that the appearance is a superficial and misleading one. For example, in this spirit he writes concerning the mathematical part of grammar: "Why do you always want to look at mathematics under the aspect of finding and not of doing? It must have a great influence that we use the words 'right' and 'true' and 'wrong' and the form of statement in calculating" (RFM, VII, #6; cf. WLC, pp. 139–40, 153–54, as recently quoted).

Compare with this stance his similar willingness, in works such as the *Philosophical Investigations* and the *Remarks on the Philosophy of Psychology*, to override the fact that first-person psychological statements relating to the present *seem* to be descriptions of mental facts, or (a less closely analogous case) his willingness to override the fact that nouns such as "number" and "meaning" *seem* to refer to entities. Also relevant in this connection is his important general distinction between "surface grammar" and "depth grammar" (PI, #664).

Here is a second possible objection: Famously, Wittgenstein is committed to a redundancy theory of truth according to which "'p' is true = p; 'p' is false = not-p" (PI, #136; cf. RFM, I, appendix III, #6; LFM, pp. 68, 188; WLC, p. 106; BT, p. 63). Does such a theory not require him to concede that grammatical principles are true or false after all?

There are, I think, two significantly different ways of construing his redundancy theory, which would require slightly different ways of formulating the objection, and then slightly different ways of answering it. On one fairly natural construal of the theory, what the theory says is that predicating truth of a proposition is always equivalent to asserting it, and predicating falsehood of a proposition always equivalent to denying it or asserting its negation. This seems to be what Wittgenstein has in mind in the following variant formulation of the theory, for instance: "To say that p is true is simply to assert p; and to say that p is false is simply to deny p or to assert ∼p" (LFM, p. 188; cf. RFM, I, appendix III, #6).

If the objection were based on this version of the theory, then a proper answer to it would be that it has already implicitly been thwarted, namely by Wittgenstein's argument that grammatical principles are (like) rules, conventions, commands, commandments, or categorical imperatives, *not assertions*.

But another interpretation of the redundancy theory is possible. It in fact seems that any adequate account of truth and falsehood ought also to make room for applications of these notions to propositions which are *not* asserted or denied (i.e., have their negations asserted), for example in truth-functional compounds such as "'p' is true v 'q' is false." So perhaps the connection between these notions and assertion is not, on Wittgenstein's considered view, really meant to be as tight as the passage just quoted above suggested. Perhaps the passage at PI, #136 (whose wording seems open to either of the two readings) really means that the *proposition* (whether asserted or not) "'p' is true" is equivalent to the *proposition* (whether asserted or not) "p" etc., not just, more specifically, that the *assertion* "'p' is true" is equivalent to the *assertion* "p" etc.

This version of the theory could allow the thwarted objection to be revived in a new form. For, to begin with a negative point, this version forgoes the tight link between truth/falsehood and assertion that was posited by the previous version, so that any objection which flows from this version will no longer be dismissable simply by pointing out that grammatical principles are not assertions. And more positively, this version might encourage taking, instead of assertedness, something more like *being a meaningful sentence in the indicative mood* as the only criterion of capacity for truth/falsehood—in other words, a criterion which grammatical principles would easily satisfy.

However, I think that this positive proposal contains a weakness which allows Wittgenstein an effective reply on behalf of his doctrine of antecedence. Breaking, for the good reason mentioned, the tight link between a sentence's capacity for truth/falsehood and assertion which was posited by the previous version of the redundancy theory need not, and should not, move us all the way to an alternative criterion as anemic (and hence as bound to be satisfied by grammatical principles) as being a meaningful sentence in the indicative mood. That it need not do so is obvious enough. That it should not do so can be seen from the following examples of meaningful sentences in the indicative mood which are nonetheless innocent of truth and falsehood: "You take route 91 and then turn off at exit 5"; "You will go to bed immediately." (Since these sentences are both implicitly imperatival in nature, neither is capable of truth or falsehood.) Available in the middle between the two unacceptable criteria which have now been tried, and free of the flaws of both, would be something more like the criterion: being a meaningful sentence in the indicative mood *which is capable of serving as an assertion (without any change in meaning)*.[30] Wittgenstein indeed sometimes seems to adopt just this sort of middle position. Consider, for example, the following passage: "The great majority of the sentences that we speak, write, and read, are statement sentences. And—you say—these sentences are true or false . . . For assertion is not something that gets added to the proposition, but an essential feature of the game we play with it" (RFM, III, #2).

But now, once the criterion has been reformulated in this more careful and defensible way, still preserving a link with assertion, albeit now an attenuated one, it seems that Wittgenstein can easily answer any objection to his doctrine which comes from this subtler version of the redundancy theory. For his position is that grammatical principles, as belonging to the family of rules, conventions, commands, commandments, and categorical imperatives, are *not* capable of serving as assertions (without changing their meaning)—any more than sentences like "You take route 91 and then turn off at exit 5" or "You will go to bed immediately."

A third potential objection is this: As we have seen, Wittgenstein's position rests on a recognition that grammatical principles are necessary. But is it not natural to suppose that to say that a principle is necessary is to say that it is necessarily *true*?

A plausible answer to this objection might run as follows. It seems fair enough to say that in ascribing necessity to grammatical principles but denying them truth or falsehood, Wittgenstein comes into conflict with a commonsense tendency to equate "necessary" with "necessarily true." However, this would in itself only pose a serious problem for him if it could be assumed that his considered position is or should be one of strict quietism, one of slavish respect for ordinary language and received common sense—which seems implausible, both exegetically and normatively.

The objector might perhaps choose to forgo reliance on that assumption and instead ground his objection on a claim that subtracting the notion of truth from the notion of necessity leaves us with a hopelessly obscure and unintelligible notion of necessity. However, in that case, it would, I think, be appropriate for Wittgenstein to reply that, on the contrary, he has provided us with a rather rich, exact, and philosophically compelling alternative account of the nature of necessity (namely, the account sketched in chapter 1 and to be further elaborated in chapter 3).

A fourth possible objection, related to the preceding one, is this: The classic semantic definition of logical validity is in terms of necessary truth-preservation between premises and conclusion. But there can certainly be logically valid inferences which involve grammatical principles as premises and conclusions—for example, "2 + 2 = 4, 4 > 3, therefore 2 + 2 > 3" or "p v ~p, therefore (p v ~p) v r." So does it not follow that grammatical principles must be capable of truth after all?

However, it seems open to Wittgenstein to argue plausibly that this is the wrong moral to draw. There may indeed be a conflict between the classic semantic definition of logical validity and his conception of grammatical principles as innocent of truth and falsehood, of just the sort pointed out by the objection. But may this conflict not instead show that the classic semantic definition of logical validity requires modification?

Strengthening such a suggestion, it might plausibly be pointed out that examples such as the two just given seem to show that the definition requires modification *anyway* (i.e., even absent a denial of truth and falsehood to grammatical principles). For when the conclusion of an argument is itself a necessary principle, as in these two examples, it seems that *any* argument to it from true premises will in consequence be necessarily truth-preserving, even arguments which are not in any normal sense logically valid—for example: "2 + 2 = 4, 4 > 3, therefore 100 + 100 = 200"; or: "p v ~p, therefore a = a."

The solution to this problem is presumably to redefine logical validity in terms of necessary truth-preservation between premises and conclusions by a form of argument *when merely contingent propositions are involved or are substituted in for necessary ones*—since, to continue with our above examples, "a = b, Fb, therefore Fa" is necessarily truth-preserving but "a = b, Fb, therefore c = d" is not; and similarly, "s, therefore s v r" is necessarily truth-preserving but "s, therefore r" is not.

But note that in developing such a solution to the problem, one has also shown that it is possible, and moreover necessary, to redefine logical validity in a way that allows grammatical principles to feature in logically valid inferences, but without the definition implying that such principles can themselves be true. In other words, one has shown in a little more detail how Wittgenstein could plausibly answer the objection by proposing a modification of the semantic definition of logical validity, and moreover one which evidently needs to be undertaken anyway.

A fifth possible objection is the following. Wittgenstein often characterizes grammatical principles as "propositions." Yet in the *Philosophical Investigations* he argues that "the use of 'proposition' and the use of 'true'" are "interwoven" (PI, #225; cf. #136), which implies that only sentences capable of being true (or false) count as propositions. So is his characterization of grammatical principles as "propositions" not implicitly inconsistent with a doctrine that they are capable of neither truth nor falsehood?

There is no *deep* inconsistency here, however. For Wittgenstein is well aware that for just this sort of reason, reference to grammatical "propositions" is misleading and can only be taken very loosely. For example, he says of formal logical principles: "One needs to remember that the propositions of logic are so constructed as to have *no* application as *information* in practice. So it could very well be said that they were not propositions at all" (RFM, I, appendix III, #20); and similarly of mathematical principles: "We are used to saying '2 times 2 is 4,' and the verb 'is' makes this into a proposition, and apparently establishes a close kinship with everything that we call a 'proposition.' Whereas it is a matter only of a very superficial relationship" (RFM, I, appendix III, #4; cf. VII, #70); "There are no true a priori propositions (mathematical propositions so called are not propositions at all)" (LC, p. 13).

A sixth possible objection might appeal to a passage in *Wittgenstein's Lectures: Cambridge 1932–1935* in which Wittgenstein seems to deny that grammatical rules are commands—"We do not call a rule about 'not' a command"—and to prefer to classify them as statements instead—"If required to classify $2 + 2 = 4$ within the rather primitive classification of utterances [into statements, commands, questions, exclamations, and instructions] I should say it is a statement, a statement about numbers" (WLC, p. 153).

There *is* a measure of inconsistency with what I am representing as his usual and considered position in this passage. However, it is much less stark than it might appear to be. For one thing, the conditional "If required . . ." is not merely rhetorical here. Wittgenstein is not saying that grammatical rules *are* statements; merely that *if* he were forced to classify them as belonging to one or other of the categories listed, then he would choose to classify them as belonging to that one. Hence (as we saw earlier) in the very same stretch of text he also says that grammatical "rules play a different role than statements" and that "it is confusing to regard rules as statements because this draws our attention to a different kind of question: Are they true or false?" (WLC, pp. 153–54).

Nor is Wittgenstein's denial in the passage quoted that grammatical rules are commands really at odds with his usual and considered position—which amounts to saying that they are in the same *family* as commands, commandments, etc. rather than that they literally are such. Indeed, the passage's emphasis on the *sui generis* character of grammatical rules— "I should say that *rule* does not fit into any of the above classifications of utterances, that it is not in the same 'style'" (WLC, p. 153)—provides valuable clarification of his usual and considered position in this respect.

The only grain of real inconsistency that remains after such closer scrutiny of the passage lies in its implication that grammatical rules are *more* like statements than commands, which is indeed at odds with Wittgenstein's usual and considered view. But this is perhaps little more than a difference of emphasis, and in any case, it is only something said in the course of an early lecture.

Seventh and finally, though, there is a set of remarks which really is rather deeply at odds with the doctrine I have attributed to Wittgenstein, and which should be mentioned in the interests of full disclosure. In the *Remarks on the Foundations of Mathematics* and the *Lectures on the Foundations of Mathematics, Cambridge 1939* Wittgenstein quite often himself applies the terms "correct" and "incorrect," "true" and "false," to grammatical principles such as those of mathematics and formal logic (see, for example, RFM, IV, #27, #44; VI, #15). Moreover, at one point in the latter work he even implies that, given the redundancy theory of truth, it is a truism that mathematical principles can be true or false because they are assertions! (LFM, p. 239; cf. RFM, I, #5; also WLC, p. 153 as just discussed.) Indeed, the main thrust of his position in that work seems to be, not that grammatical principles fail to be true or false or to be assertions, but instead merely that their truth or falsehood must not be thought to consist in the sort of relatively straightforward correspondence to reality or failure of such that constitutes the truth or falsehood of empirical propositions (LFM, pp. 239–46; cf. RFM, I, #156, as quoted earlier).

Such passages and strands in the texts seem to me anomalous. Rather than attempt an exegetical squaring of the circle, I would simply point out that it is easy enough to understand why Wittgenstein would have been tempted in this contrary direction on occasion. First, his quietist side, the side of him which wants to say that ordinary language and common sense are all right just as they are, obviously provides powerful incentives in this direction. For, of course, we do ordinarily call principles such as those of mathematics and formal logic true or false and classify them as assertions (cf. RFM, VII, #6, and WLC, pp. 139–40, as recently quoted).

Second, at the same time that he has been erecting one major obstacle to allowing grammatical principles the status of truths or falsehoods—namely, their new classification as similar to commands or categorical imperatives rather than assertions, a classification motivated by the need to explain their necessity—he has also been busy dismantling two others—namely, the *Tractatus*'s classification of them as senseless, a position which survives as late as *Wittgenstein's Lectures: Cambridge 1930–1932* but is subsequently abandoned; and the *Tractatus*'s correspondence theory of truth (T, 4.063), a position which Wittgenstein subsequently replaces with his redundancy theory of truth. Neither of these obstacles had in fact prevented him from classifying grammatical principles— that is, principles of formal logic—as true or false in the *Tractatus* (see T, 4.46). But they both obviously stand in very deep tension with doing so. And that the early Wittgenstein had himself realized this can be seen from his contrary position in

notes dictated to Moore in 1914: "Logical propositions are neither true nor false" (N, p. 109).

Third, the sort of vacillation between incompatible positions which we encounter here is fairly frequent in the later
Wittgenstein (some further examples to be discussed in this
essay concern the essential sociality of meaning [chapter 3]
and the limits of language [chapter 6]). I would suggest that
he indulges in this sort of vacillation in large part because he
supposes it to be reflective of a vagueness or fluidity in the
relevant everyday concepts, and hence excused by his principled tolerance of such conceptual vagueness or fluidity (a position which I shall discuss and criticize in chapter 6).

Let us turn now to the fourth and final component of Wittgenstein's doctrine that grammar is in a sense arbitrary by
taking up the second of the two questions posed earlier:
What is his view concerning the correctness or incorrectness,
the truth or falsehood, of the *empirical* or *factual* claims made
within alternative "true-false games" constituted by alternative grammars?

Presented merely with the first component of Wittgenstein's doctrine of arbitrariness, the diversity thesis, one might
be tempted to assume that his position would be somewhat
as follows: In at least some cases, the empirical claims which
are made possible by certain grammatical principles (namely,
through the constitution of the concepts required for their
articulation) will be correct in a way in which those made
possible by other, alternative grammatical principles are not,
since the former empirical claims will be capable of grasping
reality as it is (or at least of doing so in a higher degree)
whereas the latter empirical claims will not (or at least only
in a lower degree). Wittgenstein rejects such a position,
however.

One rather strong indication that he must reject it lies in
his recently explained view that grammatical principles are
never correct or incorrect. For if certain grammatical principles made possible empirical claims which were capable (or
more capable) of grasping reality as it is, whereas other, alter-

native grammatical principles only made possible ones which were incapable (or less capable) of doing so, then this would constitute a clear sense in which the former grammatical principles were correct (or at least more correct) and the latter incorrect (or at least less correct).

However, one does not need to rely solely on such indirect evidence. For Wittgenstein also rejects the position in question explicitly at various points, often incorporating this rejection into his doctrine that grammar is in a sense arbitrary. Thus in the *Philosophical Investigations* he dismisses the idea that "certain concepts are simply the right ones, and that *having different ones would mean not realizing something that we realize*" (PI, p. 230; emphasis added); in *The Big Typescript* and the *Philosophical Grammar* he argues in explicit connection with his doctrine of arbitrariness that "as long as we remain in the province of the true-false games *a change in grammar can only lead us from one such game to another, and never from something true to something false*" (BT, p. 161; PG, I, #68; emphasis added); and in *The Big Typescript*, the *Philosophical Grammar*, and *Zettel* he writes, again in explicit connection with his doctrine of arbitrariness, that "if you follow grammatical rules other than such-and-such ones, that does not mean you say something wrong, no, you are speaking of something else" (BT, p. 167; PG, I, #133; Z, #320).

Similarly, concerning the weaker possibility that one grammatical principle might at least furnish empirical claims which were *more* accurate than those furnished by another, the *Philosophical Investigations* rejects this on the ground that a comparison of degrees of accuracy only makes sense *within* a particular grammatical system (PI, p. 225).

This still leaves the interesting question of what positive characterization Wittgenstein wants to give of empirical or factual claims made within "true-false games" that are alternatives to ours, because constituted by alternative grammars, when those empirical or factual claims meet the standards of success set by their different grammars.

One preliminary point which can be made with confidence is that he will want to say that they have different senses from

any claims which can be made within our games, since grammar is constitutive of sense (hence the remark quoted above
that "if you follow grammatical rules other than such-and-
such ones . . . you are speaking of something else"). There
can therefore be no question of their literally either agreeing
with or contradicting any of our empirical or factual claims.

But beyond that Wittgenstein's position is less clear. Since
the question posed is an obvious, and obviously important,
one to ask, it seems reasonable to suspect that there may be a
principled reason for this obscurity. I would suggest that it
may be something like the following: On the one hand, the
doctrine of Wittgenstein's mentioned earlier that understanding a grammatical principle requires *commitment* to it in addition states that this commitment must be exclusive of alternative grammatical principles—which entails that, strictly
speaking, we can never understand an alternative grammar or
the factual propositions which it constitutes. On the other
hand, Wittgenstein's redundancy theory of truth (and falsehood)—in either its cruder, assertional or its more sophisti-
cated, propositional version—seems to entail that in order to
apply the concept of truth or falsehood one must at least
understand the proposition to which one applies it. Putting
these two considerations together motivates a conclusion that
one is in principle debarred from ever applying the concept of
truth or falsehood to factual propositions constituted by alternative grammars.

However, if this *is* Wittgenstein's line of thought, then it is
a dubious one. For one thing, as we shall see later (chapter 7),
the doctrine that understanding grammatical principles requires an exclusive commitment to them is philosophically
implausible. But even if it were not implausible, there is also a
fatal weakness in the premise concerning the redundancy theory: Just as (we saw earlier) a defensible version of the redundancy theory needs to make room for our ability to predicate
truth of unasserted but otherwise thought propositions if it is
to be at all plausible, likewise it needs to make room for a
further ability which we no less clearly possess to predicate,
and indeed assert, truth or falsehood of propositions whose

identity we happen not to know, and even of propositions which we are unable to understand. For it clearly makes perfectly good sense for us to say such things as "I do not know what George Bush told his children, and I wonder whether it was true" or "I do not know what George Washington told his children, but whatever it was, (I know that) it was true"; and even "I do not know what the theory of relativity says and am unable to understand it, but it may be true" or "I do not know what the theory of relativity says and am unable to understand it, but (I am sure that) it is true." Indeed, a plausible case could probably be made that it is in such applications of the concept of truth that its real *point* lies. Whether, and if so exactly how, a redundancy theory could be made flexible enough to accommodate such cases need not concern us here, but that it must be if it is to be defensible seems clear. And this undermines any prospect of using the theory in the manner of the above argument to preclude predicating or asserting truth or falsity of the (allegedly) always non-understood factual claims constituted by grammars which are alternatives to one's own. For if the theory must be made to accommodate such things as entertaining the question whether, or even asserting that, the theory of relativity is true or false even when one is unable to understand the theory of relativity, then it will surely thereby also be made to accommodate entertaining the question whether, or even asserting that, factual claims which are constituted by alternative grammars but which one is unable to understand are true or false.

Setting aside this illusory obstacle to pursuing the question any further, then, how might Wittgenstein answer it? There are several possible positions for him to take here. One would be simply to multiply truths, as it were—that is, to acknowledge that all of the factual claims made within alternative "true-false games" which meet the standards of success set by their games are simply true. Such a position is arguably suggested by some of Wittgenstein's remarks already quoted above: that a change of grammar can "never [lead] us from something true to something false," and that it "does not mean you say something wrong, no you are speaking of something else." Since, as I recently pointed out, a difference in their grammars ensures that factual claims do not literally agree with *or contradict* each other, there is no danger that such a stance would entangle Wittgenstein in contradictory factual commitments.

An alternative position would be that the successful factual moves made within "true-false games" other than our own are not simply true, but instead "true" in a sense peculiar to the games within which they occur, a sense no doubt analogous to that of our term "true," but not identical with it.[31] There are some indications that Wittgenstein is indeed attracted to such a position. Thus one might understand the contrast which he draws in *The Big Typescript*, the *Philosophical Grammar*, and *Zettel* between cookery, which has a single end independent of its rules that sets the standard of success and failure for both the rules and the moves of the activity, and chess-like-games or language-games, which have no such single or independent end but instead have the standards of success and failure in the activity defined by their varying rules alone, as proscribing any notion of a single common end such as truth simpliciter in terms of which moves from different language-games could be evaluated (while, at the same time, if *no* notion of "truth" were applicable to them *at all*, then how could Wittgenstein envisage different "true-false games"?). Also, if we accord a degree of precision to Wittgenstein's metaphor of a language-*game*, then it seems plausible to infer from it that what is recognized as "success" or "failure," "truth" or "falsehood," in one language-game is not going to have quite the same character as what is recognized as such in another, and that such terms will therefore have significantly different senses in application to different language-games.

In addition, Wittgenstein sometimes makes comments which suggest more explicitly that a variation in grammar brings with it a variation in concepts of "truth" and "falsehood." For example, in the *Remarks on the Foundations of Mathematics* he advances such a position in connection with variations in logical and mathematical grammar: "'But may there not be true propositions which are written in [Russell's] symbolism, but are not provable in Russells' system?'—'True propositions,' hence propositions which are true in *another* system, i.e. can rightly be asserted in another game. Certainly; why should there not be such propositions . . . ? The question is quite analogous to: Can there be true propositions in the language of Euclid, which are not provable in his system, but are true?—Why, there are even propositions which are provable in Euclid's system, but are *false* in another system. May not triangles be—in another system—similar (*very* similar) which do not have equal angles?—'But that's just a joke! For in that case they are not "similar" to one another in the same sense!'—Of course not; and a proposition which cannot be proved in Russell's system is 'true' or 'false' in a different sense from a proposition of *Principia Mathematica* . . . If you assume that the proposition is provable in Russell's system, that means it is true *in the Russell sense* . . . If the proposition is supposed to be false in some other than the Russell sense, then it does not contradict this for it to be proved in Russell's system. (What is called 'losing' in chess may constitute winning in another game.)" (RFM, I, appendix III, #7–8). Similarly, in *On Certainty* Wittgenstein says that our apparently-empirical principle that the earth has existed during the last hundred years may involve "the determination of a concept" (in other words, may be grammatical), and he then goes on in elaboration of this suggestion to argue that "if I speak of a possible mistake here, this changes the role of . . . 'truth' in our lives" (OC, #138). Also, in that work he says of other principles of the same sort, "This statement appeared to me fundamental; if it is false, what are 'true' and 'false' any more?!" (OC, #514; cf. #515).

It might seem that the redundancy theory of truth would conflict with adopting such a position, and would argue for preferring the previous one. For if the linguistic role of uses of "true" is equivalent to simple assertions (on the cruder version of the theory) or to simple propositions apt for assertion (on the subtler version), then in either case does this not preclude variations in the concept "true" across alternative language-games?

However, it at least seems clear that Wittgenstein himself sees no such conflict, since the long passage from the *Remarks on the Foundations of Mathematics* recently quoted is immediately preceded by a statement of the redundancy theory (in its cruder version) (RFM, I, appendix III, #6). And his implication that there need be no conflict indeed seems correct, on reflection. For variations in the concept "true" could quite well derive from corresponding variations between alternative language-games in the practice (and concept) of "assertion" (or of using "propositions") itself, and it does not seem implausible to suppose that transitions between alternative language-games might involve variations of the latter sort.

A final possible position would be a synthesis of the two previous ones: Certain types of grammatical variation will not be extreme enough to render our usual notion of truth inapplicable to the factual claims involved (when they are successful), so that in these cases the first sort of characterization will apply—they are simply true. Other types of grammatical variation will indeed be extreme enough to make our usual notion of truth inapplicable to such claims, so that in these cases the second sort of characterization will apply—they are only "true."

The point just made concerning the redundancy theory might argue for adopting such a hybrid position, indeed in a specific version: If, as seems likely sometimes to occur, the transition from our grammar to an alternative one involves no change in the practice (or concept) of assertion (or of using propositions), then our concept of truth will continue to be applicable, and we should say that successful factual claims are simply true. If, on the other hand, as also seems likely sometimes to occur, the transition does involve a change in the practice (and concept) of assertion (or of using propositions), then only a variant concept of "truth" will be applicable, and we should only say that successful factual claims are "true."[32]

Such, then, are the main outlines of Wittgenstein's doctrine that grammar is in a sense arbitrary. To summarize the doctrine's central components: (1) Grammatical principles always have alternatives (the "diversity thesis"). (2) There is never any possibility of justifying or refuting grammatical principles (in their competition with alternatives). (3) Grammatical principles are neither correct nor incorrect, neither true nor false. (4) The factual claims that are made possible by one grammar never outdo those that are made possible by another, alternative grammar in virtue of being able to capture reality as the latter cannot, or being able to capture it more accurately than the latter.

We should now turn to consider the sense in which Wittgenstein understands grammar to be *non*-arbitrary.

3

The Sense in Which Grammar Is Non-Arbitrary

ACCORDING to Wittgenstein, grammar is also in a sense *non*-arbitrary (Z, #358; PI, #520, p. 230; WL, p. 70; LC, p. 49).

This thesis involves a rejection of the notion which the idea of grammar's arbitrariness may easily bring with it—especially in the German, where the word *willkürlich* (arbitrary) is etymologically connected to *Wille* (will) and *küren* (to choose, elect) in a transparent way—that a person can in general simply choose to adopt any particular grammar from among those that are possible, or can simply by choice turn any old empirical or factual sentence, sentence currently excluded by grammar, or otherwise meaningful-looking sentence into a grammatical principle (accepting inevitable consequences for its meaning).

Admittedly, Wittgenstein does at points seem to embrace such views himself—in particular, that a person's acceptance of a particular grammatical principle rather than possible alternatives is a matter of choice (see, for example, RFM, III, #27; V, #20; VI, #7; OC, #87, #245-46, #251, #362), and that a person can simply by choice make any empirical or factual sentence into a grammatical principle (see, for example, RFM, VII, #74).

Accordingly, he has sometimes been interpreted in this way, perhaps most famously by Michael Dummett in his essay "Wittgenstein's Philosophy of Mathematics."[1]

However, this is not Wittgenstein's considered position. On

the contrary, his considered position is that a person's adoption of a particular grammar, and the ability of sentences to
serve as grammatical principles, are heavily *constrained*.[2]

That this is so constitutes the vitally important second limb
of Wittgenstein's quasi-Kantian explanation of the nature of
necessity (mentioned in chapter 1).

The constraints in question are of several distinguishable sorts
(as I mentioned in chapter 1, they are not only more naturalistic but also more complex than their Kantian counterpart).
First of all, according to Wittgenstein, one is normally constrained to a particular range of grammars, or even to a particular grammar, in exclusion of possible alternatives, either
by one's very *human nature* or by one's upbringing within
specific *social practices and traditions*, so that adopting the particular range of grammars, or grammar, in question is not a
matter of choice or decision for one in any usual sense of
these words.

Thus, concerning, first, constraint by *human nature*, in the
Philosophical Grammar Wittgenstein remarks, "So is the calculus something we adopt arbitrarily? No more so than the
fear of fire, or the fear of a raging man coming at us" (PG, I,
#68; cf. BT, p. 160); in the *Remarks on the Foundations of Mathe-
matics* he implies that if people "inferred" in a sufficiently deviant way, this would not count for us as "inference" or "thinking" at all, "And thinking and inferring (like counting) is . . .
bounded for us, not by an arbitrary definition, but by natural
limits," including the fact that a person "can't *think* it . . . he
can't fill it with personal content; he can't really *go along with
it*—personally, with his intelligence" (RFM, I, #116; cf. #131);
in *On Certainty* he says that our acceptance of grammatical
principles is "as it were, . . . something animal" (OC, #359);
and in the *Philosophical Investigations* he implies that the fact
that we proceed in fundamental mathematical operations,
such as counting, in the way that we do, and thereby possess
the mathematical grammar that we do, instead of in imaginable alternative ways which could ground alternative mathematical grammars, is comparable to the naturalness with

which we follow a gesture of pointing in the direction from the wrist to the fingertip rather than vice versa (PI, #185; cf. WLC, p. 188: that we proceed as we do here is "a fact of nature"; BT, p. 48: "lies in human nature").[3]

Concerning, next, constraint by *social practices and traditions*, in the *Philosophical Investigations* Wittgenstein remarks, "Compare a concept with a style of painting. For is even our style of painting arbitrary? Can we choose one at pleasure? (The Egyptian for instance.)" (PI, p. 230; cf. LFM, p. 143); in *On Certainty* he characterizes our acceptance of grammatical principles as "a form of life" (OC, #358), and our "picture of the world" (which consists of our grammatical principles, or at least the apparently-empirical ones) as "the *inherited background* against which I distinguish between true and false" (OC, #94; emphasis added); and in the *Remarks on the Foundations of Mathematics* he says of our adoption of logical principles that "the laws of inference can be said to compel us; in the same sense, that is to say, as other laws in human society. The clerk who infers as in (17) [i.e., correctly, as in the example at RFM, I, #17] *must* do it like that; he would be punished if he inferred differently. If you draw different conclusions you do indeed get into conflict, e.g. with society" (RFM, I, #125; cf. VI, #30).[4]

As the first and last passages here (those on Egyptian painting and the clerk) suggest, this subjection of a person's grammar to constraint by social practices and traditions seems for Wittgenstein to be in part merely causal and normative in much the same, familiar ways in which the subjection of a person's own norms and behavior to constraint by societal-traditional aesthetic, moral, etiquette, and legal norms commonly is.

But Wittgenstein also conceives the constraint to be stronger. For it is a consequence of his famous rule-following argument that grammar is of its very essence a product of an ongoing social practice. Thus the *Philosophical Investigations* draws the following conclusion from that argument: "Is what we call 'obeying a rule' something that it would be possible for only *one* man to do, and to do only *once* in his life?—This is of course a note on the grammar of the expression 'to obey a rule.' It is not possible that there should have been only one occasion on which only one person obeyed a rule . . . To obey a rule, to make a report . . . are *customs* (uses, institutions)" (PI, #199; cf. RFM, VI, #21, #32, #34, #39–45).[5]

When Dummett gives the interpretation of Wittgenstein's position mentioned earlier, he in particular overlooks this social-constraint aspect of it. For example, Dummett writes that "Wittgenstein's idea" is "that one [note Dummett's choice of the singular!] has the right simply to *lay down* that the assertion of a statement of a given form is to be regarded as always justified, without regard to the use that has already been given to the words contained in the statement," and he characterizes Wittgenstein as committed to the view that "it may be that the form of words we use to tell [a particular man] the facts has a different sense as a result of his having adopted some logical law which we do not accept."[6]

But there is also a further important group of constraints. This group cuts especially against the notion that one could simply turn any old empirical or factual sentence, sentence currently excluded by grammar, or otherwise meaningful-looking sentence into a grammatical principle at will (even allowing for a change in its meaning).

This further group of constraints may perhaps best be approached via reflection on the following passage from the *Philosophical Investigations*: "'So does it depend wholly on our grammar what will be called (logically) possible and what not—i.e., what that grammar permits?'—But surely that is arbitrary!—Is it arbitrary?—It is not every sentence-like formation that we know how to do something with, not every technique has an employment [*Verwendung*] in our life; and when we are tempted in philosophy to count some quite useless thing [*etwas ganz Unnützes*] as a proposition, that is often because we have not considered its application [*Anwendung*] sufficiently" (PI, #520; cf. PG, I, #82; BT, p. 76).

This passage is somewhat ambiguous: Is Wittgenstein saying that the empirical sentences for which grammar has

determined a logical space may nevertheless lack an employment (*Verwendung*) in our lives and an application (*Anwendung*) and therefore fail genuinely to express propositions, to
have a meaning? Or is he rather saying that grammatical sentences may *themselves* lack an employment in our lives and an
application and therefore fail genuinely to express propositions, to have a meaning?

Some closely related passages at *Philosophical Grammar*, I,
#82 tend to favor the former interpretation. But their formu-
lation is too different for this to be a decisive consideration.
And speaking for the latter interpretation are the above passage's equation of the sentences whose propositionality is in
question with "techniques," and its characterization of them
as the sorts of things that *philosophers* are inclined mistakenly
to treat as propositions, both of which are absent from the
corresponding passages in the *Philosophical Grammar*, and
both of which strongly suggest that it is *grammatical* sentences
themselves that are at issue. It therefore seems reasonable to
think that the second of the two interpretations captures at
least part of what Wittgenstein means here: grammatical sentences may lack an employment in our lives and an application and therefore fail genuinely to have a meaning.

Read in this way, the above passage can be seen to be drawing limits to the arbitrariness of grammar by pointing out that
not every sentence which we choose to have express, or
which appears to express, a grammatical principle can really
succeed in doing so, since however we choose, and however it
appears, it may still fail to be meaningful. And the passage
indicates two reasons *why* it may nevertheless fail to be meaningful: it may lack an employment in our lives and it may lack
an application.[7]

This points towards a more general constraint on the arbitrariness of grammar; for the requirement which Wittgenstein implies here, that a sentence must have an employment
in our lives and an application if it is to be meaningful, can be
seen as following from a more general requirement which he
embraces: that in order to be meaningful, a sentence must
have a *use*. Thus in *The Big Typescript* an earlier version of the

above passage in fact occurs immediately after the remark, "The use of the proposition, that is its sense" (BT, p. 76).

It is probably too well known to require extensive illustration here that the later Wittgenstein is generally prepared to identify the meaning of a form of words with its use. As representative of many passages which could be drawn on to illustrate this, consider the following famous passage from the *Philosophical Investigations*, for example: "For a *large* class of cases—though not for all—in which we employ the word 'meaning' [*Bedeutung*] it can be defined [*erklären*] thus: the meaning of a word is its use [*Gebrauch*] in the language" (PI, #43; cf. BT, p. 76, as just quoted).[8]

Much less obvious than Wittgenstein's commitment to this doctrine, however, is the exact sense of the term "use" that is involved in its identification of meaning with use, and hence the exact force of the doctrine. Like many of the later Wittgenstein's central terms, this one proves, on closer inspection, to have a somewhat complex and surprising sense, to be a rather heavily theory-laden term of art (albeit that Wittgenstein would himself have been extremely uneasy about acknowledging this).

Without making any claim to exhaustiveness, I would suggest that in the doctrine of meaning as use the word "use" carries, or comes to carry, at least the following five implications (which I shall present here as a sort of hierarchy of levels of increasing strength):

(1) There is a purely negative implication that, as consisting in the use of words, "meaning," despite its misleading substantive form, *does not consist in a kind of object*—in particular, not in the referents of meaningful words, not in mental images, and not in so-called abstract objects such as Platonic forms. (Consider, for example, BB, pp. 1, 4, 5; PI, #120.)

(2) There is a more positive implication that, as consisting in the use of words, "meaning" instead consists in the *function*, or role, of a form of words in language. (Consider, for example, OC, #64; PI, #120; RFM, I, appendix I, #16.) As one would expect given Wittgenstein's conception of grammar explained in chapter 1, for him this function in turn essentially

consists in, or at least essentially involves, conformity to grammatical *rules*. (Thus he writes at one point that the "functions [of words] appear to us expressed in the rules which apply to the words" [BT, p. 32], and elsewhere he goes as far as to equate the use that constitutes meaning with grammatical rules: "the grammar (the use)" [BB, p. 23; cf. WLC, p. 3; RFM, I, #130].)

(3) There is a further positive implication that, as consisting in the use of words, "meaning" consists in a function in language of a form of words which involves *the achievement of practical purposes*. (Consider, for example, Wittgenstein's frequent analogy between meaningful words and tools or instruments, in such passages as PG, I, #31 and PI, #569; his inclusion of such questions as why a sentence is important, and what it matters to me, under the general question of how it is used at OC, #38; his remark at RPPI, #266 that "the usefulness [*Nutzen*], i.e. the use [*Gebrauch*], gives the proposition its special sense"; and his observation at LWPPI, #291: "Meaning, function, purpose, usefulness—interconnected concepts.")

(4) There is a further positive implication that, as consisting in the use of words, "meaning" consists in a form of words' practical function in language *performed within an enduring practice*. (Consider, for example, PI, #199, as quoted earlier; RFM, VI, #21, #32, #34, #43.)

(5) Finally, there is a further positive implication that, as consisting in the use of words, "meaning" refers to a form of words' practical function in language performed within an enduring practice which is *social*. (Consider, for example, PI, #199, as quoted earlier, where, note, Wittgenstein equates *Gebräuche* with unequivocally social *Institutionen*, and where *Gebrauch* incorporates something like the meaning of its cognate *Brauch*, meaning an established social custom [a word from which it was indeed not clearly distinguished in everyday German before the nineteenth century]; also RFM, VI, #39–45, where, for example, he suggests that the question whether there could be only one man who followed a rule is like the question, "Can one man alone engage in commerce?")[9]

Now I would suggest that the two conditions on the meaningfulness of a grammatical sentence mentioned at *Philosophical Investigations*, #520—that the sentence have an employment in our lives and an application—should be understood as implications of level (3) of Wittgenstein's equation of the meaning of a form of words with its use: its possession of a function in language which *achieves practical purposes*. Hence Wittgenstein writes at one point concerning the grammatical principles of mathematics that "the usefulness, i.e. the use, gives the proposition its special sense . . . And insofar as a rule is often given in such a way that it proves useful, and mathematical propositions are essentially akin to rules, usefulness is reflected in mathematical truths" (RPP1, #266; cf. RFM, I, #4).

One may therefore understand the constraint on the arbitrariness of grammatical principles implied at #520 as really a special case of the following more general constraint: Not every form of words which we choose to have express, or which appears to express, a grammatical principle can do so simply in virtue of this choice or this appearance; in order to do so, it must, when so adopted, have a *use* in the complex sense sketched above, on pain of otherwise lacking a meaning.

Consequently, Wittgenstein would, I think, say that the *human nature* and *social practices and traditions* constraints on people's adoption of grammatical principles discussed earlier in this chapter both in part constrain that adoption by constituting conditions on the very meaningfulness of people's use of the grammatical sentences in question (*human nature* in virtue of level (3) of use and hence meaning, *social practices and traditions* mainly in virtue of levels (4) and (5)). A passage which illustrates this position is the following one from the *Remarks on the Foundations of Mathematics*, where Wittgenstein is discussing what would happen if calculating were to become "confused" in the sense of coming to lack the sort of support from human nature that consists in a person's normally reaching the same result when he repeats a calculation and the sort of support from society that consists in people moreover normally reaching the same results as each other in calculation: "Calculating would lose its point, if *confusion* supervened. Just as the use of the words 'green' and 'blue' would lose its point. And yet it seems to be nonsense to say— that a proposition of arithmetic *asserts* that there will not be confusion.—Is the solution simply that the arithmetical proposition would not be *false* but useless, if confusion supervened? Just as the proposition that this room is 16 feet long would not become *false*, if rulers and measuring fell into confusion. Its sense, not its truth, is founded on the regular working of measurements" (RFM, III, #75).

However, having noted this more general constraint, I shall not attempt to pursue all of the avenues to which it points, but shall instead concentrate on the one mentioned at #520. Consider, then, once again, the reference at #520 to the need in which grammatical sentences stand of *an employment (Verwendung) in our lives* and *an application (Anwendung)* if they are to be meaningful. I have suggested that this need should be seen as a consequence of Wittgenstein's position that in order to have a meaning, a form of words must have (because meaning just consists in) a *use*, in a sense implying (among other things) a function in language which *achieves practical purposes*. It is perhaps self-evident enough that the condition that grammatical sentences must have *an employment in our lives* can be seen as such a consequence. What, though, of the condition that they must have *an application*? I suggest that this too can be seen as such a consequence, for the general reason that if they were to lack an application they would be incapable of serving practical purposes.

What exactly does Wittgenstein mean here by an "application," though? The sort of application that a grammatical sentence belonging to our "true-false games" must have in order to be meaningful is, in Wittgenstein's conception of it, a matter of at least the following three things:

(i) He believes that any meaningful grammatical sentence must be articulated by means of concepts which have a use in empirical or factual claims as well. As he puts this idea in the *Remarks on the Foundations of Mathematics*, "Concepts which occur in 'necessary' propositions must also occur and have a meaning in non-necessary ones" (RFM, V, #41). As he applies this idea to the grammatical principles of mathematics in particular: "I want to say: it is essential to mathematics that its signs are also employed in *mufti*. It is the use outside mathematics, and so the *meaning* of the signs, that makes the sign game into mathematics" (RFM, V, #2; cf. LFM, p. 268); "What does it mean to obtain a new concept of the surface of a sphere [i.e., in a geometrical proof]? How is it then a concept of the surface of a *sphere*? Only insofar as it can be applied to real spheres" (RFM, V, #4). Or to give an example from arithmetic, the concept "2" occurs not only in grammatical principles, such as "$2 + 2 = 4$" and "$2 - 1 = 1$," but also in factual propositions, such as "There are only 2 apples left on the tree" and "Here are 2 more blankets." Or to give one from logic, the concept "v" or "or" occurs not only in grammatical principles, such as "$p \lor \sim p$," but also in factual propositions, such as "He ate the cake or he gave it to someone else who did."

(ii) Wittgenstein also believes that a grammatical sentence belonging to our "true-false games" must—to borrow one of his favorite metaphors—*channel* empirical or factual propositions if it is to be meaningful. That is, it must unconditionally require or forbid certain forms of empirical or factual description which would otherwise seem optional. Thus, in relation to the grammatical principles of mathematics, he writes that "arithmetic bars a particular kind of description and conducts description into other channels" (RFM, VII, #3). We have already seen an example of how he envisages this: Once a person has accepted as a part of arithmetical grammar the principle that $25 \times 25 = 625$, if he counts a collection of objects by one means (say, by setting them up in an array of 25 rows each containing 25) and gets the result that there are 25×25 of them, but then counts them by another means (say, one by one) and gets the result that there are not 625 of them (but, say, only 624), the option, which would otherwise have appeared open, of simply leaving his description of the situation at that—of saying that the objects made up 25×25 though not 625 (but instead 624)—is excluded. Turning to other areas of grammar, Wittgenstein similarly expresses the view that formal logic "gets its whole sense simply from its presumed application to propositions," by which "I don't mean *logical* propositions" (RFM, IV, #14). In other words, if the grammatical principles of formal logic did not channel factual propositions as they do—by, for example, excluding as an option the simultaneous acceptance of factual proposition p arrived at as the result of one method of testing and factual proposition ~p arrived at as the result of another—then they would not have a sense. Again, in *On Certainty* he remarks in connection with the apparently-empirical principles which he there assigns to grammar that one might understand these as if they "were hardened and functioned as channels for such empirical propositions as were not hardened but fluid" (OC, #96), and he gives the following example of an apparently-empirical principle performing this function: "We form the *picture* of the earth as a ball floating free in space and not altering essentially in a hundred years . . . and this picture now helps us in the judgment of various situations" (OC, #146). But, by contrast, he suggests that sentences of the same class which do *not* perform such a function are to be rejected as meaningless—"We expunge the sentences that don't get us any further" (OC, #33)—and he identifies as prime candidates for this fate the sentences "Perhaps I have been to the moon" and "I have a body": "The supposition that perhaps I have been [to the moon] would strike me as *idle*. Nothing would follow from it, nothing be explained by it. It would not tie in with anything in my life" (OC, #117);[10] "I don't know how the sentence 'I have a body' is to be used" (OC, #258).

Principles (i) and (ii) are a major source of Wittgenstein's occasional tendency towards revisionism in mathematics. Thus principle (i) is a source of his skepticism about Cantor's proof of the existence of non-denumerable sets by means of the diagonal argument: "What can the concept 'non-denumerable' be used for?" (RFM, II, #12; cf. V, #5, #7). And principle (ii) is a source of his inclination to skepticism about the "Multiplicative Axiom," or Axiom of Choice, which he identifies as a mathematical proposition lacking the sort of function in regulating factual claims that is in question in principle (ii) (see RFM, V, #25). Hence he writes that "if you did not understand *any* mathematical proposition better than you understand the Multiplicative Axiom, then you would *not* understand mathematics" (RFM, VII, #33; cf. II, #35; V, #25).[11]

Principle (i) may be more problematic than it appears at first sight, and arguably requires more careful formulation than Wittgenstein usually gives it. In particular, as he normally states it (for example, at RFM, V, #41), it seems too liberal in one way, and too illiberal in another. Concerning, first, excessive liberality:[12] Unless some further restriction is placed on the *sorts* of factual propositions in which a concept occurring in a grammatical sentence must have a use, and the *ways* in which it must have a use in them, it seems that this condition will be trivially satisfiable in a manner that Wittgenstein would presumably want to, and arguably ought to, avoid. For instance, if occurrences of a concept in psychological factual sentences such as "So-and-so reflected on Xs" (note that the word "X" is *used* here, not merely mentioned) are good enough to count, then presumably "Cantor reflected on non-denumerable sets" will count as a use of the concept "non-denumerable" in a factual sentence and will satisfy the condition. Or if occurrences of a concept in true negative factual sentences such as "There are no Xs in the world of physical objects" are good enough to count, then presumably "There are no non-denumerable sets in the world of physical objects" will count as a use of the concept "non-denumerable" in a factual sentence and will satisfy the condition. Or if occurrences of a concept in false positive factual sentences such as "There are Xs in the world of physical objects" are good enough to count, then presumably "There are non-denumerable sets of physical objects" will count as a use of the concept "non-denumerable" in a factual sentence and will satisfy the condition. So Wittgenstein arguably needs to make his condition more restrictive in a way that excludes such factual uses as these.

Still, this problem could perhaps be solved by stipulating that the factual uses required must include non-psychological ones, and, among them, true positive sentences, sentences which state or imply the actual occurrence of the object or property in question and which are moreover true.[13] Indeed, one might see Wittgenstein's own example of the sphere (RFM, V, #4) as pointing in the direction of this sort of refinement.

Concerning, next, excessive illiberality: Another potential problem is the likelihood that certain concepts in the mathematical and logical parts of grammar which Wittgenstein would want to, or ought to, consider legitimate may lack any *direct* use in factual propositions (at least once the class of relevant factual uses has been suitably restricted to cope with the previous problem), although their occurrence in grammatical principles is such as to give them an *indirect* relation to factual propositions of a sort that at least satisfies the spirit, even if not the letter, of Wittgenstein's condition. For example, it may be that the concept of a Gödel number has no use in merely factual propositions (of the relevant sort), but that it does nonetheless relate indirectly to factual propositions—for instance, to ones concerned with certain limitations on the abilities of computers which we are proposing to construct.

If this is correct, then presumably Wittgenstein needs to liberalize his condition in order to accommodate suitable indirect relations to factual propositions along with direct factual uses (of the relevant sort). Indeed, he himself sometimes seems inclined to move in this direction. For example, he writes at one point of "transitions, bridges from . . . fanciful to non-fanciful applications" (RFM, VII, #32; cf. #33).

In sum, principle (i) seems problematic as it stands, but the prospects of finding remedies for its weaknesses look fairly good.

(iii) For Wittgenstein the requirement that grammatical principles must have an application if they are to be meaningful is also a requirement that the factual judgments whose conceptual form they constitute, and which they regulate, *not prove too recalcitrant* when so regulated. This is the source of his position in the *Remarks on the Foundations of Mathematics* that mathematical laws rest on (although due to their status as grammatical rules they do not *express*) certain empirical regularities—such empirical regularities as, for example, our rarely finding in practice that by counting a particular group of objects by two different methods we arrive by one method at the result that there are 25 × 25 of them and by the other that there are only 624 of them; our almost always finding that when such discrepancies *do* arise they can be eliminated by recounting; and our almost always finding that when they do so we can discover an independently verifiable, or at least plausible, empirical explanation for them (consider, for example, RFM, VII, #1, #18). In the absence of such empirical regularities, mathematical sentences would lose their use and hence their sense. This is another facet of Wittgenstein's thought in a passage which I quoted earlier: "Calculating would lose its point, if *confusion* supervened. Just as the use of the words 'green' and 'blue' would lose its point. And yet it seems to be nonsense to say—that a proposition of arithmetic *asserts* that there will not be confusion.—Is the solution simply that the arithmetical proposition would not be *false* but useless, if confusion supervened? Just as the proposition that this room is 16 feet long would not become *false*, if rulers and measuring fell into confusion. Its sense, not its truth, is founded on the regular working of measurements" (RFM, III, #75; cf. I, #37). Wittgenstein is making the same point in connection with apparently-empirical principles of grammar when he writes in *On Certainty* that "what stands fast . . . is . . . held fast by what lies around it" (OC, #144). Thus he says there that a significant grammatical sentence of this type, like the one which bids us consider the earth as a ball, "proves itself everywhere" (OC, #147), but that if such a grammatical sentence of mine "were contradicted on all sides . . . then in that case the foundation of all judgment would be taken away from me" (OC, #614) and "I could not go on with the old language-game any further" (OC, #617).

It will be recalled that in chapter 2 we encountered an argument of Wittgenstein's to the conclusion that grammatical principles cannot be justified (or refuted) in terms of their faithfulness (or unfaithfulness) to facts. The main thrust of that argument could be put in the form of the following dilemma: Since any reference to facts presupposes grammatical principles which constitute its concepts and regulate its content, *either* the grammatical principles presupposed in a given reference to facts will include those which are supposed to be justified or refuted by that reference, in which case this presupposition will make such a justification viciously circular and such a refutation self-defeating, *or* they will exclude them, in which case the reference to facts will rest on grammatical principles other than those to be justified or refuted and there will inevitably be a conceptual incommensurability between it and the latter, so that once again justification or refutation will be thwarted.

Nevertheless, we can now see that for Wittgenstein there is a sense in which grammatical principles *may* properly be said to be responsible to facts (hence his remark at OC, #248 that "one might almost say that [the] foundation-walls are carried by the whole house"): If grammatical sentences had no application to facts in the sense of either (i) not having their concepts used in factual judgments, or (ii) not having a regulative role vis-à-vis factual judgments, or (iii) having such a role but vis-à-vis factual judgments which proved too recalcitrant for the role to be performed smoothly, then the grammatical sentences in question would lack use and hence meaning.

It is for this reason that Wittgenstein can, despite his rejection of the notion that grammatical principles are justifiable or refutable by appeal to facts (and indeed in a context in which he is arguing strongly for that rejection), nonetheless make the following claim on behalf of a sense in which grammar is non-arbitrary: "Yes, but has nature nothing to say here? Indeed she has—but she makes herself audible in another way. 'You'll surely run up against existence and non-existence somewhere!' But that means against *facts*, not concepts" (Z, #364).

Similarly, we saw in chapter 2 that Wittgenstein rejects the notion that one can justify grammatical principles in terms of their success in realizing purposes, their usefulness; but we can now see that he nonetheless thinks that grammatical principles *are* in a way required to be useful—namely, as a condition, not of their merit, but of their very existence, their very meaningfulness.

However, it is important in interpreting these constraints on the arbitrariness of grammar to resist a likely temptation to misunderstand the character and to exaggerate the strength which they have for Wittgenstein.

As we have seen, he believes that alternative grammatical principles for "true-false games" are always possible and conceivable, if not indeed actual. Consequently, the same holds for empirical or factual propositions whose senses they constitute as well: alternatives are always possible and conceivable, if not indeed actual, here too. Therefore, the mere fact that *we* do not have an empirical or factual application for a putative grammatical principle is no sufficient ground at all, in Wittgenstein's view, for concluding that it lacks one and is for that reason senseless. Thus, as we have seen, he writes: "These people are acquainted with reddish green.—'But there *is* no such thing!'—What an extraordinary sentence.—(How do you know?)" (Z, #362; cf. #369).

Nor may we assume that Wittgenstein equates the practical purposes which a form of words must serve if it is to have a use and hence a meaning (the practical purposes which also make it necessary that grammatical principles have an application if they are to be meaningful) with *our* practical purposes. Thus recall his insistence in *The Big Typescript* and the *Philosophical Investigations* on the *diversity* of purposes served by linguistic practices (as quoted in the previous chapter), and recall that (as we saw there) for him this diversity importantly includes differences between our purposes with grammatical principles and concepts and the purposes which other people who use alternative grammatical principles and concepts have with theirs.

4

Some Modest Criticisms

THE PRECEDING DESCRIBES what I take to be Wittgenstein's official position concerning a sense in which grammar is arbitrary and a sense in which it is non-arbitrary. I would like now to suggest some criticisms of this position, however—criticisms which, if valid, would by no means destroy it, but would require some significant revisions in it.

For convenience' sake, I will structure these criticisms as an ascending serial critique concerning the five levels of the doctrine of meaning as use which were distinguished in the previous chapter. Along the way, some other aspects of Wittgenstein's theses of grammar's arbitrariness and non-arbitrariness will come in for criticism as well, though.

Several levels of the doctrine of meaning as use, indeed arguably all of them, seem vulnerable to a certain sort of *internal* criticism. The internal criticism in question derives from Wittgenstein's official conceptual quietism, his official commitment to *leaving ordinary language as it is*. In this spirit, the *Blue Book* tells us that "ordinary language is all right" (BB, p. 28); the *Philosophical Grammar* that "we are not justified in having any more scruples about our language than the chess player has about chess, namely none" (PG, I, #77), that "the task of philosophy is not to create a new . . . language, but to clarify the use of our language, the existing language" (PG, I, #72); and the *Philosophical Investigations* that "philosophy may in no way interfere with the actual use of language; it can in the end only describe it" (PI, #124), that the confusions which it is philosophy's task to clear up do not require that it reform language (PI, #132).

This commitment to leaving ordinary language as it is creates a problem for the doctrine of meaning as use generally. It is not even clear that the doctrine stays completely faithful to our ordinary concept of meaning at levels (1) and (2), i.e., when construed in a minimalist way as saying only that meaning is not any kind of object but instead a function of words in language. For example, it seems arguable that the ordinary language concept of meaning conflates what Frege in "On Sense and Reference" for the first time carefully distinguished as meaning (*Sinn*) and reference (*Bedeutung*), and what Wittgenstein himself distinguishes similarly (see, for instance, BT, pp. 34, 250; WLC, p. 3—though note Wittgenstein's—for our present purposes, somewhat revealing—shift in terminology: *Bedeutung* [meaning] and *Träger* [referent]), and hence does involve an implication that meaning is an object, namely a referent.

Indeed (though the fact is not well known), Wittgenstein himself sometimes concedes points of this general sort. For example, when he first developed the doctrine of meaning as use, especially in *Wittgenstein's Lectures: Cambridge 1932–1935*, he was inclined to concede that, even merely in excluding the notion that meaning was a mental image, the doctrine amounted to a departure from the ordinary meaning of the term "meaning," a selective accentuation of one strand of the term's ordinary meaning to the neglect of other strands, rather than simply a reflection of the term's ordinary meaning (see WLC, pp. 44, 47–48, 121).

But certainly, the more additional specificity Wittgenstein builds into the relevant concept of use and thereby of meaning when defined as use—and, as we saw in the previous chapter, he ultimately builds in a great deal: not only that use is not an object but a function of words in language (levels (1) and (2)); but also that this is a function which achieves practical purposes, or is useful, including, in the case of grammatical principles, having an application of the complex threefold sort recently explained (level (3)); that it does so within an enduring practice (level (4)); and moreover that this practice is a social one (level (5))—the less plausible it becomes for him to claim that his own concept of meaning is simply our everyday one.

Let us turn first to level (3), his incorporation of usefulness—and hence, in the case of grammatical principles, empirical application of the complex threefold sort—into the very concept of use and hence of meaning. As we saw in the previous chapter, this incorporation plays a central role in his nonarbitrariness thesis. However, it seems problematic, both for internal reasons of the sort just described and for external ones.

To begin with internal criticism: It is surely hard to believe that our ordinary language concept of meaning includes requirements of the sort of usefulness, and, as an essential part of this in the case of grammatical principles, the sort of complex threefold empirical application, in question. In particular, it seems easy enough to think of sentences which serve a "grammatical" function for people who accept them but which lack the third component of such empirical application, namely smoothness in the regulation of empirical judgments, and which hence lack usefulness in Wittgenstein's full-blooded sense, yet which most competent speakers of English (unless they have already been "got at" by philosophers!) would nonetheless unequivocally classify as meaningful rather than meaningless (albeit while perhaps criticizing them on *other* grounds, such as falsehood, unknowability, fancifulness, or uselessness itself).

Think, for example, of such fundamental theological doctrines as the doctrine of God's omnipotence, omniscience, and perfect benevolence, with its implication that (in Leibniz's notorious expression) this is the best of all possible worlds, or the doctrine of transubstantiation, the doctrine that bread and wine change into Christ's body and blood during the Holy Communion service. (Lest these examples seem too far removed from what Wittgenstein has in mind with "grammar," note his remark in the *Philosophical Investigations*: "Theology as grammar" [PI, #373].) These theological doctrines arguably do fulfil Wittgenstein's first two conditions of empirical application: the concepts which they employ also have application in factual judgments (for example, concerning the first doctrine, people make factual claims such as "*God* said unto Moses . . . ," "Jones is *powerful*," "Jones is *knowledgeable*," "Jones is *benevolent*," and "Smith is *completely* innocent"; or, concerning the second doctrine, people make factual claims about "X *changing into* Y," and about *bread, wine, body, blood, Christ*, and the *Holy Communion service*); and the doctrines also regulate factual judgments (by, for example, proscribing our saying that such and such events were simply bad, or that such and such a substance was at such and such a time on Sunday merely a piece of bread). But the doctrines arguably fail to fulfil Wittgenstein's third condition, namely smoothness in such regulation—as Voltaire vividly and pointedly reminds us in *Candide* where the former doctrine is concerned, and as can be readily verified for the latter doctrine too by asking people in the ordinary way to identify the substances involved at relevant points in a Holy Communion service (to which their answer will tend to be: Why, simply bread and wine of course!).[1] In this way, at least, the doctrines also lack the sort of full-fledged usefulness that Wittgenstein has in mind. And yet most competent speakers of English would certainly not be at all inclined, prephilosophically, to say that these doctrines were therefore *meaningless* (which, note, for one thing, would also require saying that they did not *differ* from each other in meaning)—however critical they might be of them on *other* grounds (grounds which, note, would typically be not only different from a charge of meaninglessness but actually inconsistent with it—for example, grounds of falsehood or fancifulness).

Indeed, Wittgenstein sometimes himself implies skepticism about the notion that the sort of full-blooded usefulness and threefold empirical application in question are essential to the meaningfulness of grammatical principles. For example, in the *Lectures on the Foundations of Mathematics, Cambridge 1939* he at one place considers the question of whether we ought

to call the activity of one of his imaginary groups with a
different logic "language," entertains the possible objection to
doing so that there seems to be no *point* in what they do, but
then, instead of *sympathizing* with this objection (as his official
position would lead one to expect), replies, "But is there a
point in everything we do? What is the point of our brushing
our hair in the way we do? Or when watching the coronation
of a king, one might ask, 'What is the point of all this?' etc."
(LFM, pp. 203–4; cf. p. 230; RFM, I, #153). Similarly, at another
place in the same text he considers the case of a person who
proposes to deviate from our usual color grammar by calling
black a reddish green, and he objects to this that the grammatical system which would result would be very impractical—presumably, in particular because its regulation of factual claims would lack smoothness. But his objection is not
that this would undermine the very sense of such an alternative grammatical system (as his official position would lead
one to expect), but *simply* that the impracticality in question
would result (LFM, p. 235). Again, in the *Remarks on the Foundations of Mathematics* he at one point distinguishes between
two sorts of facts on which calculating is founded, "the . . .
ones that make it possible" and "those that make it a useful
activity," and says that "the connection with *the latter* consists
in the fact that the calculation is the picture of an experiment
as it practically always turns out" (RFM, VII, #78)—thereby
implying (contrary to his official position) both that usefulness is not a condition of the meaningfulness of grammar,
and that in particular smoothness in the regulation of factual
claims is not a condition of its meaningfulness but only of its
usefulness.[2]

So far this has been no more than an *internal* criticism of part
of Wittgenstein's non-arbitrariness thesis. For it in fact seems
quite implausible that we should accept his commitment to
conceptual quietism (for reasons which are in part emerging
here but which will be added to in chapter 6). In other words,
while it is evident that the aspect of his conception of grammar's non-arbitrariness just discussed collides with his com-

mitment to conceptual quietism, it also seems clear that the latter ought to be sacrificed *anyway*, so that there is little prospect of seeing in this collision itself a good philosophical argument against the former.

However, this internal criticism can easily be converted into a compelling external criticism as well. Suppose that one in the end rejects Wittgenstein's unattractive strict conceptual quietism in favor of the following arguably more attractive position: Modifying everyday concepts is sometimes acceptable and indeed desirable, but it should respect what is already determinate in our everyday linguistic intuitions unless there is a compelling justification for not doing so.[3] In that case, the internal criticism which we have considered can easily be turned into a plausible external one along the following lines: The external criticism in question again rests on the observation that such an elaborate incorporation of conditions into the concept of use, and hence meaning, as Wittgenstein undertakes accords ill with our everyday concept of meaning. But, unlike the internal criticism, it then frames its objection, not in terms of this being unacceptable *per se*, but instead in terms of it (a) involving a rather *high degree* of violence to our everyday linguistic intuitions, and especially (b) lacking any compelling *justification*.

Deciding the exact point, along a continuum of possibilities, at which Wittgenstein's incorporation of conditions becomes unacceptable in these two respects would no doubt be a large and difficult task. But the following two points seem plausible. On the one hand, concerning levels (1) and (2), the degree of violence to our everyday linguistic intuitions seems modest and, above all, there seem to be compelling justifications for excising reference from the everyday concept of meaning. These justifications lie, for example, in the obvious and widely recognized fact that many non-referring terms (i.e., terms which are non-referring by function), for example "and" and "not," are nonetheless meaningful (this theme is central to the *Philosophical Investigations*, where it forms a large part of Wittgenstein's attack on the Augustinian model of language, set up as a target at PI, #1), and the equally obvious and widely recognized fact that even referring terms (i.e., ones whose function is to refer, whether or not they successfully fulfil it) are often meaningful despite entirely lacking referents—consider, for example, the terms "Zeus" and "centaurs," which never did have referents—or despite having lost them—consider, for instance, the term "Napoleon," whose referent has ceased to exist (see PI, #40).

By contrast, it seems fairly clear that, judged by the light of this new principle governing conceptual revision, at least the third component of empirical application, smoothness in the regulation of factual claims, would have to be excluded from the conditions incorporated into the very concept of meaning (as applied to grammatical principles), and that the overarching concept of usefulness incorporated (of which threefold empirical application was a part in relation to grammatical principles) would have to be deflated correspondingly, in order for Wittgenstein's incorporation of conditions to become acceptable. For, as we saw above in connection with the theological examples, that third component seems to stand in sharp contradiction with our linguistic intuitions; and moreover, it seems to do so without being furnishable with any compelling justification.

The criticism just developed in effect amounts to a call for pruning back Wittgenstein's non-arbitrariness thesis, for deflating the full-blooded usefulness and threefold empirical application that he takes to be conditions of the very meaningfulness of grammatical principles. However, it might well also encourage a compensating pruning back of the *arbitrariness* thesis. For if an aspect of full-blooded usefulness and threefold empirical application, such as smoothness in the regulation of factual claims, cannot defensibly stand as a condition of the very meaningfulness of grammatical principles, might it not be retained as a criterion of their relative *value* instead? And in that case, would it not be reasonable to say, pace the arbitrariness thesis (as explained in chapter 2), that grammatical principles *can* sometimes in a sense be justified or refuted over against their alternatives, and indeed precisely in the light of empirical facts and usefulness?

At some points in the texts this indeed seems to be Wittgenstein's own position. One example is the passage from *Wittgenstein's Lectures on the Foundations of Mathematics, Cambridge 1939* recently cited where he objects to a color grammar, incompatible with ours, which classifies black as a reddish green and consequently produces various impracticalities, saliently including lack of smoothness in the regulation of factual judgments, not that these impracticalities would destroy the very meaningfulness of the grammar in question, but instead simply that they would *result*. Another example is a passage from the *Remarks on the Foundations of Mathematics* in which he says that recalcitrant experience might make us reject such a mathematical axiom as the parallel postulate of (modern) Euclidean geometry (in favor of an alternative geometrical grammar): "But might not experience determine us to reject the axiom?! Yes. And nevertheless it does not play the part of an empirical proposition" (RFM, IV, #4).

Indeed, even if one allowed that Wittgenstein's full-blooded usefulness and threefold empirical application *were* internal to the meaning of grammatical principles in the way he officially holds them to be, so that all grammatical principles had to achieve a certain minimum of these things in order even to exist (in order even to be meaningful), one might still find such a criterion of the relative value of alternative grammars attractive, and hence want to qualify the arbitrariness thesis's denial of the possibility of ever justifying or refuting a grammatical principle over against alternatives (in terms of empirical facts or usefulness). For full-blooded usefulness and empirical application of the threefold sort seem clearly to be things that come in *degrees*. So such an internality to meaning would still leave room for the possibility of justifying (or refuting) one grammatical principle over against another, alternative one in certain cases, namely according as the former's full-blooded usefulness and threefold empirical application, in par-

ticular the smoothness of its application to facts, were *greater*
(or less) than the latter's.

To put the thought in very crude, but perhaps helpfully
vivid, terms: Whatever the amount of full-blooded usefulness
and threefold empirical application necessary for meaningfulness might be, say n units, there could presumably arise a
situation in which two competing grammatical principles
both achieved that amount and hence were both meaningful,
but one of them *just* achieved it whereas the other one *over-
achieved* it, say with $n + 1$ units.

Or to give an imaginary example which may illustrate the
point slightly less crudely: We ourselves accept the grammatical principle $2 + 2 = 4$, and it proves useful and enjoys empirical application in Wittgenstein's threefold sense. But suppose some tribe of people, who were in other respects very
much like us, were instead to accept the following more complicated alternative: $2 + 2 = 4$ except between 7:00 and 7:01
on Sunday mornings, during which time $2 + 2 = 3$. Presumably, such an alternative principle would still be pretty
useful and would still enjoy a high degree of empirical application in the threefold sense. But it would be a *little* less useful
and a *little* less empirically applicable than our counterpart
principle, in particular because for one minute each week it
would fail to apply smoothly to the facts, so that the tribe had
to invoke ad hoc hypotheses in order to explain away the
apparent discrepancies. (Only a *little* less useful and empirically applicable, mind you. After all, only one minute's worth
of experience is affected each week—and early on a Sunday
morning at that, when, like us, most members of the tribe are
still asleep!) So might one not say that, while both grammatical principles are meaningful, ours is more justified than
theirs?[4]

However, the departure from the spirit of Wittgenstein's
arbitrariness thesis which either form of this revision would
involve would arguably be much less dramatic than it might
initially seem. It might initially appear that the arbitrariness
thesis would hereby be seriously defanged. But contrary to
that appearance: First, there would be no implication in ac-

cepting either version of this revision that *all* or even *many* grammatical disputes could be decided in favor of one of the disputing parties over the other by means of the proposed criterion. For competing grammars might measure up more or less equally well in terms of it, or not be meaningfully comparable in terms of it. Second, Wittgenstein's important qualification concerning his non-arbitrariness thesis, that the usefulness and empirical application in question in the thesis are not restricted to *our* purposes or *our* experience, would still stand unabated. Besides being important in its own right, this also exacerbates the problem just alluded to that it might often be impossible to make a meaningful comparison. Third, even when diversities in purposes and in types of experience are allowed for in this way, and indeed in part precisely *because* they are allowed for in this way, the proposed criterion of full-blooded usefulness and threefold empirical application would have a decidedly *subjective* character, in that it could not plausibly be claimed to be shared as a measure of the relative value of grammatical standpoints by *all* grammatical standpoints (let alone by all possible ones). Think, for example, of the sort of theological standpoint recently discussed. Besides in itself attenuating the sense in which advancing this criterion would deflate the spirit of the arbitrariness thesis, this might also do so by constituting a reason for restricting the criterion's function of deciding between competing grammars still further, namely to cases in which two grammatical standpoints *did* both happen to accept the criterion.

Indeed, once all of these qualifications have been taken into account, the departure from the spirit of Wittgenstein's arbitrariness thesis which either version of this revision would involve might in the end seem *so* modest that it might reasonably be wondered whether such a revision could possibly be of much significance at all. However, I suggest that it *is*, for the following reason. Even if, as seems likely, these qualifications make the proposed criterion of relative value effectively inapplicable to the great majority of contests between competing grammars, as well as in an important sense only subjective, there remains one very important subset of such contests to which the qualifications do not make the criterion inapplicable, namely contests in which we ourselves (with our strong empiricist and pragmatic leanings) confront a choice within an area of discourse among two or more alternative grammars between which we find ourselves torn.

As we shall see in chapter 6, Wittgenstein and we seem to confront a particularly important contest of just this sort in connection with the grammars of such concepts as "language," "meaning," and "thought."

The above points concerning level (3) of Wittgenstein's concept of use and hence of meaning have focused mainly on a specific component of the full-blooded usefulness invoked there, namely smoothness in the regulation of factual claims by grammatical principles. But analogous points could be extended to further aspects of that usefulness.

Wittgenstein evidently conceives the usefulness which he holds to be required for meaningfulness in (3) to consist in a realization of purposes which goes beyond merely realizing principles as ends in themselves. This can be seen, for example, from his treatment of it as essentially involving an empirical application of the threefold sort in the case of grammatical principles.

However, it in fact seems quite doubtful that our ordinary linguistic intuitions concerning meaning require of a grammatical (or other) principle that it be useful in the sense of fulfilling purposes beyond itself in order to be meaningful. (Think again of certain theological doctrines, for example.)

Indeed, as we have already seen, Wittgenstein himself sometimes implies such skepticism—for example, when he responds defiantly to the objection to calling an alternative logic "language" that it seems to have no point, "But is there a *point* in everything we do? What is the point of our brushing our hair in the way we do? Or when watching the coronation of a king, one might ask, 'What is the point of all this?' etc." (LFM, pp. 203–4).

It therefore seems likely that Wittgenstein's incorporation of this sort of usefulness into the very concept of use and hence meaning will run into internal and external problems similar to those that were raised above concerning his incorporation of smoothness in regulating factual claims.

Similarly again, noting this, and in consequence refraining from such an incorporation, might well make it attractive to adopt such usefulness as a criterion of the relative *value* of competing grammatical principles instead, in further qualification of the arbitrariness thesis's denial of the relative justifiability or refutability of alternative grammars.

Indeed, as we have already seen, Wittgenstein sometimes himself seems to embrace such a position, for example when he criticizes the proposal to call black a reddish green on the grounds that this would be very impractical (LFM, p. 235; cf. BT, p. 173).

Again similarly, this move might, moreover, be attractive even if the incorporation in question went ahead, since even if a certain minimum of such usefulness was required for meaningfulness, presumably there could still be differences in the degree of it achieved beyond that minimum which could constitute grounds for differential evaluations of competing grammatical principles.

Similarly again, if such a criterion of their relative value were adopted (in either version), then its limitation of the arbitrariness thesis would, however, be modest, since there would be many contests between competing grammatical principles in which both competitors measured up about equally well by this standard or failed to be meaningfully comparable in terms of it; the specific purposes in question would be highly variable from one grammatical standpoint to another; and indeed such usefulness would itself be a subjective criterion not shared by all grammatical standpoints.

Finally, and again similarly: Despite a danger that these qualifications might make the proposed criterion vacuous, they arguably do not. For the criterion at least promises to find application to one important class of contests, namely those in which we ourselves (with our pragmatic leanings) confront a real choice between alternative grammars within an area of discourse.

And once again, as we shall see in chapter 6, this in particular seems to occur for Wittgenstein and us in connection with the important case of such concepts as "language," "meaning," and "thought."[5]

Criticisms analogous to those raised above against level (3) of Wittgenstein's concept of use and hence of meaning can also be raised against levels (4) and (5), his incorporation of *enduring practice* and moreover *social* practice into his concept of use and hence of meaning.

To begin with an internal criticism: There certainly seems to be little *prima facie* plausibility to the notion that our everyday concept of meaning implies an *enduring practice*, and still less to the notion that it implies an enduring *social* practice. On the face of things, we can coherently imagine an intelligent creature who understands meanings being created by God, produced by a chance confluence of atoms, or whatnot just for a few instants, and then destroyed immediately afterwards (cf. RFM, VI, #34: the "two-minute man"), or—even more easily—a radical variant of Robinson Crusoe who, though quite alone in the world from birth, nonetheless comes to understand and express meanings.

It might reasonably be protested that this consideration falls short of decisiveness against Wittgenstein because there may be commitments in our ordinary language concept of meaning which lie buried beneath the surface, as it were. Indeed, does not Wittgenstein himself arrive at the internality of enduring social practice to meaning via a long and involved argument, the rule-following argument, which aims at uncovering just such buried commitments?[6]

However, I would suggest that appealing to this argument only postpones, and indeed aggravates, the problem rather than solving it. On a plausible interpretation of Wittgenstein's *official intentions* in the rule-following argument, he conceives the argument as a serial critique, on grounds of a sort of implicit incoherence, of a set of *merely philosophical* concept(ion)s of meaning all of which share the common feature that they would in principle make meaning autonomous of enduring social practice; a critique which then warrants and culminates in an inference to what he takes to be our *ordinary language* concept(ion) of meaning as something that essential involves enduring social practice, as a concept(ion) free of the incoherence in question.[7] But it seems reasonable to object that such an argument, rather than removing, in the end only delays and exacerbates Wittgenstein's prima facie conflict with ordinary language: along with his false imputation to ordinary language of a concept(ion) of meaning which implies enduring social practice (here undiminished), he now also evinces a failure to realize that the philosophical concept(ion)s which he serially criticizes are all, in their common feature of avoiding that implication, attempting to make theoretical sense of something that really *is* characteristic of ordinary language's concept(ion) of meaning, namely a contrary implication that meaning is at least in principle something autonomous of enduring social practice, something that even a solitary individual could achieve, indeed probably even an instantaneous one.[8]

This is not to say that the rule-following argument must therefore be worthless; perhaps the implicit incoherence which it purports to identify in the concept(ion)s serially criticized is genuine, and its inference to an incoherence-free concept(ion) of meaning as essentially involving enduring social practice consequently justified. But in order for the argument to be liberated from its hermeneutical errors about ordinary language so that such a core as this could be salvaged, it would need to be reconstrued in something more like the manner of Saul Kripke's famous reading: namely, as an argument which criticizes as implicitly incoherent a series of attempts to give theoretical content to *ordinary language's* concept(ion) of meaning as something in principle autonomous of enduring social practice, and which infers from this critique to a *novel* concept(ion) of meaning framed in terms that essentially involve enduring social practice, as a way of escaping that incoherence.[9]

Whether a version of the argument recast along such lines could really work is another matter (as will become clear below, I am in fact skeptical). The essential point for now is just that, when one pursues levels (4) and (5) of the conditions which Wittgenstein incorporates into the concept of use, and hence of meaning, beyond their prima facie conflict with our ordinary language concept of meaning, to the rule-following argument which is supposed to justify their incorporation, it seems that this argument has no real prospects of showing that the conflict was *merely* prima facie.[10]

Turning next to external criticism of Wittgenstein's incorporation of levels (4) and (5) into his concept of use and hence of meaning: If the points made above were correct, then incorporating enduring social practice into the concept of meaning would certainly involve a good deal of *violence to our everyday linguistic intuitions*. In this case, though—in contrast to the case of smoothness in the regulation of factual claims, for example—there seems to be at least some hope that a *justification* for the violence might be forthcoming, namely in the form of the rule-following argument, modified à la Kripke. However, whether such a justification can really work is another matter, and I am skeptical that it can.

There are several potential points of vulnerability in the Wittgenstein-Kripke argument. One of these lies in the weakness of its case against the possibility that grasping a rule or understanding a meaning is something potentially achievable by a solitary individual, perhaps even an instantaneous one, but radically *sui generis*.[11]

My own reservations instead stem mainly from an intuition that neither Wittgenstein nor Kripke has done justice to the alternative suggestion, which they both consider but reject, that grasping a rule, or understanding a meaning, consists in having—potentially individual, and potentially even instantaneous—*dispositions*.

More specifically, their objections to this suggestion seem to me to rest on various misunderstandings of the concept of a disposition, albeit misunderstandings which are contrary in nature (Wittgenstein's involving an unacceptably crude realism about dispositions, whereas Kripke's involve an implausible anti-realism about them). This is a large and difficult topic which can only be touched on here, but the following points seem to me important.

Wittgenstein himself raises the dispositional suggestion in connection with the rule-following argument, but rejects it, as follows: "If one says that knowing the ABC is a state of the mind, one is thinking of a state of a mental apparatus (perhaps of the brain) by means of which we explain the *manifestations* of that knowledge. Such a state is called a disposition. But there are objections to speaking of a state of mind here, inasmuch as there ought to be two different criteria for such a state: a knowledge of the construction of the apparatus, quite apart from what it does" (PI, #149; cf. WLC, pp. 91–92; BT, p. 109).

This passage is not easy to interpret. One fundamental feature of it which is clear, though, is that it involves a certain realist assumption about dispositions, namely that the concept of a disposition essentially refers not only to characteristic behavior (whether actual or counterfactual) but also to a state producing it. Thus Wittgenstein implies here that to identify knowing the ABC with a disposition would be to identify it with a state of the brain or of a (putative) mental apparatus.[12] This realist assumption about dispositions, while certainly controversial, seems very plausible to me, and it is not on this score that I would find fault with Wittgenstein's dismissal of the dispositional suggestion.

What is Wittgenstein's case for rejecting the dispositional suggestion? One point which he seems to have in mind is an epistemic one along roughly the following lines: For the reason just mentioned, to identify knowing the ABC—or analogously, grasping a rule, or understanding a meaning—with a disposition would be to identify it with some state of the brain or of a (putative) mental apparatus. Now, we often know that someone knows the ABC—or grasps a rule, or understands a meaning. But it seems that all that we really know about in this area is his behavior, not states of his brain or (putative) mental apparatus. For, where knowledge of *other* people is concerned, surely all one really knows about them is their behavior, and where *self*-knowledge is concerned, according to Wittgenstein's distinctive account of first-person psychological reports these do not in fact express knowledge at all (PI, #246). So when we know that someone knows the ABC—or grasps a rule, or understands a meaning—this must in fact be knowledge concerning his behavior, not knowledge of some state of his brain or (putative) mental apparatus.

This point does not seem very compelling, however. For one thing, Wittgenstein's unusual theory that first-person psychological reports do not express knowledge seems quite questionable; perhaps they do express knowledge after all, and in particular knowledge of what are in fact brain states or states of a mental apparatus (whether or not they are known *as* such). For another thing, even if Wittgenstein were right that no such direct knowledge of brain states or states of a (putative) mental apparatus is available, might there not still be *indirect* knowledge of them? If not knowledge by acquaintance, then why not knowledge by description? In particular, might one not know of their presence under some such description as "the state which produces this pattern of behavior"?[13]

But Wittgenstein also has a subtler point in mind in the passage quoted, albeit one which in the end again fails. His subtler point again begins from the assumption that to identify knowing the ABC—or grasping a rule, or understanding a meaning—with a disposition would be to identify it with a state of the brain or of a (putative) mental apparatus. But the objection is now that this would conflict with the close conceptual ties which knowing the ABC—or grasping a rule, or understanding a meaning—has to characteristic (linguistic) behavior: Such an identification would force one to say, falsely, that in possible worlds in which the state in question occurred but (say, due to different natural laws obtaining) the wrong sort of behavior happened, knowing the ABC—or grasping the rule, or understanding the meaning—nonetheless took place; and conversely, it would force one to say, again falsely, that in possible worlds in which the right sort of behavior occurred but (say, again due to different natural laws obtaining) the state in question was absent, knowing the ABC—or grasping the rule, or understanding the meaning—did not take place.

However, this subtler point is still objectionable. First, to the extent that it assumes that characteristic behavior *alone* is sufficient to constitute knowing the ABC—or grasping a rule, or understanding a meaning—so that a possible world in which such behavior occurred but there simply was no producing state would still be a possible world in which knowing the ABC—or grasping the rule, or understanding the meaning—took place, it seems vulnerable to a strong contrary intuition that there is a difference between merely exhibiting the behavior characteristic of knowing the ABC—or grasping a rule, or understanding a meaning—and *really* doing so.

Second, this subtler point assumes that if the concept of a disposition involves realist reference to a state or states, it must therefore also (i) pick out the state(s) in question *rigidly* (to use Kripke's term), i.e., pick out the same state(s) in all possible worlds, and (ii) by contrast involve only *contingent* reference to characteristic behavior. But these are both non sequiturs. For it is quite consistent, and more plausible, to suppose that, while the concept of a disposition does indeed refer in a realist manner to a state or states, the state(s) in question is (are) picked out *non*-rigidly, whereas by contrast the reference to characteristic behavior is *necessary*: more specifically, that the concept of a disposition to X is the concept of "the state(s) apt to produce X-ing" (where this definite description should be construed non-rigidly, as is usual with definite descriptions).

Kripke's case against equating the grasp of a rule or the understanding of a meaning with a disposition is quite different, indeed quite contrary in spirit—but no more convincing. He raises two main objections.

First, he objects that the concept of a disposition could not account for the normativity of meaning: the notion of grasping a rule or understanding a meaning essentially allows for the possibility of a (systematic) *discrepancy* between the subject's grasp or understanding, on the one hand, and his actual (linguistic) behavior, on the other, whereas the concept of a disposition does not allow for any such (systematic) discrepancy.[14]

However, it seems to me that, on the contrary, it is in fact an essential part of our concept of a disposition to X—or of a state apt to produce X-ing—that (systematic) non-manifestation of the behavior which is typical of the disposition is perfectly consistent with nonetheless having the disposition, just so long as one of an (indefinitely large and collectively unspeciable, but severally recognizable) set of possible explanatory-excusing conditions is realized. This essential feature of dispositional concepts is evident even in the case of such mundane physical dispositions as salt's solubility in water. For example, a particular piece of salt may (systematically) fail to dissolve when put in water because it happens to be coated with a thin plastic film, but nonetheless still be water-soluble.[15]

To put this point in a slightly different way which serves to reveal the likely source of Kripke's error, we need to distinguish (as Kripke does not) between two different senses in which a notion of "characteristic behavior" applies to dispositional concepts: "characteristic behavior" in the sense of behavior *typical* of the disposition, for example, in the case of salt's water-solubility, salt's actually dissolving when put in water; and "characteristic behavior" in the sense of behavior *consistent* with the disposition, which in the case of salt's water-solubility would include not only salt's actually dissolving when put in water but also such things as its failing to do so when appropriate explanatory-excusing conditions are present, such as the thin plastic coating.[16] It is only the latter sort of "characteristic behavior" that must occur in order for a disposition to be present, not the former.

Consequently, the concept of a disposition, far from excluding, precisely includes the sort of possibility of (systematic) discrepancy that Kripke rightly takes to be essential to grasping rules or understanding meanings. Far from being an embarrassment for the dispositional theory, therefore, the normativity of grasping rules and understanding meanings, and the possibility of (systematic) discrepancy which this essentially involves, on closer inspection look like a strong argument in *favor* of the theory.

Kripke's second objection is that whereas grasping rules and understanding meanings involve a certain sort of infinitude—for example, my understanding of the function " + 1" essentially encompasses an infinite number of argument-value pairings, many of which are much larger than any that I ever will or could consider—our dispositions, by contrast, are merely finite—for example, proceeding along the series of larger and larger argument-value pairings for " + 1," at some point I will cease to have a disposition to give the correct pairing, and will instead be disposed to give up, or die, or whatnot.[17]

However, it seems not in fact to follow from the circumstance that a person or thing is subject to the sorts of mental or physical limitations to which Kripke appeals here, that the person's or thing's dispositions must therefore be similarly finite, as Kripke takes it to. Even in the case of mere physical things, one can at least imagine having good reason to attribute an infinite disposition to a thing despite knowing that it will at some point in fact fail to realize the infinite performance in question due to encountering obstacles of some sort or due to only existing for a finite length of time, namely insofar as one can identify a mechanism in the thing which *would* produce the infinite performance in question if the obstacles were removed and the thing went on existing. In such a case, the obstacles and the finite duration of the thing would in effect be treated as just more explanatory-excusing conditions.

Imagine, for example, that we were to discover that nature itself produced physical "counting machines" with mechanisms which on inspection appeared apt for printing out the whole sequence of the positive integers in order in decimal notation (or, to be more exact, for doing something that was physically indistinguishable from that), but that we also knew that these "counting machines" would at some point meet such obstacles as running out of material to print on and that they would be subject to normal wear and tear and therefore of only finite duration. Might we not nonetheless indeed reasonably ascribe to them dispositions to print out the whole sequence of the positive integers in order in decimal notation (or rather, to do something that was physically indistinguishable from that)?

Or, lest it be suspected that the infinitary character of rule-following and understanding is somehow being illicitly smuggled into such an example rather than accounted for by it (I take that not in fact to be the case), consider the following slightly less fanciful example. (Assuming, for the sake of the example, Newtonian physics but minus the complication of strictly *universal* gravitation,) although we could no doubt say with a high degree of certainty that any object which was presently moving through space at uniform velocity in a straight line and with no force impinging upon it would at some point or other become subject to a force which caused it to change speed, change direction, be destroyed, or some combination of these things (namely, when it came into proximity to, or collided with, other objects in space), it does not seem that this fact would preclude our truly ascribing to such an object, in accordance with the law of inertia, a *disposition* to continue moving with uniform velocity in a straight line forever.[18]

In short, both of Kripke's main arguments against the dispositional theory seem to fail on closer inspection.[19]

Another potential Achilles' heel in the rule-following argument, modified à la Kripke, is that even if there *were* the sort of problem with the conception of individualistic and instantaneous rule-following or understanding which the argument alleges there to be, it seems doubtful that an appeal to enduring social practice could provide any sort of solution to it.[20] But since the thrust of the above considerations has been that there is no such problem in the first place, we may perhaps spare ourselves the task of pursuing this further potential line of criticism here.

Because the rule-following argument, modified à la Kripke, thus fails, it seems likely that in the end an external criticism analogous to, albeit more circuitous than, that leveled earlier against incorporating smoothness in regulating factual claims into the very concept of meaning (as applied to grammatical principles) will apply against incorporating enduring social practice into the very concept of meaning as well: not only would such an incorporation involve significant violence to our everyday linguistic intuitions concerning meaning, but in addition the violence in question would lack any compelling *justification*.

The above criticisms of the rule-following argument undercut the component of Wittgenstein's non-arbitrariness thesis which depicts conformity to social practices and traditions as essential to the very meaningfulness of a person's employment of grammatical sentences.

However, Wittgenstein's non-arbitrariness thesis could still legitimately and plausibly appeal to the *weaker* version of his conception that social practices and traditions constitute a constraint on the arbitrariness of grammar (discussed near the start of chapter 3): the simple claim that our adoption of grammatical principles is normatively and causally constrained by our social practices and traditions (much as our adoption of ethical or aesthetic norms is, for example).

PART TWO

The Diversity Thesis

5

Alternative Grammars? The Case of Formal Logic

THE FINAL CHAPTERS of this essay—chapters 5, 6, and 7—will address some issues which arise in connection with the first component of the doctrine that grammar is in a sense arbitrary: the thesis that for every grammatical principle in every area of the grammar that constitutes our "true-false games," alternative but in some degree similar grammatical principles, and hence alternative but in some degree similar concepts, either actually exist or are at least possible and conceivable (the "diversity thesis").

The diversity thesis is fundamental to Wittgenstein's position concerning the arbitrariness of grammar. If it were removed, the remaining components of his doctrine that grammar is in a sense arbitrary and the various components of his doctrine that it is in a sense non-arbitrary would at least take on very different characters (a fact which the reader can easily verify by reviewing them).

Up to this point I have argued without much qualification that the Williams-Lear reading of Wittgenstein's position, which attributes to him a denial of the diversity thesis (or perhaps, rather, a denial of its intelligibility), is diametrically opposed to his official intentions. I believe this to be true. However, as I hinted earlier, somewhat more could be said on behalf of the Williams-Lear reading than they themselves find to say on its behalf or than we have yet seen. For Wittgenstein's commitment to the diversity thesis at least seems to be jeopardized by a number of further features of his position. Chapters 5, 6, and 7 will identify and consider three such features. I hope to show, though, that in the end they do not really undercut the diversity thesis either exegetically or philosophically.

It will be recalled that the later Wittgenstein's diversity thesis centrally includes the case of formal logic, and that in this connection he advocates, for example, the possibility of a logic which lacks the law of double-negation elimination and even a logic which disregards the law of contradiction.

However, the early Wittgenstein of the *Tractatus* had argued that it was impossible for propositions, language, or thought to violate classical logic (T, 3–3.032, 3.1).[1] And he had implied (albeit obscurely) an argument of roughly the following sort in support of that position: All of the classical logical truth-functions ("not," "and," etc.) are in a sense internal to each proposition (for example, each proposition essentially contains the possibility of being negated), and conformity to all of the classical logical laws and rules of inference is in turn internal to the truth-functions (for example, respecting the law of double-negation elimination, or inferring p from $\sim\sim p$, is internal to negation), so that conformity to all of the classical logical laws and rules of inference is ultimately internal to any given proposition (T, 3.42, 5.44, 5.47, 5.4731, 5.5151, 6.124; N, pp. 15, 27, 29, 31–32, 36, 94, 118).[2]

Similarly (and this is the crucial point for our present purposes), the later Wittgenstein often seems to continue to imply that if a form of words is properly to be described as a proposition, a part of language, or an expression of thought at all, then it *must* be used in conformity with classical logical laws and rules of inference. Consider, for example, the following statements from the *Remarks on the Foundations of Mathematics*: "Logic . . . shows us what we understand by 'proposition' and by 'language'" (RFM, I, #134; cf. WLC, p. 140); "The propositions of logic are 'laws of thought,' 'because they bring out the essence of human thinking'—to put it more correctly: because they bring out, or show, the essence, the technique of thinking. They show what thinking is" (RFM, I, #133; cf. #116, #131); "The reason why [logical inferences] are not brought into question is not that they 'certainly correspond to the truth'—or something of the sort—no, it is just this that is called 'thinking,' 'speaking,' 'inferring,' 'arguing'" (RFM, I, #156; cf. #116).

And similarly again, the later Wittgenstein often seems to continue to imply an argument for this position like his earlier one. Thus he argues that it belongs to the very essence of propositions that the truth-functions ("not," "and," etc.) apply to them: "We call something a proposition when *in our language* we apply the calculus of truth-functions to it" (PI, #136; cf. PG, I, appendix 5; BT, pp. 63, 85). And he also implies that applying the truth-functions to propositions essentially involves using the latter in conformity with classical logical laws and rules of inference. For instance, he writes: "Not letting a contradiction stand is something that characterizes the technique of our employment of our truth-functions. If we do let the contradiction stand in our language-games, we alter that technique—as, if we departed from regarding a double negative as an affirmative" (RFM, VII, #27; cf. #30).[3]

To illustrate this general argument with a specific example: As the first passage quoted in the previous paragraph implies in context, propositionality essentially involves a possibility of negation (PI, #136: "We have: 'p' is true = p; 'p' is false = not-p. And to say that a proposition is whatever can be true or false amounts to saying: we call something a proposition when *in our language* we apply the calculus of truth-functions to it"). But Wittgenstein also goes on to argue in the same work that conformity to the law of double-negation elimination is internal to negation (PI, p. 147: "It looks as if it followed from the nature of negation that a double negative is an affirmative. (And there is something right about this . . .)").

Not surprisingly, therefore, a number of recent commentators—including Gordon Baker and Peter Hacker, James Conant, and David Cerbone—have taken such a position to be the later Wittgenstein's bottom line concerning logic.[4]

But this position of Wittgenstein's, first embraced in his

early period and then apparently retained in his later period as well, seems to entail that it must, after all, be *false* to suppose, as the diversity thesis does, that there could be alternatives to the classical logical laws and inferences. For, to the extent that any form of words had the appearance of articulating such an alternative, or of being used in conformity with such an alternative, it would ipso facto constitute no proposition, fail to be language, and express no thought.

Accordingly, one of the recent commentators just mentioned—Cerbone—has attempted to read the later Wittgenstein's apparent imaginary examples of logical deviance as ones which are in fact ultimately intended to lead to the moral that the very notion of such deviance is implicitly incoherent (in effect, as though they worked on the same model as the "soulless tribe" example discussed earlier).[5]

Nor would conclusions of this sort be restricted to the case of formal logic. For the later Wittgenstein also at points seems to imply a similar position concerning mathematics. For instance, in the *Lectures on the Foundations of Mathematics, Cambridge 1939*, immediately after articulating a version of the position concerning logic described above, he goes on to draw the following comparison with his imaginary example of people who sell wood at a price proportionate to the area that it happens to cover: "Think of the case where people have a queer way of calculating a price for the wood: we might not be inclined to call it calculation at all" (LFM, p. 214; cf. RFM, III, #83).

Wittgenstein also hints at an argument for this position concerning mathematics that is closely analogous to his argument in the logical case: Such concepts as, for example, that of *quantity* belong to the very essence of calculation, but possessing them requires a large measure of conformity to standard mathematical practice (see, for example, RFM, I, #143–50; PI, pp. 226–27).

Once again, this position seems to entail that it must after all be false to suppose, as the diversity thesis does, that there could be alternatives to standard mathematics.

Accordingly, Cerbone has attempted to read the later Wittgenstein's apparent examples of mathematical deviance in the same way as he attempts to read his apparent examples of logical deviance: as ultimately in fact intended to lead to the moral that the very notion of mathematical deviance is implicitly incoherent.[6]

There is thus a prima facie threat to the diversity thesis here—certainly, to its attribution to the later Wittgenstein, and perhaps also to its philosophical viability. And this threat extends beyond the case of formal logic to encompass that of mathematics as well.

It is possible that the later Wittgenstein does on occasion incline to positions of the sort in question as his bottom line (the ambiguous nature of his later writings makes this not altogether unlikely). However, I think that his considered positions on formal logic and mathematics are—and moreover, rightly are—in a sharply contrary spirit, and consistent with his commitment to the diversity thesis in its full force.

A first clue that his considered positions cannot be as the above may have suggested can be seen from the fact that Cerbone's reading of his intentions with his examples of logical and mathematical deviance is clearly untenable as exegesis. Pace Cerbone, it is quite clear from Wittgenstein's discussion of the wood-sellers, and of the analogous case of logical aliens, at *Remarks on the Foundations of Mathematics*, I, #143–52 (and again at *Lectures on the Foundations of Mathematics, Cambridge 1939*, pp. 202–4) that although he believes that the wood-sellers' concepts are different from ours; that what they do is not quite what we call paying, calculating, etc.; and even that we do not literally understand them—and correspondingly in the case of logical aliens: that the logical aliens' concepts are different from ours; that what they do is not quite what we call thinking; and that we do not literally understand them—*he nonetheless believes that they are engaging in genuine alternative practices*. His bottom line about the wood-sellers in the text is: "We should presumably say in this case: they simply do not mean the same by 'a lot of wood' and 'a little wood' as we do; and they have a quite different system of payment from us" (RFM, I, #150). It is *not* that they do not mean anything and have no system at all.

The same exegetical point applies to Wittgenstein's other examples of mathematical and logical deviance as well. For example, his bottom line concerning the imaginary example of people who (roughly speaking) measure with elastic rulers is that "what is here called 'measuring' and 'length' and 'equal length,' is something different from what we call those things. The use of these words is different from ours, but it is *akin* to it" (RFM, I, #5). He does *not* say, imply, or even leave open as a possibility that it is a non-use, a mere illusion of a use.

Similarly, when he considers the imaginary example of people who (roughly speaking) believe that "twice two [is] five," he indeed implies that they would not mean by these words quite what we mean by them, that what they were doing would not strictly speaking be what we call calculating, and perhaps even that we would not literally understand them; but *he also implies that they nonetheless have a genuine alternative practice*. Thus the example (which in this case is short enough to quote in full) reads as follows: "But what would *this* mean: 'Even though everybody believed that twice two was five it would still be four'?—For what would it be like for everybody to believe that? [The context which precedes this passage on the page shows that Wittgenstein's main point here is that such a change in people's judgments would also entail a change in the meanings of the words involved.]—Well, I could imagine, for instance, that people had a different calculus, or a technique which we should not call 'calculating.' But would it be *wrong*? (Is a coronation *wrong*? To beings different from ourselves it might look extremely odd.)" (PI, pp. 226–27).

The same exegetical point applies to the logical example of people who do not accord a double negation its usual meaning, instead treating it either as meaningless or as equivalent in meaning to a single negation: Wittgenstein initially presents this example as an illustration of the fact that "we can easily imagine human beings with a 'more primitive' logic, in which [there is] something corresponding to our negation"

(PI, #554), and he neither states nor implies any retraction of this characterization in the course of the example (for instance, along the lines of saying that the people in question did *not* have a more primitive logic or anything corresponding to our negation after all).

Noting this feature of the texts should prompt us to reconsider the later Wittgenstein's apparent positions that classical logic is internal to propositions, language, and thought, and standard mathematical practice to calculation. For if such positions really were his bottom line, then one *would* expect a reading of his imaginary examples of logical and mathematical deviancy like Cerbone's to be right. (From now on, I shall focus mainly on the case of formal logic, but most of the points I will be making would have close analogues for the mathematical case as well.)

It is perhaps worth beginning with a historical point. The secondary literature which sees the position that classical logic is internal to thought, etc. as the later Wittgenstein's bottom line usually also implies that this position is a recent invention—due originally to Kant,[7] or even to Wittgenstein himself.[8] Nothing could be further from the truth, however. In fact, this position concerning the nature of classical logic is the oldest of the old, virtually coeval with the invention of formal logic itself. For it was Aristotle who first introduced it, namely in *Metaphysics*, book gamma, where he argued in defense of the law of contradiction that (1) it is impossible to believe contradictions true, and moreover (2) in order to mean or understand anything one must believe the truth of the law of contradiction (and where he then went on to sketch more briefly and cryptically what is probably intended to be a similar argument in support of the law of excluded middle). Such a position has continued to be popular in the modern period as well. In particular, Kant did indeed embrace a version of it (as was mentioned in chapter 1), and so too did the early Wittgenstein (as we saw above).[9]

Now, as I implied earlier, it is possible that, like the early Wittgenstein before him, the later Wittgenstein was occasionally tempted to continue with a version of this old position on the nature of formal logic as his bottom line. However, in his more considered reflections on the subject he instead makes it a *target*, developing at least two forceful lines of counterargument which aim to *deflate* it. (As he formulates them, these two lines of counterargument are somewhat at odds with each other, and the second of them is moreover presented in two somewhat inconsistent versions. But with a dash of interpretive charity they can be united into a single consistent and cogent contrary position.)

In short, the later Wittgenstein, far from being a champion of a new conception of logic here, is really a subverter of the oldest of the old.[10]

Wittgenstein's most prominent line of deflating counterargument aims to prevent the putative internality of classical logic to propositions, language, and thought from undermining his diversity thesis as applied to logic by arguing, in effect, that even if classical logic *is* internal to propositions, language, and thought, people might still very well reject it and embrace alternative logical principles, namely by doing *something like* expressing propositions, using language, and thinking. This is the moral that we are supposed to draw from his suggestion that even if adherence to the law of contradiction is essential to propositionality, it might still be possible to accept Russell's paradox, namely through recourse to something supra-propositional: "Why should Russell's contradiction not be conceived as *something supra-propositional*, something that towers above the propositions and looks in both directions like a Janus head?" (RFM, IV, #59; emphasis added).[11]

An analogous point concerning the mathematical case lies behind the remark which we recently saw Wittgenstein make in connection with his imaginary example of a deviant mathematics in which (roughly speaking) people believe that twice two is five, "I could imagine . . . that people had a different calculus, or a technique which we should not call 'calculating.' But would it be *wrong?*" (PI, pp. 226–27); behind his statement that we can "imagine a human society in which calculating quite in our sense does not exist" (RFM, VII, #19); and behind his remark, "It is a good way of putting things to say: 'this order . . . is unknown to this calculus, but not to that one.' What if one said: 'A calculus to which this order is unknown is not really a calculus'? (An office system to which this order is unknown is not really an office system.) It is—I should like to say—for practical, not for theoretical purposes, that the disorder is avoided" (RFM, III, #83).

This line of deflatory counterargument shows that even if the passages quoted earlier in which Wittgenstein implies the internality of classical logic to propositions, language, and thought express his real position, that position does not in his view require any real taming of the diversity thesis in application to logic.

It also suggests, however, that the diversity thesis needs to be interpreted in a way which we might not at first have anticipated: its point is not *simply* that alternative grammatical principles and concepts are always possible if not actual, but rather that alternative grammatical principles and concepts *or things relevantly like them* are always possible if not actual. This no doubt introduces an element of vagueness into the thesis (for what constitutes *relevant* similarity?). However, Wittgenstein's sympathetic treatment of vagueness in the *Philosophical Investigations* and elsewhere shows that he would not consider that to be in itself a vice. And such a position may be reasonable. Moreover, he could fairly claim to have shown with *sufficient* clarity what would and what would not count here by means of the many real and imaginary examples which he has provided.

It is a natural extension of this line of deflating counterargument to add that if we were to find people rejecting classical logic and yet still doing *something like* expressing propositions, using language, and thinking, then our concepts of "proposition," "language," and "thought" could be changed in such a way as to cover the activities of these people as well as the activities which already fall under them (concepts like "grammar" and "concept" being changed correspondingly, so that it became possible to restate the diversity thesis in its original simple verbal form and now have it apply to what these people did).

Thus in the *Philosophical Grammar* Wittgenstein remarks on
cases in which a change in practice may "broaden (alter) the
concept of language" (PG, I, #71). And note that one does not
have to read his assertion that "logic . . . shows us what we
understand by 'proposition' and by 'language'" (RFM, I,
#134) with the emphasis on "proposition" and "language,"
but may instead read it with the emphasis on "we."

This ready possibility that we might modify our current
concepts of "proposition," "language," and "thought" in
response to encountering deviant logical practices which,
though not strictly examples of, are nonetheless relevantly
similar to, what we currently call propositions, language, and
thought, in order to have the concepts in question cover those
practices as well, is part of Wittgenstein's point when he says
of a certain contradictory statement, "If the question is
whether this is a statement at all, I reply: You may say that it's
not a statement. Or you may say it *is* a statement, but a useless one" (LFM, p. 209; cf. pp. 230–31, for a similar remark
concerning "calculation"); when he argues concerning a violation of the law of excluded middle or bivalence, "One may
. . . very well say that the proposition 'If . . . then . . .' is
either true, or false, or undecided . . . One treats the matter
under these three headings. I divide the field of possibilities
into three parts. It will perhaps now be said: a *proposition*
divides into *two* parts. But why? Unless that is part of the
definition of a proposition. Why shouldn't I also call something a proposition that makes a threefold division?" (RPP1,
#272); and when he refers to our "alter[ing] the form of our
thinking, so as to alter what we call 'thinking'" (RFM, IV,
#29).

Note that this first line of deflating counterargument thus
not only aims to defend the diversity thesis but also (non-
essentially) invokes a specific application of it, namely to such
concepts as "proposition," "language," and "thought."

Another, less prominent but no less important, line of deflating counterargument is found in a set of remarks which show
that Wittgenstein is really far more skeptical that classical
logic is internal to our usual concepts of "proposition," "lan-

guage," and "thought" than the passages quoted at the start of this chapter may have suggested.

In this connection, consider again the passages recently quoted in which he says of a certain contradictory utterance, "You may say it's not a statement. Or you may say it *is* a statement," and of treating a proposition as having three possible values (true, false, and undecided) instead of the usual two, "It will perhaps now be said: a *proposition* divides into two parts. But why? Unless that is part of the definition of a proposition. Why shouldn't I also call something a proposition that makes a threefold division?" For, in addition to implying the point mentioned above that it is possible to revise such concepts as "proposition" from excluding to accommodating classical illogicality, these passages also imply (in tension, but perhaps not inconsistency, with that) that it is indeterminate *now* whether such concepts exclude or accommodate classical illogicality. One also gets a strong hint of this sort of skepticism from the following passage in the *Remarks on the Foundations of Mathematics*, where, after articulating the doctrine of internality, Wittgenstein goes on to deflate it in a certain way: "'Then according to you everybody could continue the series as he likes; and so infer *any*how!' . . . If you say that, while he may indeed *say* it, still he can't *think* it, then I am only saying that that means, not: try as he may he can't think it, but: it is for us an essential part of 'thinking' that—in talking, writing, etc.—he makes *this sort* of transition. And I say further that the line between what we include in 'thinking' and what we no longer include in 'thinking' is no more a hard and fast one than the line between what is still and what is no longer called 'regularity'" (RFM, I, #116). His position in such passages as these seems to be that there is really no clear fact of the matter as to whether or not classical logic is internal to propositionality, language, and thought—that this is a grey area. Thus he also says at one point: "You may say that logic gives you some of the most important characteristics of what's called thinking, . . . etc. And there is no clearcut distinction; there are things which we should not know whether or not to call calculating or thinking" (LFM, p. 231).

But Wittgenstein also sometimes embraces an even stronger (and strictly speaking incompatible) form of skeptical deflation of the doctrine that classical logic is internal to thought, implying that even in the case of the law of contradiction (and, one may reasonably infer, therefore in the cases of other classical laws and inferences as well) there really is no internality to thought. Consider, for example, the following exchange in *Wittgenstein's Lectures on Philosophical Psychology 1946–47*: "[*Norman*] *Malcolm*: Suppose that [Smith] always said self-contradictory things . . . Would you take that as a test that he had wrongly represented his thought? *Wittgenstein*: On what evidence? On the ground that most people who said that didn't think it, i.e. is the proposition contingent? . . . Or on the ground that they can't think that? But they *can*" (WLPP, p. 248).

It seems to me that even this stronger skeptical deflation of the doctrine that classical logic is internal to thought is probably justified—even for the law of contradiction, and certainly therefore for other classical laws and inferences as well. Let me make a few observations in support of such a view.

To begin with, it is important to emphasize, especially in light of the heavy weight of tradition behind the doctrine and the contrary assumption which this can create, that the doctrine has very little *prima facie* plausibility, even in the case of the law of contradiction. This remains true even when one has set aside cases of merely *implicit* self-contradiction, and instead focused exclusively on *explicit* self-contradictions (as the doctrine no doubt intends). Consider, for instance, the sorts of explicit rejections of and deviations from the law of contradiction which we find in philosophers such as Heraclitus, Plato, and Engels. Prephilosophically, we are surely quite strongly inclined to say that these are examples of logically inconsistent *thoughts* (not non-thoughts)—no doubt ill justified, false, indeed necessarily false thoughts, but *thoughts* nonetheless.[12]

Nor is this point significantly weakened by noting, as Hilary Putnam does,[13] that one can draw a distinction between the meaningfulness of an illogical utterance and its expressing a thought, and can therefore concede the former while denying the latter. Assuming, as seems plausible, that such a distinction can indeed in principle be drawn, a move of this sort would certainly give our commonsense intuitions about the cases in question here *some* of what they want, but surely not *all* of it. For example, when Plato in the *Republic* tells us in some detail that and how appearances have contradictory properties, we prephilosophically want to say that he is expressing not just words with meanings but also contradictory *thoughts* (albeit no doubt poorly justified, false, and indeed necessarily false ones). This contrasts sharply with certain *other* types of utterances which really *do* lend themselves plausibly to the sort of compromise description that Putnam is advocating—for instance, to borrow an example of Wittgenstein's from another context, "Mr. S. came to today's redness."

It would therefore require some sort of non-obvious, compelling *argument* in order to establish the doctrine in question in the face of our contrary prephilosophical intuitions. But, while the doctrine's champions have certainly offered arguments from time to time, these invariably prove to be unconvincing upon inspection.

Consider, for instance, Aristotle's case for his claims that (1) it is impossible to believe contradictions true, and moreover (2) in order to mean or understand anything, one must believe the truth of the law of contradiction.[14]

Aristotle's general strategy seems to be to argue at length for (1), and then infer (2) more or less directly from his case for (1). The latter step may seem very problematic at first sight. One apparent problem with it concerns its shift to speaking of conditions of *meaning or understanding*. However, this problem is addressed by some of the specific details of Aristotle's case for (1) (see below). Another apparent problem with it concerns the appearance of a crass non sequitur in inferring from people's inability to believe contradictions to their having to believe the law of contradiction.[15] However, such an inference does not seem unreasonable if, as is likely, what Aristotle has in mind in (2) is *implicit* belief in the law of contradiction. For a person's consistent inability to believe any contradictions, as affirmed by (1), might indeed reasonably be taken to show that he has (or perhaps even that he must have) an implicit belief in the law of contradiction. Also, even without (2), (1) would by itself constitute a strong case for the law of contradiction being in a sense internal to thought. So, in short, we may focus on Aristotle's case for (1).

Aristotle has two main arguments for (1), both of which, however, are deeply problematic. First, he argues that beliefs in two contradictory sentences are themselves contrary properties of a person and therefore cannot both belong to a person at the same time (1005b26–32). But this argument just begs the original question, which is in effect precisely whether or not such beliefs *are* contrary properties of a person.[16]

Second, Aristotle argues (roughly) that in order to mean anything by one's words, and hence in order to think—or as he also vividly puts it, in order to avoid being "like a vegetable"—one must signify a subject, a (type of) substance, which requires that one signify some *one* thing, by which he means the essence of a (type of) substance, for example in the case of the subject "man" "two-footed animal," but that one would *fail* to signify one thing to the extent that one also signified the negation of the thing in question, for example "not a two-footed animal" (1006a11–1007a35).

But this argument is again deeply problematic. A somewhat tempting line of objection is that it implicitly assumes a highly questionable philosophy of language and metaphysics, including theses to the effect that all meaning and thought must ultimately refer to subjects, or substances, that all substances have essences, that in order to refer to subjects or substances one has to signify their essences, and so on. However, this sort of objection could perhaps be addressed by recasting the argument more simply and plausibly in terms of the attractive thesis that understanding any word requires having certain unequivocal analytic beliefs connected with it (for example, understanding the word "bachelor" requires having an unequivocal belief that all bachelors are unmarried), so that to the extent that one undermined one's claim to possess such unequivocal beliefs by also believing opposites (for example, that it is not true that all bachelors are unmarried) one would ipso facto also undermine one's claim to understand words.

A deeper problem with the argument (either in its original or in this reconstructed version) is the following different and more glaring one: Even if the argument were as successful as possible, it would only show that in order to mean or think anything, a person must have *some* beliefs which are not contradictory. But this would fall far short of establishing (1), which says that a person cannot believe *any* contradictions (and would provide no basis at all for inferring (2) either).

What about Kant, the man whom some of the secondary literature mistakenly touts as the inventor of the doctrine of internality? Kant certainly does embrace the doctrine. For example, he writes in the *Critique of Pure Reason* that formal logic "contains the absolutely necessary rules of thought without which there can be no employment whatever of the understanding" (A 52/B 76). However, so far from being its inventor, he merely takes it over uncritically and carelessly from the tradition which Aristotle had inaugurated, neither clearly recalling Aristotle's position and case nor substituting anything better of his own. This can be seen from the following facts: First, Kant leaves it unclear whether he is committing himself only to versions of Aristotle's conclusion (1) or also to versions of Aristotle's conclusion (2). Second, Kant neither recalls Aristotle's arguments for (1) and (2) nor substitutes for them any argument of his own, let alone any better argument, instead simply advancing whichever of these principles he means to advance as a sheer dogma. Third, as was mentioned in chapter 1, Kant's commitment to this doctrine is largely motivated by an assumption that modal facts, including the necessities of formal logic, must ultimately be reducible to non-modal ones, to actualities (an assumption which is most explicit in his precritical essay *The Only Possible Proof of God's Existence*, and which is visible in his critical explanations of the other two types of necessity that he recognizes: analytic necessity consists in *the containment of a predicate-concept in a subject-concept*, synthetic a priori necessity in *the idealist fact of mind-imposition*). What non-modal fact constitutes the necessity of the principles of formal logic? Answer: Their being constitutive of the very nature of thought. However, there is an obvious problem here which Kant overlooks, namely that this explanation *itself implicitly includes a modal claim*: as he himself puts it in the above quotation, "there *can* be no . . ." Indeed, the explanation *must* do so in order to avoid collapsing into a type of psychologism about logic that he himself strongly opposes. This shows that the explanation cannot as it stands satisfy the aforementioned assumption which motivated offering such an explanation in the first place. It also suggests that in order to solve this problem Kant would have had to arrive at some conclusions which would at the very least have greatly surprised him. For, obviously enough, the solution cannot be that the residual necessity in question is *logical* necessity. But nor would Kant be at all inclined to classify it as *synthetic a priori* necessity (since, for one thing, this would deprive formal logic of its validity for *all* thought, not just human[-like] thought, given that Kant always explains synthetic a priori necessity in terms of the imposition of the principles involved by *minds like ours*). And so the only plausible tack for him to have taken would have been to say that it was an *analytic* necessity grounded in truth-in-virtue-of-meaning, or the containment of a predicate-concept by a subject-concept—in other words, to say that it was a necessity constituted by the fact (roughly) that the subject-concept "thought" implicitly contains the predicate-concept "conforms to classical logical principles."[17] But saying this would have amounted to conceding to analyticity (in the sense of truth-in-virtue-of-meaning, or the containment of a predicate-concept by a subject-concept) a sort of primacy over logic which would at least have greatly surprised Kant (who commonly, rather, seeks to explain analyticity in terms of logic, specifically in terms of the law of contradiction).[18]

What about Wittgenstein's own argument in terms of the meanings of the truth-functions (sketched earlier in this chapter)? In the end, this argument fails too, it seems to me. Certainly, its second step—the step which states that (apparent) violation of or opposition to classical logical laws and inferences would undermine the usual meanings of the truth-functions—is a very plausible one.[19] But this would only show that violation of or opposition to classical laws and inferences entailed either the meaninglessness of the truth-functions *or a change in their meanings*—it would not show that it entailed their meaninglessness *simpliciter*. Indeed, Wittgenstein in the *Philosophical Investigations* himself implies just that: "If we change the rules [governing the word 'not'], it now has another meaning (or none)" (PI, p. 147). So if we were to reach the desired conclusion, we really would need the first step of the argument as well, the claim that "we call something a proposition when . . . we apply the calculus of truth-functions to it"—which, of course, in order for the argument to work, would have to mean: we *only* call something a proposition when we apply the calculus of truth-functions to it *in their usual, classical meanings*.[20] But now, how plausible is this claim that something only counts as a proposition insofar as it is used in accordance with the truth-functions in their usual, classical meanings? Why should we suppose that if the truth-functions were to take on somewhat different meanings (constituted by somewhat different logical laws and inferences) then those meanings would necessarily be incapable of articulating propositions? At this point Wittgenstein's argument runs dry. Indeed, he himself argues in other contexts, rather to the contrary, that such concepts as "proposition" are very vague and fluid, so that it is unclear (and not merely in an epistemic sense) exactly what is required in order for something to instantiate them (see, for example, WLC, pp. 12, 20; PG, I, #65). Moreover, that skepticism is warranted here can perhaps be seen from the well-known fact that it is far from clear that *ordinary language* (commonly) employs the truth-functions of classical logic.[21] For we would surely not want to deny that ordinary language sentences express propositions.

   Another problem with the argument is that the later Wittgenstein is officially, and moreover plausibly, committed to skepticism about its implication that because classical logic is internal to the truth-functions and hence to propositionality, *it is therefore also internal to language and thought*. For, whereas the early and even the middle Wittgenstein had indeed equated language and thought with propositionality (see, for example, T, 3.1, 3.2, 3.5, 4, 4.001; BT, p. 54), the later Wittgenstein does not; he does not believe that language and thought need to involve the use of propositions at all. For example, the primitive language-game which he imagines at *Philosophical Investigations*, #2—"Slab!" "Beam!" etc.—does not involve propositions, truth, or truth-functions at all, but is nonetheless described by him as a "primitive *language*" (PI, #2, emphasis added; cf. #6), and is presumably therefore understood by him to involve a sort of thought as well.[22]

The later Wittgenstein sometimes also implies a different and quicker line of reasoning to the conclusion that apparent violations of or oppositions to classical logic inevitably fail to express propositions, language, or thought: they lack a *use*, and hence, since meaning is use, a meaning (see, for example, LFM, p. 224). However, as we saw earlier, the sort of heavy theoretical loading of the notion of "use" which such an argument would require would make the doctrine that meaning is use a very dubious one—both by Wittgensteinian lights and for independent reasons. And accordingly, Wittgenstein himself in more considered remarks contradicts such a line of reasoning—for example, when he responds to the objection to calling an alternative logic "language" that there is no *point* in it: "But is there a *point* in everything we do? What is the point of our brushing our hair in the way we do? Or when watching the coronation of a king, one might ask, 'What is the point of all this?' etc." (LFM, pp. 203–4). Moreover, it is far from clear that deviant logic *does* in general lack a use. For example, common sense frequently seems to violate the law of excluded middle in connection with vague predicates in what appear to be useful ways ("Is this a river or not?" "Well, neither, it's in between"; "Is Hegel a religious thinker or not?" "One can't really say yes or no"). And fairly plausible proposals are made from time to time to employ one or another deviant logic for serious theoretical purposes—for example, to employ a deviant logic which rejects either the law of ex-

cluded middle or the distributive law (the law which says p &
(q v r) ⊃ (p & q) v (p & r)) in quantum mechanics.

In sum, I would suggest that the doctrine of classical logic's
internality to thought is one which has been living more on
its venerable antiquity and illustrious ancestry than from any
intrinsic merits, and that even Wittgenstein's most severely
skeptical stance towards it is therefore justified.

To conclude. As I mentioned earlier, Wittgenstein's way of
developing these two lines of deflatory counterargument en-
tangles him in certain minor inconsistencies: the first line of
deflating counterargument assumes that classical logic really
is internal to our concepts of proposition, language, and
thought, whereas the second one calls this into question or
even denies it; and the second one sometimes says that there
is no determinate fact of the matter, but at other times implies that there is and that it is that classical logic is not in fact
internal to these concepts.

However, as I also suggested earlier, these inconsistencies
are relatively superficial, and with a dash of interpretive charity this whole deflatory side of Wittgenstein's reflections on
the subject can be cast into a self-consistent and cogent form.
That form would be roughly as follows: Even if classical logic
is internal to propositions, language, and thought, that still
does not preclude alternative logics occurring in practices
which would be relevantly similar to propositions, language,
and thought, and which our concepts of proposition, language, and thought might reasonably be modified to cover.
But it is in fact at best indeterminate whether classical logic *is*
internal to propositions, language, and thought, and indeed
probable that it is not. Consequently, there is no case to be
made on the basis of a doctrine of the internality of classical
logic to propositions, language, and thought for retracting or
pruning back the diversity thesis.[23]

Finally, this may be a suitable place to conclude payment on a
promissory note which I issued in chapter 1 concerning Witt-

genstein's reasons for rejecting Kant's explanations of logical and analytic necessity and for consequently generalizing Kant's explanation of synthetic a priori necessity in terms of mind-imposition and our constraint to it to cover logical and analytic necessity as well.

As we have seen, Kant had explained *logical* necessity in terms of a version of precisely the doctrine of classical logic's internality to thought which has been considered above. But we can now see that, despite a superficial appearance of sympathy with such an explanation, the later Wittgenstein is really in deep disagreement with it. This is because he is skeptical about the doctrine of internality itself, and moreover believes that even if the doctrine were true, that would still not preclude people engaging in logical practices which deviated from classical logic, for, even if we resisted calling those practices thought, they might still be relevantly similar to thought, and might reasonably come to be covered by a modified version of our concept of thought. Consequently, if classical logic really does have a substantial sort of necessity, as Wittgenstein agrees with Kant that it does, then this requires some different and better explanation.

An illuminating paragraph for this stance of Wittgenstein's is *Remarks on the Foundations of Mathematics*, I, #116. There he takes up the proposal that conforming to classical rules of inference is internal to what we call "inferring" and "thought," shows some sympathy with it, but implies the two deflating caveats that (1) "the line between what we include in 'thinking' and what we no longer include in 'thinking' is [not] a hard and fast one" and (2) this proposal might seem to make such conformity rest on "an arbitrary definition." However, he also responds to these two caveats by saying that ultimately such conformity rests rather on "natural limits corresponding to the body of what can be called the role of thinking and inferring in our life," which he explicates in terms of classical laws of inference compelling us like other social laws, being supported rather than opposed by empirical regularities ("other practical consequences"), and being dictated rather than opposed by our psychological nature (in other words, in terms of just the sorts of constraining factors which were discussed in chapter 3). The paragraph is worth quoting at some length:

> "Then according to you everybody could continue the series [i.e., the chain of inferences—cf. #113] as he likes; and so infer *anyhow!*" In that case we shan't call it "continuing the series" and also presumably not "inference." And thinking and inferring (like counting) is of course bounded for us, not by an arbitrary definition, but by natural limits corresponding to the body of what can be called the role of thinking and inferring in our life.
>
> For we are at one over this, that the laws of inference do not compel him to say or to write such and such like rails compelling a locomotive. And if you say that, while he may indeed *say* it, still he can't *think* it, then I am only saying that that means, not: try as he may he can't think it, but: it is for us an essential part of "thinking" that—in talking, writing, etc. he makes *this sort* of transition. And I say further that the line between what we include in "thinking" and what we no longer include in "thinking" is no more a hard and fast one than the line between what is still and what is no longer called "regularity."
>
> Nevertheless the laws of inference can be said to compel us; in the same sense, that is to say, as other laws in human society. The clerk who infers as in (17) [i.e., correctly, as in the example at #17] *must* do it like that; he would be punished if he inferred differently. If you draw different conclusions you do indeed get into conflict, e.g. with society; and also with other practical consequences.
>
> And there is even something in saying: he can't *think* it. One is trying e.g. to say: he can't fill it with personal content; he can't really *go along with it*—personally, with his intelligence. It is like when one says: this sequence of notes makes no sense, I can't sing it with expression. I cannot *respond* to it. Or, what comes to the same thing here: I don't respond to it.

Concerning next *analytic* necessity, Kant notoriously wavers between explaining this in terms of logical law (more specifically, the law of contradiction) and explaining it in terms of a Kantian version of truth-in-virtue-of-meaning (more specifically, containment of a predicate-concept in a subject-concept).[24] Obviously, insofar as Kant invoked the former explanation to account for analytic necessity, Wittgenstein would make the same criticisms of this explanation as we just saw him implying for the case of logic itself. But nor is Wittgenstein any more sympathetic to an explanation of analytic necessity in terms of truth-in-virtue-of-meaning. For, as we saw in chapter 2, he thinks that the notion of truth-in-virtue-of-meaning rests on a false picture of the nature of meaning and of its relation to the principles which traditionally get classified as analytic. As he puts it: "The rules constitute the meaning and we are not responsible to it . . . How is the meaning of 'negation' defined, if not by the rules? $\sim\sim p = p$ does not follow from the meaning of 'not' but constitutes it"; "The rules do not *follow from* the idea . . . ; *they constitute it*" (WLC, pp. 4, 86; cf. PI, p. 147; RFM, I, #2, #10; VII, #42; LFM, pp. 184, 190 ff., 282). Hence truth-in-virtue-of-meaning (or more specifically, the containment of a predicate-concept in a subject-concept) will not do as an explanation of the necessities which have traditionally been classified as analytic either.[25]

Pace Kant, therefore, the necessity of logical principles and the necessity of so-called analytic principles are for Wittgenstein no less a prima facie mystery than the necessity of so-called synthetic a priori principles. It is this realization that motivates him to generalize Kant's explanation of the necessity of so-called synthetic a priori principles in terms of mind-imposition and our constraint to it to cover both of the former types of necessity as well.

6

Alternative Grammars? The Limits of Language

IN THIS CHAPTER and the next I turn to some further features of Wittgenstein's position which pose prima facie threats to his diversity thesis. In the present chapter my concern is with two sets of passages which seem to imply that grammatical diversity is either altogether impossible or at least severely limited in the scope of its possibility because of certain (non-logical) conditions on properly calling something a language, a thought, a proposition, a concept, etc. These two sets are as follows.

(A) There are a number of passages in which Wittgenstein suggests that concepts such as "language," "thought," "proposition," and "concept" are restricted to the languages in which we learn them, in the sense that we can only legitimately apply them to something to the extent that the something in question is also expressible in our own languages. Such passages would eliminate altogether the possibility of grammatical principles and concepts alternative to ours, because they imply that nothing could legitimately be called a "concept" unless it was identical to a concept which we already possess, and because, by implying this, they also imply that anything which is by definition constitutive of concepts, as grammatical principles are, must also be something which we already possess.

For example, in the *Philosophical Grammar* (1932–34) Wittgenstein writes concerning the question, in what sense the languages which I have learned seem to have "led me beyond themselves": "How did I come by the concept 'proposition' or the concept 'language'? Only through the languages I've learned.—But in a certain sense they seem to have led me beyond themselves, since I'm now able to construct a new language, for instance to invent new words.—So this construction too belongs to the concept of language. But only if I so stipulate . . . 'But language can expand.'—Certainly, but if this word 'expand' has a sense here, then I know *already* what I mean by it. I must be able to specify how I imagine such an expansion. And what I can't think, I can't now express or even hint at. And in *this* case the word 'now' means: 'in this calculus' or 'if the words are used according to these grammatical rules' . . . It would be quite correct to add in thought the rider: 'It is not as if I was able to transcend my own thought,' 'It is not as if I could sensibly transcend what has sense for me.' We feel that there is no way of smuggling in by the back door a thought I am debarred from thinking directly" (PG, I, #71; cf. BT, pp. 55–56).

A similar position seems to be presupposed in the following passage from Wittgenstein's *Remarks on Frazer's "Golden Bough"* (1931 and later): "One could very easily invent primitive practices for oneself, and it would be pure luck if they were not actually found somewhere. That is, the principle according to which these practices are arranged is a much more general one than in Frazer's explanation and *it is present in our own minds, so that we ourselves could think up all the possibilities.*—We can easily imagine, for example, that the king of a tribe is kept hidden from everyone, but also that every man in the tribe must see him" (RFGB, pp. 65–66; emphasis added). For by "practices" here Wittgenstein evidently means not only the *behavior* of the participants in the activities in question, but also the *meanings* that their behavior has for them (as can be seen from the example which he gives at the end of the quoted passage)—so that his claim that we can think up all the possible practices for ourselves and that we have their principle present within our own minds implies that we already have all the conceptual resources which people engaging in these practices could have.

(B) A little less extremely, at *Philosophical Investigations* (1945–49), #206–8, Wittgenstein discusses the topic of "following a rule" and considers in connection with it an imaginary case in which we come as explorers to the people of an unknown country who have an entirely strange "language" and set about trying to interpret it by means of observing their behavior: "Let us imagine that the people in that country carried on the usual human activities and in the course of them employed, apparently, an articulate language. If we watch their behavior we find it intelligible, it seems 'logical.' But when we try to learn their language we find it impossible to do so. For there is no regular connection [*kein regelmäßiger Zusammenhang*] between what they say, the sounds they make, and their actions; but still these sounds are not superfluous, for if we gag one of the people, it has the same consequences as with us; without the sounds the actions fall into confusion." Wittgenstein asks whether or not we should say that these people have a language, and he gives the emphatic reply: "There is not enough regularity [*Regelmäßigkeit*] for us to call it 'language.'" He then goes on to try to define more closely the following of a rule (*Regel*) which he takes to be essential in order for a form of verbal behavior to count as language, and the absence of which in the verbal behavior of the people imagined in the example makes it wrong for us to credit them with a language: "Then am I defining [*erkläre*] . . . 'rule' [*Regel*] by means of 'regularity' [*Regelmäßigkeit*]?'¹—How do I define the meaning of 'regular' [*regelmäßig*], 'uniform,' 'same' for anyone?—I shall define these words for someone who, say, only speaks French by means of the corresponding French words. But if a person has not yet got the *concepts*, I shall teach him to use the words by means of *examples* and by *practice*.—And when I do this I do not communicate less than I know myself. In the course of this teaching I shall show him the same colors, the same lengths, the same shapes, I shall make him find them and produce them, and so on. I shall, for instance, get him to continue an ornamental pattern uniformly when told to do so.—And also to continue progressions. And so, for example, when given: . .. ... to go on: ...."[2]

Interpreting this passage is difficult. It does not impose such a strict condition on calling a form of verbal behavior "language" (and hence on calling it an expression of "concepts" or "grammatical principles") as the passage from the *Philosophical Grammar* quoted under (A). It does not, that is to say, require that the verbal behavior in question be fully translatable into our existing languages if it is to be properly so called. Nevertheless, it does still seem to impose a pretty strict condition on calling a form of verbal behavior "language" (and hence on calling it an expression of "concepts" or "grammatical principles"). And in this way, although it does not exclude the possibility of alternative grammatical principles and concepts altogether, as the passages in (A) appear to, it does impose a significant limitation on the range of possible grammatical and conceptual variations.

The strict condition in question lies in what it has to say concerning language and regularity. Note, to begin with, that when Wittgenstein writes that in the case of the people imagined in the example "there is no regular connection between what they say . . . and their actions" and that this absence of regularity undermines the propriety of describing their verbal behavior as language, the absence of regularity that is at issue is evidently an absence of regular correlations between their verbal behavior, their other behavior, *and features of their environment* which would enable us to interpret what they say. This is evident from the fact that he is alluding to a principle which he enunciated a few lines earlier that "the common behavior of mankind is the system of reference by means of which we interpret an unknown language" (PI, #206); for, clearly, in order to be plausible, this principle must mean the common behavior of mankind *in conjunction with features of the environment in which it occurs.* Now to turn to the point of substance: Had Wittgenstein in our passage suggested merely that any form of verbal behavior properly called "language"

must *in fact* relate in regular ways to the remaining behavior of its users and what *they* recognize as features of their environment, then his suggestion would perhaps have been fairly uncontroversial, and would have imposed no very substantial restriction on the possibility of conceptual or grammatical variation. But what he actually seems to be suggesting is a good deal more controversial and restrictive: he seems to be suggesting that any form of verbal behavior properly called "language" must be such that *we can recognize* a regular relation in which it stands to the remaining behavior of its users and to what *we* recognize as features of their environment (cf. PI, #237). And he seems to mean to justify this suggestion with the argument that, since our concept of regularity is one which we learn with reference to regularities which our own conceptual resources make it possible for us to recognize (the regularities we recognize in objects of the same color, of the same length, or of the same shape, and in sequences like . ..
... ., for example), the extension of the concept of regularity could not include regularities which our conceptual resources did *not* enable us to recognize.

His remarks are perhaps too vague to allow any very confident conclusions about the precise strength and character of the substantial restrictions on possible conceptual and grammatical variations which would follow from them. But these might well include, for example, such a requirement as that any verbal expression, in order to be legitimately described as a part of language, or as the expression of a concept, must at least have the same *extension* as some concept of our own. And that would be a pretty significant restriction. For example, it would probably preclude our attributing to another people, and indeed the very possibility of their possessing, "thick" ethical concepts or elusive concepts similar in general nature to our own concepts of "irony" or "comicality" which we ourselves happen to lack and for which we are unable to provide even extensional equivalents, despite the fact that in the absence of this restriction we would have been strongly inclined to say that they did or at least could possess such concepts.

These (A) and (B) passages may seem to lend hope to the Williams-Lear reading of Wittgenstein's intentions. To be sure, a champion of the diversity thesis, faced with this challenge, might reply that the thesis still has the sort of "If not language, then why not *schm*language?" loophole available to it that we saw Wittgenstein exploiting in relation to formal logic in chapter 5. But since Wittgenstein's point in passages (A) and (B) seems to be not only that our concept of language *does* rule out counting the forms of behavior in question as language but also that it is somehow *right* to do so, such a reply would not be exegetically convincing.

However, the exegetical cause of the diversity thesis is far from lost here. For not only are passages (A) and (B) indirectly contradicted by the many passages in which Wittgenstein expresses commitment to the diversity thesis (as adumbrated in chapter 2), but in addition they are directly contradicted and counterbalanced by two sets of precisely corresponding and precisely contrary passages.

(A1) Corresponding to but contradicting (A): In *Zettel* (mainly 1945–48) we encounter a passage virtually identical to the first part of the passage from the *Philosophical Grammar* quoted above under (A), in which Wittgenstein again raises the question of the languages that I have learned having apparently "led me beyond themselves." He again writes: "How did I come by the concept 'proposition' or the concept 'language'? Only through the languages I've learned.—But in a certain sense they seem to have led me beyond themselves, since I'm now able to construct a new language, for instance to invent words.—So this construction too belongs to the concept of language. But only if I want to fix the concept that way" (Z, #325). However, whereas, as we saw, the passage from the *Philosophical Grammar* went on to "fix the concept" of language in a restrictive way which firmly excluded the possibility that there should be grammatical principles or concepts which were alternatives to those found in our languages, *Zettel* makes the opposite choice, fixing it in such a way as to allow the possibility of alternative grammatical

principles and concepts. Admittedly, the work seems undecided about the question of such a possibility at one or two
points, as for example when Wittgenstein writes in response
to the suggestion that the conception of a "bluish yellow"
signifies "a *no thoroughfare*": "But what is the right simile here?
That of a road that is physically impassable, or of the non-
existence of a road? I.e. is it one of physical or of mathematical impossibility?" (Z, #356). But for the most part the work
instead "fixes the concept" of language quite decidedly in
such a way as to allow the possibility of alternative grammatical principles and concepts. Consider, for example, Wittgenstein's reference there to a language-game which "we cannot
learn" containing the principle "Red is complex" (Z, #338–
39); his remark there (quoted earlier): "These people are acquainted with reddish green.—'But there is no such thing!'—
What an extraordinary sentence.—(How do you know?)" (Z,
#362); his response there to skepticism about the possibility
of people experiencing colors in accordance with a conceptual
system different from, and more finely discriminating than,
ours: "Could people without absolute pitch have guessed at
the existence of people with absolute pitch?" (Z, #369); and
finally, his remarks there (again quoted previously) that "an
education quite different from ours might also be the foundation for quite different concepts" (Z, #387), and that in this
way "*essentially* different concepts are imaginable" (Z, #388).

(B1) In the *Remarks on the Foundations of Mathematics*, part
VI (1943–44), Wittgenstein imagines an encounter with an
alien people which seems to be in all essential respects identical in character to the encounter imagined at *Philosophical
Investigations*, #206–8 and presented under (B). In particular,
it is again an encounter in which we are said to find ourselves
unable to arrive at any understanding of their (verbal) behavior due to our inability to identify regularity or rule-following
in that behavior: "Suppose . . . there were a tribe whose people apparently had an understanding of a kind of regularity
which I do not grasp. That is, they would also have learning
and instruction . . . If one watches them one would say that
they follow rules, learn to follow rules. The instruction

effects, e.g., agreement in actions on the part of pupil and teacher. But if we look at one of their series of figures we can see no regularity of any kind" (RFM, VI, #45).[3] In the corresponding example from the *Philosophical Investigations*, it will be recalled, Wittgenstein's verdict was that (1) our inability to recognize regularity, to identify any rule followed, showed that there *was no* regularity, no rule followed, since our concept of regularity or rule-following is learned by reference to examples of it which we can recognize as such and hence can only have application where such recognition is possible for us, and (2) for this reason the behavior in question could not properly be called linguistic, since language requires regularity or rule-following. In this example from the *Remarks on the Foundations of Mathematics*, on the other hand, his verdict is quite different: "What should we say now? We *might* say: 'They appear to be following a rule which escapes us,' but also, 'Here we have a phenomenon of behavior on the part of human beings, which we don't understand'" (RFM, VI, #45). Note that *neither* of the two alternative responses which he suggests here implies a denial that the behavior in question is regular or follows a rule (and hence a denial that it could be linguistic) like the denial which he issued and argued for in his verdict in the *Philosophical Investigations* passage. Instead, the two alternatives suggested are that we should respond to our inability to find any regularity in the behavior in question, any rule followed, either by judging that the behavior nevertheless *is* regular, *does* follow a rule (and hence: *might* be linguistic), or by adopting an agnostic attitude on the matter and resting content with the assessment that we do not understand the behavior. This passage from the *Remarks on the Foundations of Mathematics*, in thus rejecting the necessary conditions which are accepted at *Philosophical Investigations*, #206–8 for properly calling a form of behavior regular or rule-governed, and hence for calling it language, by the same token rejects the consequent substantial restriction on the scope of possible conceptual and grammatical variations which *Philosophical Investigations*, #206–8 seems to imply.

In short, as far as straight exegesis is concerned, passages

(A) and (B) cannot overturn the claim that Wittgenstein is committed to the diversity thesis in favor of saying that he is committed to something more like the Williams-Lear position as his considered view, for they not only face indirect opposition from the many passages which express the diversity thesis itself (as adumbrated in chapter 2) but are also directly contradicted and counterbalanced by the corresponding but contrary evidence of passages (A1) and (B1).[4]

What, though, of the *philosophical* questions that are at stake here? What ought we to say about the important philosophical disagreements between (A) and (B), on the one hand, and (A1) and (B1), on the other?

These disagreements obviously turn on, or at least centrally involve, a question about the nature of, and the proper conditions for applying, a family of concepts which includes the concepts "language," "thought," "proposition," "concept," etc. The restrictive side—(A) and (B)—imposes certain heavy conditions on the propriety of describing something as "language," "thought," "proposition," "concept," etc. and thereby eliminates or limits the possibility of alternative grammars and concepts. By contrast, the liberal side—(A1) and (B1)—denies the appropriateness of those heavy conditions, and thereby avoids eliminating or limiting the possibility of alternative grammars and concepts. An obvious first step to take towards assessing the philosophical disagreements here might therefore be to consider more closely Wittgenstein's views concerning the disputed concepts in question and others from the family to which they belong.

One striking and crucial feature of his position concerning this family of concepts is a belief that in their ordinary state they are all *vague* or *fluid*. Consider, for example, his following statements: (1) "The concept of a living being has the same indeterminacy as that of a language," "Language is a fluid concept" (Z, #326; PG, I, #65; cf. PG, I, #76, #139; WLC, p. 12; BT, pp. 53 ff.; and PI, #65 ff., where, however, the question of the vagueness or indeterminacy of the concept of a language is not clearly distinguished from such separable ques-

tions as those of its "family-resemblance" character and of a
certain technical sense in which Wittgenstein's rule-following
argument implies that *all* concepts, merely including this one,
are indeterminate in relation to new applications). (2)
"'Thinking' is a fluid [*fließender*] concept" (PG, I, #65; cf.
RFM, I, #116). (3) "The concept 'proposition' itself is not a
sharp one" (OC, #320; cf. PG, I, #69, #76; BT, pp. 53 ff.;
WLC, pp. 12, 20, where, however, this question is once again
conflated with that of "family-resemblance"). (4) "'Concept'
is a vague concept" (RFM, VII, #70; cf. BrB, p. 104 on "meaning"; WLC, pp. 21, 48 on "sense" and "meaning"; Z, #154 on
"sense" and "meaning" again). (5) "'Understanding' is a vague
concept" (RFM, VI, #14; cf. PG, I, #5; WLC, p. 48). (6) "Our
use of the words 'rule' and 'game' is a fluctuating [*schwan-
kender*] one (blurred at the edges)" (PG, I, #55; cf. BT, pp. 58–
59, 172).

What exactly does Wittgenstein mean when he says that
these concepts are vague or fluid? As I have indicated in a
couple of cases above, he does not always clearly distinguish
his central thesis here from such different claims as that
concepts belonging to this group are "family-resemblance"
concepts,[5] and that all concepts are, as a consequence of his
rule-following argument, in a certain technical sense indeterminate in relation to new applications. However, abstracting
from that conflation of ideas, one can, I think, distinguish two
main components of the vagueness or fluidity that he has in
mind here. The first component consists in the ordinary use
of such terms as "language," "thinking," "proposition," "concept," "understanding," and "rule" being in important respects *indeterminate*, in the sense that competent speakers will
come across cases of (linguistic) behavior in relation to which,
even after careful reflection in the light of ample evidence,
they are unsure whether or not these terms should be applied; if questioned on the matter, they will be inclined to
shrug their shoulders.[6] The second component consists in the
ordinary use of these terms being in important respects *inconsistent*, in the sense that competent speakers will encounter
cases in relation to which, even after careful reflection in the

light of ample evidence, they disagree with each other or even with themselves concerning whether or not the terms should be applied, some(times) saying "Yes," some(times) saying "No."[7] A concept may of course be both indeterminate and inconsistent in the same respect: when asked whether or not it applies, competent speakers will sometimes shrug their shoulders, sometimes say "Yes," and sometimes say "No."[8]

Wittgenstein's position here rests on a (plausible) assumption that such characteristics of *judgments* affect the nature of the very *concepts* involved as well. In this connection, recall passages like the following: "We say that, in order to communicate, people must agree with one another about the meanings of words. But the criterion for this agreement is not just agreement with reference to definitions, e.g., ostensive definitions—but *also* an agreement in judgments. It is essential for communication that we agree in a large number of judgments" (RFM, VI, #39; cf. PI, #242).

When understood in the twofold way explained above, Wittgenstein's thesis of the vagueness or fluidity of the family of concepts with which we are concerned in their ordinary use seems very plausible.[9] Empirical studies strongly support the view that the ordinary use of concepts from this family is in important respects indeterminate and inconsistent in the senses defined above.[10]

This thesis of Wittgenstein's seems to me of great philosophical importance, for reasons which extend well beyond the particular issue with which we are concerned here. For example, it suggests that a certain method much favored by recent philosophers of language, such as Kripke and Putnam, for attempting to decide such central questions in the philosophy of language as the nature of the reference of proper names and natural kind terms (Kripke) or the nature of meaning and its relation to features of the external world (Putnam), namely by scrutinizing our "linguistic intuitions" concerning these matters, may well be doomed. For these seem likely to be just the sorts of areas in which our ordinary usage of the relevant semantic terms will have the types of indeterminacy and inconsistency that Wittgenstein describes, so that attempting to adjudicate such questions by appeal to our "linguistic intuitions" will, if carried out conscientiously and accurately, lead to an impasse (the illusion of determinate results coming merely from the philosopher's partiality for certain such intuitions over other ones, engendered by his own theoretical commitments).[11]

Now my suggestion in connection with our topic here is of course that the disputes between (A) and (B), on the one hand, and (A1) and (B1), on the other, concern another such area, and that this is why we find Wittgenstein torn in his answers to the questions involved: his ambiguity reflects a vagueness or fluidity that pertains to the relevant concepts in their ordinary use.

One might plausibly speculate—though doing so is not really essential for our purposes here—that this present-day indeterminacy and inconsistency in our ordinary intuitions concerning whether, for example, as (A) says, "language" is of its nature restricted to concepts which *our* language can express, or, as (A1) says, "language" may also apply to concepts which our language cannot express, arose in something like the following way: Such concepts as "language," "concept" (or "meaning"), and so forth originally developed in societies which were both inward-looking and intellectually static (at least as far back as their historical memories reached), so that it was natural for them to define these concepts in restrictive ways. But as societies became better acquainted with other societies and their very different linguistic and conceptual resources, and also with intellectual innovation occurring among their own members, the impact of these empirical experiences, together with interests of accurately understanding other societies and of permitting rather than precluding intellectual innovation in their own, led them to more liberal redefinitions of the concepts in question. The result is that, collectively, we are today the inheritors of both restrictive and liberal intuitions concerning these concepts.

Assuming that this account of the nature of the disputes between (A) and (A1) and between (B) and (B1) is broadly correct, what would and what should Wittgenstein's considered response to this situation be?

As has already been mentioned, Wittgenstein generally presents himself as a conceptual quietist, a philosopher who would not dream of changing ordinary language, but who only seeks to clarify its grammar and thereby guard against other philosophers' misunderstandings of it. This is the Wittgenstein who says that "ordinary language is all right" (BB, p. 28), that "we are not justified in having any more scruples about our language than the chess player has about chess, namely none" (PG, I, #77), that "the task of philosophy is not to create a new . . . language, but to clarify the use of our language, the existing language" (PG, I, #72), that "philosophy may in no way interfere with the actual use of language; it can in the end only describe it" (PI, #124), that the confusions which philosophy is to clear up do not require that it reform language (PI, #132), and so forth.

Accordingly, but more specifically, Wittgenstein defends the *vagueness* or *fluidity* of ordinary language; in his view, the philosopher should accept this. The *Philosophical Investigations* famously develops an extended case in support of such a position (see especially PI, #71, #79–81, #88, #99–100).

Accordingly again, but more specifically still, Wittgenstein says many things which suggest that his response to the sort of vagueness or fluidity which he perceives in our ordinary concepts of "language," "thinking," "proposition," "concept," "understanding," and "rule" will remain faithful to these principles, that he will simply leave these concepts as he finds them: vague or fluid. For example, in the *Philosophical Grammar* he writes, "When I talk about language . . . I must speak the language of everyday" (PG, I, #77), and even more explicitly, "The use of the words 'proposition,' 'language,' etc. has the haziness of the normal use of concept-words in our language. To think this makes them unusable, or ill-adapted to their purpose, would be like wanting to say 'the warmth this stove gives is no use, because you can't feel where it begins and where it ends'" (PG, I, #76). Similarly, in the *Philosophical Investigations* he repeats the former remark, that in talking about language "I must speak the language of everyday" (PI, #120), at the conclusion of an extended defense of the use of vague concepts (PI, #71 ff.) which was originally prompted as a response to a charge that he has failed to define the essence of language (PI, #65). Further remarks in a similar vein can be found in the *Blue Book* (BB, pp. 25–28).

We may therefore understand Wittgenstein's ambiguities between (A) and (A1), and between (B) and (B1), as of a piece with this stance, as a principled attempt to stay faithful to corresponding indeterminacies and inconsistencies in our ordinary language intuitions about what constitutes "language," etc.

However, this conceptual quietism, its application to the vagueness or fluidity of ordinary concepts generally, and its application to that of the family of concepts with which we are here concerned in particular, are ultimately unacceptable positions—both in fact and by Wittgenstein's own lights.[12]

In order to see one reason why, recall that the notion of vagueness or fluidity in the ordinary-language use of terms that is in question here comprises two main components: indeterminacy and inconsistency.

Now Wittgenstein's inclination to allow his own use of terms generally, and his use of such terms as "language," "thinking," "proposition," "concept," etc. in particular, the same sort of vagueness or fluidity that they have in ordinary language may just possibly be acceptable where *indeterminacy* is concerned. Perhaps it *is* all right—both in fact and by Wittgenstein's own lights—for a philosopher to shrug his shoulders in response to the question of whether such and such a behavioral phenomenon is a language, thinking, a proposition, a concept, etc. in the same cases in which the competent user of ordinary language shrugs his. On the other hand, perhaps not. For, since the philosopher's shrugs are not merely shrugs of epistemological agnosticism, but signify that there is no real fact of the matter, his indulgence in them evidently involves contravening the law of excluded middle. That *might* be acceptable, both in fact and to Wittgenstein. On the other hand, it is not at all clear that it is, either in fact or to Wittgenstein.[13]

But what about *inconsistency*? Given that the vagueness or fluidity of ordinary language, both generally and in connection with the terms just mentioned in particular, also includes inconsistency, Wittgenstein's commitment to conforming to ordinary language and its vagueness or fluidity, both generally and in this connection in particular, also implies an endorsement of *inconsistency*. Wittgenstein no doubt tends to overlook this fact through failing to distinguish clearly between the two main components of his notion of vagueness or fluidity as I have done here (and through conflating them with such further notions as family-resemblance and the sort of technical indeterminacy posited by the rule-following argument). But the implication in question comes into the open at points. For example, Wittgenstein writes in one passage, "It may seem queer to say that we may correctly use either of two forms of expression which seem to contradict each other, but such cases are very frequent" (BB, p. 29). And the contradictions between passages (A) and (B), on the one hand, and (A1) and (B1), on the other, are an example of his accepting this implication in the particular area with which we are presently concerned. However, this implication is surely *not* acceptable, either in general or in the present case in particular, either in fact or by Wittgenstein's own lights. For self-contradiction is unacceptable in fact. And (whatever his position concerning the existence or possibility of alternative logics) Wittgenstein is clearly no friend of self-contradiction either: "'Then are you in favor of contradiction?' Not at all; any more than of soft rulers" (RFM, VII, #15).

Nor can the conceptual quietist side of Wittgenstein escape this problem by retaining ordinary language's contradictions—for example, between (A) and (A1) or between (B) and (B1)—only *verbally*, while avoiding their contradictoriness through carefully distinguishing two (or more) uses or meanings of the key terms involved, and distributing these across the two sides of the "contradictions"—so that, for example, position (A) would in effect implicitly be about "language₁," whereas position (A1) would implicitly be about "language₂." This would be no solution to the problem at all, because it would amount to a covert violation of the commitment to adhere to ordinary language and its vagueness or fluidity that is under discussion here. For, as Wittgenstein says at one point, "A sharper concept would not be the same concept" (LWPP1, #267; cf. PG, I, appendix 8; BT, p. 175).[14] In addition, it would have further serious drawbacks: for example, it would be highly confusing, and it would amount to an evasion of what at least seems to be an intellectual responsibility to *decide* the disputes that have surfaced—and both of these things for naught, since, as was just mentioned, the underlying motive of staying faithful to ordinary language has been violated anyway.

In short, Wittgenstein's official conceptual quietist approach seems unacceptable both in general and as a way of responding to the cases with which we are concerned here in particular.[15]

Fortunately, however, the later texts also contain a second, albeit much less vocal and less well-known, Wittgenstein alongside the conceptual quietist Wittgenstein described above. This second Wittgenstein is *not* in principle opposed to departing from ordinary language in his own use of the terms required for the statement of his philosophical views—at least to the extent of eliminating some of the vagueness or fluidity (the indeterminacy and inconsistency) which their ordinary use has. To this extent at least, he is prepared to change their grammar or the concepts which they express (recall: "A sharper concept would not be the same concept"). Consider, for instance, the following passage from the *Philosophical Grammar*: "If we wish to draw boundaries in the use of a word, in order to clear up philosophical paradoxes, then alongside the actual picture of the use (in which as it were the different colors flow into one another without sharp boundaries) we may put another picture which is in certain ways like the first but is built up of colors with clear boundaries between them" (PG, I, #35).[16] And consider also this remark from *Zettel*: "Our investigation does not try to *find* the real, exact meaning of words; though we do often *give* words exact meanings in the course of our investigation" (Z, #467). This second Wittgenstein is especially prominent in *Wittgenstein's Lectures: Cambridge 1932–1935*.[17]

This less vocal Wittgenstein would in particular have no real reservations about eliminating from such terms as "language," "thinking," "proposition," "concept," etc. some of the vagueness or fluidity which he believes their use to have in ordinary language, when it comes to employing them in the statement of his own philosophical position. Consider, for example, the following points which he makes concerning one of these terms: "The word 'proposition' does not signify a sharply bounded concept. If we want to put a concept with sharp boundaries beside our use, we are free to define it, just as we are free to narrow down the meaning of the primitive measure of length 'a pace' to 75 cm" (PG, I, #69); "There is an ambiguity in the use of the word 'proposition' which can be removed by making certain distinctions. I suggest defining it arbitrarily rather than trying to portray usage" (WLC, p. 11).

Indeed, it seems that, whether or not he is happy to acknowledge the fact, Wittgenstein is heavily committed to undertaking at least this much conceptual revision in relation to some of the terms from this family. Consider, for example, how he could possibly uphold his central doctrine that *meaning* (one of the terms belonging to this family) is *use*, in the complex sense of "use" which we saw this doctrine to involve in chapter 3, without conceding that the doctrine entails the adoption of a less vague or fluid use of the term "meaning" than it has in ordinary language. Accordingly, in work from the period 1932–35 he occasionally concedes that this doctrine amounts to the adoption of a less vague or fluid use of the term "meaning" than the one that it has in ordinary language (see, for example, WLC, pp. 44, 47–48).

This other side of Wittgenstein's thought casts a new and rather different light on the ambiguities in his writings between the restrictive uses of such terms as "language,"

"thought," "proposition," and "concept" represented by the
(A) and (B) passages and the liberal uses of the same terms
represented by the (A1) and (B1) passages: it allows us to see
the two sides of these ambiguities as, not so much the (unacceptable) inconsistencies of Wittgenstein the conceptual quietist, but rather (or, if we are being stricter and less charitable
in our exegesis, perhaps: also) incompatible alternative choices
between relatively precise uses of these terms introduced in
order to replace the vague or fluid uses which they have in
ordinary language.

To expand on that suggestion: No mere direct examination
of ordinary language will give us determinate, consistent answers to the question at issue between (A) and (A1) of
whether or not such words as "language" can properly be
applied to verbal behavior not translatable without conceptual residue into the languages known to us who use these
words, or to the question at issue between (B) and (B1) of
whether or not such words as "language" can properly be
applied to verbal behavior in which we who use these words
cannot find a certain sort of regularity. Ordinary usage is
vague or fluid here in the sense that speakers who are competent in the use of such words as "language" judged by all the
usual criteria will, if asked these questions, either shrug their
shoulders or give inconsistent answers. What is needed in
order to yield answers to these questions is instead the adoption of a use of such words as "language" which is more determinate and consistent than the use that they have in ordinary language (while at the same time preserving those
aspects of the latter use which *are* already determinate and
consistent). To put it in terms of one of Wittgenstein's metaphors, sharp boundaries will be drawn here which "will be
related to the fluctuating boundaries of the natural use of
language in the same way as sharp contours in a pen-and-ink
sketch are related to the gradual transitions between patches
of color in the reality depicted" (PG, I, #76; cf. PI, #76).

Nor does there seem to be much reason to assume that it
will be possible to find some particular precise use of such
words as "language," involving a particular way of answering

the questions at issue between (A) and (A1) and between (B) and (B1), which will be even *better* grounded in, *more* favored by, the vague or fluid use of ordinary language than a number of incompatible alternative precise uses entailing contrary answers to the same questions. Consider in this connection what Wittgenstein says of a rather similar case in which a concept which loses its use for certain reasons gets replaced by a more appropriate analogue: "I am at liberty to choose between many uses, that is, between many different kinds of analogy. One might say in such a case that the term . . . hasn't got one legitimate heir only" (BB, p. 62).

The adoption of a particular more precise use of such words as "language" here will therefore represent a *choice* in the sense that with it "we *give* words exact meanings" and do not "*find* the real, exact meaning of words" (Z, #467)—neither an exact meaning found straightforwardly in ordinary language (since the meaning found in ordinary language is not exact) nor an exact meaning found by discovering which exact meaning ordinary language favors (since the vague or fluid use of ordinary language favors no particular exact meaning over incompatible exact alternatives).

Accordingly, the answers to the questions at issue between (A) and (A1) and between (B) and (B1) will amount to a choice in the same sense. Thus in connection with the question disputed between (A) and (A1), Wittgenstein actually says in the key passages that the way in which the languages I have learned have "led me beyond themselves" is something that holds "only if I want to fix the concept [of language] that way" (PG, I, #71; Z, #325).

It seems to me that this sense in which Wittgenstein sometimes implies that the answers to the vital questions disputed by (A) and (A1) and by (B) and (B1) turn on a choice is an insight as important and sound as the one on which it rests (that the ordinary language use of terms belonging to the family "language," "thinking," "proposition," "concept," etc. is vague or fluid, indeterminate and inconsistent).

In short, I propose that we should see the inconsistencies between (A) and (B), on the one hand, and (A1) and (B1), on the other, as not so much Wittgenstein the conceptual quietist's warm embrace of the confusions of ordinary usage, but rather (or, if we are to be exegetically strict and uncharitable, perhaps: also) this less vocal Wittgenstein's more philosophically interesting and forgivable vacillation in choosing between alternative ways of *eliminating* areas of confusion in our ordinary language use of these terms and thereby settling the important questions disputed between the two sides of the inconsistencies.

But how exactly should this choice be made? Must not a choice in favor of *one* use of the terms "language," "thinking," "proposition," "concept," etc. which remains faithful to what is already determinate and consistent in their ordinary language use, but which at the same time achieves greater precision with respect to areas in which their ordinary language use is vague or fluid, rather than *another*—and hence, in favor of one answer to the questions at issue between (A) and (A1), and between (B) and (B1), rather than another—be justified by *reasons*? And if so, by what *sorts* of reasons? And *which* choice do they justify?

At certain points Wittgenstein seems to hint that such a choice *indeed can and should* be based on reasons, and that these are reasons of utility relative to various purposes which one might have in, say, drawing a boundary between linguistic and non-linguistic behavior. Thus the *Philosophical Grammar* and the *Philosophical Investigations* both contain the following remark: "To say 'This combination of words makes no sense' excludes it from the sphere of language and thereby bounds the domain of language. But when one draws a boundary it may be for various kinds of reason. If I surround an area with a fence or a line or otherwise, the purpose may be to prevent someone from getting in or out . . . or it may show where the property of one man ends and that of another begins; and so on. So if I draw a boundary line that is not yet to say what I am drawing it for" (PG, I, #137; PI, #499). Similarly but conversely, the *Philosophical Grammar* says that the decision to accept an apparently senseless form of words as meaningful, and hence as a part of language, leaves one a choice as to how to do this, how to understand the form of words, a choice which, however, is bounded by, among other things, "various types of utility" (PG, I, #81).

On the other hand, these remarks are noticeably diffident and vague, and there is also a rather prominent strand in the texts which seems designed to undercut the idea that there is a set of purposes which could constitute reasons for, say, drawing the boundary around the linguistic in one way rather than another. Thus in the *Philosophical Grammar* immediately after the former passage Wittgenstein goes on to write: "Language is not defined for us as an arrangement fulfilling a definite purpose . . . Language is of interest to me as a phenomenon and not as a means to a particular end" (PG, I, #137; cf. PI, #501). Moreover, on reflection, it is pretty clear *why* Wittgenstein is bound in his more official moods to resist the idea that reasons of utility could justify, say, drawing the boundary around the linguistic in one way rather than another. For, after all, a decision to draw it in one way rather than another could in his eyes only be a decision in favor of one grammatical principle—one grammar and concept of "language"—rather than an alternative; and as such, according to his official doctrine of the arbitrariness of grammar (as explained in chapter 2), this is supposed to be a decision which cannot be justified (or refuted). Hence Wittgenstein writes at one point in the *Philosophical Grammar*, in an even more emphatic rejection of the idea of basing a choice of the kind in question on a justification by reasons, in which he reveals precisely the source of concern just mentioned: "I would like to say: 'I must *begin* with the distinction between sense and nonsense. Nothing is possible prior to that. I can't give it a foundation'" (PG, I, #81). In short, Wittgenstein's official position seems to preclude making this sort of choice on the basis of reasons.[18]

However, I suggested in chapter 4 that Wittgenstein ought quite generally to revise his official stance against the possibility of ever justifying or refuting alternative grammars in competition with one another, that he ought to treat aspects of the full-blooded usefulness and threefold empirical application which he himself rather implausibly regards as conditions of the very meaningfulness of grammatical principles, in particular smoothness in the regulation of empirical judgments and usefulness in realizing purposes, as instead (or also) criteria of their relative value, and hence as possible grounds for justifying or refuting them when they stand in competition with each other. And I would accordingly suggest that this general moral applies to the contests between alternative grammars for such words as "language" with which we are concerned here in particular, and that it is therefore the former set of passages quoted above in which Wittgenstein hints that such contests might properly be settled in light of reasons of utility (presumably including smoothness in the regulation of empirical judgments) that represents his better philosophical assessment, rather than the latter set of passages in which he contradicts this.

So Wittgenstein's best position is that reasons should guide the sort of choice in question here. But which reasons? And which choice do they justify?

As we saw in chapter 4, and again above, the sorts of reasons that this side of Wittgenstein considers relevant to such choices seem to be ones of *utility*, or usefulness in realizing purposes, including in particular *smoothness in regulating empirical judgments*. These also seem to be appropriate sorts of reasons.

Now I would suggest that if one *does* accept utility and smoothness in regulating empirical judgments as criteria here, then they tell pretty strongly in favor of choosing the liberal grammar for such terms as "language" reflected in (A1) and (B1) over the restrictive grammar for them reflected in (A) and (B). The following considerations support this.

First and foremost, empirically informed interpretive investigations of the languages and texts of historically and culturally remote peoples which have been undertaken in modern times by such disciplines as classical scholarship, anthropology, history of ideas, and linguistics seem to have established that such peoples possess many concepts which are fundamentally discrepant with our own, and indeed some which are not even capturable extensionally by our own. The criterion of a grammar's *smoothness in regulating empirical judgments* therefore seems to tell strongly in favor of defining such concepts as "concept" and "language" in liberal ways which permit their application in cases where one cannot find conceptual equivalence, and even in cases where one cannot find co-extensiveness, between an encountered use of symbols and the conceptual resources of one's own language, instead of defining them in restrictive ways which proscribe this.

In addition, the criterion of *utility*, or usefulness in realizing purposes, arguably affords further reasons for making the same choice. As we recently saw, even in the passages in which he seems inclined to endorse an appeal to such a criterion in order to ground choices of the sort in question here, Wittgenstein is extremely vague about what sorts of purposes should set the standard. There is an important theoretical point to such vagueness: it quite properly dissuades us from assuming that the potentially relevant purposes are limited in number to one or a few, or that they are somehow given independently of us and our varying and mutable interests. However, that point granted, clearly if this criterion were to be employed as such at all, it would need to be specified more closely in some way. I want to suggest that the following two purposes are attractive candidates here, and that (assuming the primary point made in the previous paragraph) they both lend further support to accepting a liberal grammar for such terms as "language" in the spirit of (A1) and (B1) instead of a restrictive one in the spirit of (A) and (B).

(i) We (have come to) value intellectual and practical innovation in our communities. History has taught us that this is inextricably bound up with deep "grammatical" or conceptual change, including conceptual change which fails even to preserve co-extensionality with existing concepts (think, for example, of the introduction of our modern concept of irony). If we were to opt for a restrictive grammar for such terms as "concept" and "language," we would inhibit such innovation for the future, since a restrictive grammar would in effect force us to classify any such innovation as mere nonsense. Therefore, opting for a restrictive grammar is a bad thing to do here.

(ii) We (have come to) place value on treating cultural "others" with respect, and, as an essential part of this, interpreting them sensitively. Experience in such areas as international relations and the human sciences has taught us that these things require an openness in our approach to understanding others which avoids both the Scylla of fundamentally assimilating their mental life to our own—and attributing the interpretive difficulties which we inevitably encounter in doing so to various sorts of confusion at their end—and the Charybdis of dismissing much of it as merely nonsense. Opting for a restrictive grammar for such terms as "language" would require us to live commuting between precisely such a Scylla and Charybdis (especially if the restriction demanded outright conceptual equivalence, but to a significant extent even if it only demanded co-extensionality—in which latter connection one might think, for example, of others' "thick" ethical concepts). Therefore, opting for a restrictive grammar is a bad thing to do here.

It thus seems to me that in the end the position represented by passages (A) and (B), and the threat which it poses to the diversity thesis, not only fail to reflect Wittgenstein's considered view as an exegetical matter but also fail philosophically.

However, before such a conclusion can be drawn with any confidence, there is still a final task that needs to be performed. For there remains one last strand of Wittgenstein's texts which might yet undermine such a conclusion, in both its exegetical and its philosophical aspects, and show that Wittgenstein really is, and moreover ought to be, committed to severely pruning back, or even felling, the diversity thesis after all. This will be the subject of the next (and final) chapter.

7

Alternative Grammars? The Problem of Access

EARLIER in this essay I said that Wittgenstein's use of actual and imaginary examples of alternative grammars and concepts was intended to show us that such alternatives are at least possible and *conceivable.* But of course there is an ambiguity lurking there. Does showing us that they are "conceivable" merely mean making it conceivable to us that there are or could be such things (and that such and such forms of behavior are or could be expressions of them), or does it in addition mean doing so through bringing us actually to *understand* some of them?

If one casts a quick glance at Wittgenstein's general statements concerning such alternatives, as quoted in chapter 2—his statements that "a language-game does change with time"; that in the context of an education quite different from ours and the quite different interests which would arise from it, "different concepts would no longer be unimaginable"; that if we imagine certain very general facts of nature to be different from what we are used to, "the formation of concepts different from the usual ones will become intelligible"; that "concepts other than though akin to ours might seem very queer to us"; and so on—it is perhaps natural to assume that he means to imply by these remarks that we might, and in some cases do, while possessing the grammar and concepts which we currently possess, come literally to understand alternatives as well. And a casual survey of the wealth of actual and imaginary examples which he gives from different areas of grammar in support of the thesis that there are or could be alternatives, examples such as were again referred to in chapter 2, may reinforce this assumption. Accordingly, many interpreters imply that he finds the literal intelligibility of alternative grammars quite unproblematic.[1]

Nevertheless, a closer inspection of Wittgenstein's texts throws this admittedly somewhat natural assumption into serious doubt.

In an important exchange in the secondary literature, Michael Dummett complained in his essay "Wittgenstein's Philosophy of Mathematics" that Wittgenstein's examples of alternative grammars (in the area of mathematics) are "thin and unconvincing,"[2] and Barry Stroud then responded in his essay "Wittgenstein and Logical Necessity" that this is *intentional* on Wittgenstein's part, that although the examples really are meant to convince us that alternative grammars are possible, Wittgenstein does not believe that this can be done, and does not aim to do it, by making the alternatives literally intelligible to us: "Wittgenstein's example are intended to oppose Platonism by showing that calculating, counting, inferring, and so forth, might have been done differently . . . But we can understand and acknowledge . . . the possibility of different ways of calculating, and so forth, without understanding what those different ways might have been."[3]

That Wittgenstein does indeed refrain from implying that alternative grammars are literally intelligible to us can be confirmed by taking a closer look at the textual evidence. Consider again, to begin with, the general statements mentioned above. It is indeed somewhat natural to read these as implying that one can achieve intellectual access to actual or imaginable alternatives. But on closer inspection, such a reading is really by no means inevitable. A claim that "a language-game does change with time" does not, strictly speaking, imply that the alternative language-games existing before and after such a change are ever literally intelligible to anyone at the same time. Similarly, to say that in the context of an education different from ours and the different interests arising therefrom, "different concepts would no longer be unimaginable" need not mean or imply that hypothesizing these changed circumstances makes the different concepts themselves "imaginable" in the sense of intelligible; it might only mean that hypothesizing them makes it imaginable that there should be different concepts. Again, the suggestion that if we imagine certain very general facts of nature to be different from what we are used to, "the formation of concepts different from the usual ones will become intelligible" need not mean that such different concepts will themselves become intelligible; it may only mean that it will become intelligible that there should be such different concepts.[4] And finally, the claim that "concepts other than though akin to ours might seem very queer to us" could, without undue violence, be understood to involve some such tacit qualification as "if we could understand them (per impossible)" or "insofar as we encountered their expressions in behavior." These general statements are thus compatible either with the position that intellectual access to alternatives is possible or with the position that it is not.

But Wittgenstein's treatment of examples tips the balance, providing strong evidence for Stroud's claim that Wittgenstein's position is really the latter. Admittedly, Wittgenstein does give a few examples of alternative grammatical principles and concepts in which he either fails to signal scruples concerning their literal intelligibility to us or perhaps even implies such intelligibility.[5] However, that small handful of cases aside, the great majority of cases strongly support Stroud's interpretation of his intentions.

In the great majority of cases Wittgenstein seems to expect no more from an example than an incomplete specification of ways in which an alternative grammar and its concepts might appear to us as we observe their behavioral manifestation but without literally understanding them. Thus as Stroud says with reference to Wittgenstein's mathematical examples: "When we look more closely at the examples, are they really as intelligible as they seemed at first? For instance, consider the people who sell wood at a price proportionate to the area covered by the pile of wood (and who respond to an attempt to show them that there is something wrong with this way of measuring amount by say spreading the logs of a pile which they consider small over a larger area with the remark, 'Yes, now it's a *lot* of wood and costs more') . . . What would the relation between quantity and weight possibly be for such people? A man could buy as much wood as he could possibly lift, only to find, upon dropping it, that he had just lifted more wood than he could possibly lift. Or is there more wood, but the same weight? . . . Also, it would be possible for a house that is twice as large as another built on exactly the same plan to contain much less wood. How much wood is bought need have no connection with how much wood is needed for building the house. And so on. Problems involved in understanding what it would be like to sell wood in this way can be multiplied indefinitely."[6]

Indeed, even such a relatively straightforward-looking example as that of the people who do not accord the double negation of a proposition its usual meaning but instead treat it as either meaningless or just a repetition of the simple negation causes problems of intelligibility when considered more closely. For example, what do these people do when presented with the two propositions "p $\supset$ ~q" and "q"? Do they have a modified version of *modus tollendo tollens* which allows them to infer "~p" from these premises directly without first inferring "~~q" from "q," or do they simply not acknowledge the inference to "~p" at all? Surely we could not really grasp what their notion of negation amounted to unless or until we had answered this and similar questions.[7]

Interestingly enough (although Stroud does not notice the fact), Wittgenstein himself makes this very point about his examples in one late passage: "We say: 'Let's imagine people who do not know *this* language-game.' But in doing so we still have no clear conception of the life of these people insofar as it differs from our own. We do not yet know what we are supposed to imagine; for the life of these people is in all other ways to correspond with ours, and it still must be determined what we would call a life corresponding to ours under these new conditions. Isn't it as if one said: There are people who play chess without the king? Questions immediately arise: Who wins now, who loses, and others. You have to make *further* decisions that you don't anticipate in that first determination" (LWPP2, p. 71; RC, III, #296).

Moreover (and this is another important point in support of Stroud's reading which he does not himself make), Wittgenstein often signals to his readers through a judicious choice of direct instead of indirect quotation, and various verbal qualifications, that an example must neither be assumed to involve our familiar grammatical principles or concepts (an obvious point, given the purpose of the examples) nor to have communicated to readers a literal understanding of whatever alternative grammatical principles or concepts may be involved. For instance, in his discussion of the people who (as one might roughly put it) sell wood by the area which it covers, he certainly begins by describing them carelessly enough as people who "sold it at a price proportionate to the area covered by the piles" (RFM, I, #149). But he avoids misleading us into thinking that we know what their concepts of quantity or payment are by using direct rather than indirect quotation to report their views concerning these subjects: "And what if they even justified [this practice] with the words: 'Of course, if you buy more timber you must pay more'?" (RFM, I, #149). And by the time we reach the end of the example, he makes it clear through explicit qualification that these people's concepts of quantity, payment, etc. are not ours, and that we must not assume that we have a literal understanding of what they are doing or thinking: "We should presumably say in this case: they simply do not mean the same by 'a lot of wood' and 'a little wood' as we do, and they have a quite different system of payment from us" (RFM, I, #150). Again, he prefaces his discussion of the people who do not accord the double negation of a proposition its usual meaning with a statement that such rules as that of double-negation elimination, which these people lack, constitute the very meaning of the negation sign, so that a change in these rules changes the meaning of the sign: "Without these rules the word ['not'] has as yet no meaning; and if we change the rules it now has another meaning (or none)" (PI, p. 147). And when he gives the example itself, he accordingly speaks with studied vagueness of "something corresponding to our negation" in order to prevent both the erroneous identification of the concept at issue with our concept of negation and the rash assumption that we understand it. Again, concerning his example in *On Certainty* of a tribe who (as we might put it carelessly) believe that people sometimes go to the moon, note his judicious choice of direct rather than indirect quotation to report their views—"But suppose that . . . we met the reply: 'We don't know *how* one gets to the moon, but those who get there know at once that they are there; and even you can't explain everything'"—and his concluding remark on this subject, "We should feel ourselves intellectually very distant from someone who said this" (OC, #108). Again, regarding his example in the *Remarks on the Foundations of Mathematics* of a people who (as we might put it carelessly) have money but exchange it for goods in an arbitrary fashion, note his judiciously flexible expression: "money, or what looks like money" (RFM, I, #53). Again, concerning his example in the same work of people who (as we might put it carelessly) measure with flexible rulers, note his careful qualification: "What is here called 'measuring' and 'length' and 'equal length,' is something different from what we call those things. The use of these words is different from ours, but it is *akin* to it" (RFM, I, #5). Such illustrations of the point could easily be multiplied.

Why, though, does Wittgenstein adopt this stance? Why does he develop what seem to be examples of alternative grammars and concepts but refrain from implying their literal intelligibility to us, and indeed imply that they are not literally intelligible to us? As we saw, Stroud's picture is that Wittgenstein intends to persuade us that there really are possible alternatives (and thereby to combat Platonism) but to do so by means of examples which perforce fall short of making the alternatives literally intelligible to us. However, such a project might well sound odd or dubious, and it might therefore seem tempting to argue that the explanandum invites a contrary explanans instead, namely one along the lines of the Williams-Lear interpretation: Wittgenstein's ultimate purpose here is not to show that such alternatives are possible, but instead to show that they are unintelligible and illusory.

In short, the feature of the texts in question can seem to constitute a good argument in support of the Williams-Lear interpretation. Strangely enough, neither Williams nor Lear makes any attempt to exploit this potential mine of textual evidence which could be used for the evidential enrichment of their evidentially impoverished interpretation. Indeed, Williams says things that contradict doing so.[8] But at least one author in this general interpretive camp has recently done so, namely Cerbone.[9]

In straightforwardly exegetical terms at least, such a move is not convincing, however. For one thing, it conflicts with the great mass of textual evidence—both general statements and specific examples—which shows that Wittgenstein is committed to the diversity thesis (as adumbrated in chapter 2). And (as we saw in chapter 5) his formulations of his imaginary examples simply do not permit the reading that his ultimate purpose with them is the negative one of showing them to be meaningless and illusory, instead of the positive one of showing them to be possible. For instance (as we saw in chapter 5), his bottom line about the wood-sellers in the text is: "We should presumably say in this case: they simply do not mean the same by 'a lot of wood' and 'a little wood' as we do; and they have a quite different system of payment from us" (RFM, I, #150); it is *not* that they do not mean anything and have no system after all.

For another thing, there is an alternative and better explanation of the feature of Wittgenstein's imaginary examples which seems to lend support to the Williams-Lear reading here, namely the fact that in these examples Wittgenstein refrains from implying that we can, and indeed implies that we cannot, literally understand the alternative grammars and concepts involved. For Wittgenstein indicates at least four reasons, four obstacles, logically independent of the sort of position that Williams and Lear ascribe to him which prevent him from claiming to have made alternative grammars and concepts literally intelligible to readers by means of his examples. These four reasons, or obstacles, are as follows (roughly in order of increasing severity).

A first, and rather mundane, one is that even if it were in principle possible to describe alternative grammars and concepts in sufficient detail to make them literally intelligible to readers, doing so would be a laborious task and is not necessary for Wittgenstein's purpose of showing readers their possibility, which can be accomplished by means of a merely partial sketch. In this spirit, Wittgenstein writes in the *Brown Book* concerning his primitive language-games: "We have only given a very sketchy description of the practices of our fictitious languages, in some cases only hints, but . . . one can easily make these descriptions more complete" (BrB, p. 102).

To illustrate the point by reference to a specific example: Perhaps, in sketching the alternative grammar and concept of "not" in which this term only has application to simple sentences, Wittgenstein rests content with a merely partial sketch that is insufficient to convey literal understanding of the grammar and concept, not necessarily because he believes that it would be impossible to give a full and determinate characterization of them which would make them literally intelligible to readers, but rather because such a task would be a large one and is supererogatory given that his philosophical purpose is merely to show that there *could* be such an alternative grammar and concept.

Second, though, Wittgenstein is in fact also skeptical that it *would* ever be possible to make an alternative grammar fully intelligible to readers through a mere description such as he provides, or could provide, in his examples. Thus in one late remark he says, "Am I not getting closer and closer to saying that in the end logic [i.e., grammar] cannot be described? You must look at the practice of language, then you will see it" (OC, #501; cf. WLPP, pp. 5–7). Wittgenstein's skepticism about this seems to be motivated by at least four considerations:

(a) The *family-resemblance* character of many concepts (for instance, the concept "game")—that is (as I would define this elusive notion), their applying in virtue of facts of some other sort but having as their extension an open class for which it proves impossible to specify necessary and sufficient conditions in terms of those facts (even in a complicated disjunctive way)—makes their use resistant to full capture in any description (see, for example, PI, #68, #78; WLC, p. 81).[10]

(b) Especially in the case of psychological concepts, the role of *criteria* presents two major obstacles to fully capturing their grammar in any description. First, the correct identification of something as a criterion that warrants applying such a concept in a particular case, for instance as a behavioral criterion of Smith's being in pain now, always essentially includes a sensitivity to complex contextual features which resists full capture in any description (see, for example, PI, p. 228; Z, #114–16, #119, #121; RPP2, #168, #206; LWPP1, #41, #920–27, #936–37). Second, even disregarding that problem, it would still be impossible to capture exhaustively in a description the numerous and diverse collection of different criteria-in-contexts which together define a particular psychological concept, because the collection's family-resemblance character forbids this (see, for example, Z, #118, #121; RPP2, #202; LWPP1, #968–73). These two concerns together lead Wittgenstein to reject the idea that one can fully describe the grammar of psychological concepts such as "to think," "to be able to count," "to pretend," and so on (see, for example, Z, #114–21 on "to think"; WLPP, p. 267 on "to be able to count"; LWPP1, #861–62 on "to pretend"; cf. LWPP1, #954 and LWPP2, pp. 89–90).[11]

(c) *Linguistic holism*, or the phenomenon of essential interdependencies between our concepts, constitutes a further obstacle to the full capture of grammar in a description for Wittgenstein.

Wittgenstein is somewhat undecided about what exact

strength to give his thesis of linguistic holism. In a moderate version, which he developed first, it merely holds that words and sentences only have their meanings in a "grammatical system" (WL, pp. 51, 53; LC, pp. 29, 36–37, 112, 114). But he later went on to develop a more radical version in which it says more ambitiously (as Donald Davidson subsequently would) that this system always encompasses a whole language: "To understand a sentence means to understand a language" (BT, p. 73; PI, #199; cf. BB, p. 5).[12] His final undecidedness between these two (or really more) possible versions of linguistic holism comes out in the following late remark (1948–49): "What am I after? The fact that the description of the use of a word is the description of a system, or systems.—But I don't have a definition for what a system is" (LWPP1, #294).[13]

Philosophically speaking, the former version of holism seems much more plausible than the latter. It is certainly easy enough to understand the *temptation* to move from the former towards the latter. For instance, if one recognizes that our color concepts form a system, one is likely also to acknowledge that this system depends on our physical-object conceptual system in various ways (as Wittgenstein arguably implies when he combats the notion that one might arrive at color concepts through inner ostensive definition), and in this way, if not indeed before, the system of our color concepts may well seem also to depend on our mathematical conceptual system (which, as Wittgenstein puts it in a passage quoted earlier, "create[s] the form of what we call facts," for example by constituting the concepts "one" and "two" which we need in order to say whether we are dealing with one physical object or two), and so on. But an unlimited linguistic holism runs into damning objections, such as the one already mentioned in chapter 2 (the "camcorder" example).

However, for present purposes, the important point is that *either* of these two versions of linguistic holism would impose severe limits on the describability of grammar. For one thing (and most obviously), they both imply that any full description of the grammar of a particular word would require a description of a whole grammatical system or language to which it belonged—which would certainly constitute a complication, and perhaps even a practical impossibility. For another thing (and less obviously), if any part of the system or language in question included family-resemblance concepts or psychological concepts with criteria, then considerations (a) and (b) would make full description of the word's grammar a strict impossibility.

(d) Wittgenstein also seems to believe that there is an essential *non-cognitive* component in all grammar and all mastery thereof which cannot be conveyed by any mere description. Thus, in *On Certainty*, where he implies grammar's resistance to description in the remark with which I began this discussion (OC, #501), he also argues that language rests on "action," "form of life," "as it were, . . . something animal" (OC, #204, #358, #359; cf. LWPP1, #913: "Words have meaning only in the stream of life"). He explicitly links this essential non-cognitive component of grammar and its mastery with the non-describability of grammar in the following passage: "There is a good sense in saying that [the primitive language-games corresponding to describing color or saying that you remember] cannot be taught by explanation. 'Apple,' in a particular tone, is a primitive expression. One could say: if the child did not express a wish, one could not do a *thing* . . . Reactions come before any explanation" (WLPP, p. 143).

That limitations on grammar's describability such as (a)–(d) are indeed among Wittgenstein's reasons for refraining from claiming to have made alternative grammars literally intelligible with his examples can be seen from the fact that he concludes the long passage quoted earlier in which he himself says about his examples exactly what Stroud says about them with a final sentence, as follows: "You have to make *further* decisions that you don't anticipate in that first determination. *Just as you also don't have an overview of the original technique, and are only familiar with it from case to case*" (LWPP2, p. 71; emphasis of final sentence added).

Third, Wittgenstein believes that, just as our confinement to a social tradition constrains us towards certain grammars and concepts (see chapter 3), so it also makes others inaccessible to us: "Compare a concept with a style of painting. For is even our style of painting arbitrary? Can we choose one at pleasure? (The Egyptian, for instance.)" (PI, p. 230).

Wittgenstein seems ambiguous between two claims here, one of which implies a very severe obstacle to access but is philosophically implausible, the other of which implies a less severe obstacle but is philosophically plausible. (a) His claim might be that it is essential to any grammar or concept that it be backed by a social tradition, and essential to one's understanding of any grammar or concept that one be part of the social tradition in question, so that in order for the alternative grammatical and conceptual possibilities gestured towards by his examples to be real, they would need to be backed by a social tradition, and even if that happened or has happened, one would need to be(come) part of the social tradition in question in order to understand them literally. Such a claim seems implausible, however, both because the social theory of meaning on which it rests is implausible (see chapter 4), and because the implication that it is impossible to achieve a literal understanding of concepts belonging to social traditions which are not one's own and which one has not joined seems false, since, for instance, the modern classical scholar seems able to arrive at a literal understanding of distinctively ancient Greek concepts (*miasma*, *mētis*, and so on). (b) Alternatively, Wittgenstein's claim might be merely that our own social tradition constitutes a causal and normative obstacle preventing our easy access to the alternative grammars and concepts of other (possible) social traditions. This is a much more plausible claim, but it also entails a much less severe and insurmountable impediment to the literal understanding of alternative grammars and concepts.

Either way, though, we can here see another reason why Wittgenstein would be reluctant to imply that his examples convey a literal understanding of alternative grammars and concepts.

Fourth, and most radically, Wittgenstein is moreover skeptical that a person could ever come literally to understand an alternative grammar and concepts, in the sense that, while retaining his literal understanding of his own grammar and concepts, he came literally to understand the alternative grammar and concepts as well, *at all*—whether through a description, through participation in another social tradition, through the careful hermeneutics of the classical scholar, *or in any other way.* For Wittgenstein espouses a doctrine to the effect that understanding any particular principle of grammar and the concepts which it constitutes (concepts which articulate it and which are made available by it for the articulation of empirical or factual propositions as well) requires that one have *a complete commitment to the principle of grammar in question of a kind making alternative uses of language to that which it prescribes unavailable to one.* (I shall call this his *doctrine of exclusive commitment.*) And this doctrine *precludes* the possibility of simultaneously understanding one's own grammar and the concepts which it constitutes and also understanding alternatives.

Thus G. E. Moore reports that already in lectures in the early 1930s, Wittgenstein insisted that meaning something by a word requires that I "commit myself," which he explained by saying that "if I commit myself, that means that if I use, e.g., 'green' in this case, I have to use it in others," "if you commit yourself there are consequences" (WL, p. 52; cf. LC, pp. 36–37).[14]

Such a position is also implied by the following passage from the *Remarks on the Foundations of Mathematics:* "So much is clear: when someone says, 'If you follow the *rule* it *must* be like this,' he has not any *clear* concept of what experience would correspond to the opposite. Or again: he has not any clear concept of what it would be like for it to be otherwise" (RFM, IV, #29; cf. Z, #442).[15]

This doctrine also plays a central role in *On Certainty.* The thesis that understanding requires a *firm commitment* to grammatical principles is fundamental to the work's anti-skeptical argument that "doubt gradually loses its sense" (OC, #56), an argument in which Wittgenstein urges, with particular reference to the apparently-factual principles which the work assigns to grammar, "If you are not certain of any fact, you cannot be certain of the meaning of your words either. If you tried to doubt everything you would not get as far as doubting anything. The game of doubting itself presupposes certainty" (OC, #114–15). Wittgenstein gives as examples of apparently-factual grammatical principles to which one must have a firm commitment if one is to understand the concepts which they contain and constitute the principles that information about the past is good grounds for what will happen in the future (PI, #481), that no one has ever been to the moon (OC, #108), and that this object before me is my hand: "If I wanted to doubt whether this was my hand, how could I avoid doubting whether the word 'hand' has any meaning? So that is something I seem to *know* after all. But more correctly: The fact that I use the word 'hand' and all the other words in my sentence without a second thought, indeed that I should stand before the abyss if I wanted so much as to try to doubt—shows that the absence of doubt belongs to the essence of the language-game, that the question 'How do I know . . .' drags out the language-game, or does away with it" (OC, #369–70;[16] cf. #456).

The thesis that the firm commitment to grammatical principles in question must moreover be of such a nature as to *exclude* alternative uses of language and hence any understanding of alternative grammars and concepts comes out when Wittgenstein says of a tribe whose people express a grammatical conviction incompatible with ours which we might be inclined to characterize as a conviction that people sometimes go to the moon, "We should feel ourselves intellectually very distant from someone who said this" (OC, #108); when he asks of someone who had a grammatical conviction incompatible with ours that, as we might be tempted to put it, "the earth has not long been," "What would he be impugning? Do I know? Would it have to be what is called a scientific belief? Might it not be a mystical one? Is there any absolute necessity for him to be contradicting historical facts? Or even geographical ones?" (OC, #236); and when he says of someone who had a grammatical convic-

tion incompatible with one's own in what one might characterize as a Last Judgment, "Suppose someone were a believer
and said: 'I believe in a Last Judgment,' and I said: 'Well, I'm
not so sure. Possibly.'. . . It isn't a question of my being anywhere near him, but on an entirely different plane, which you
could express by saying: 'You mean something altogether different, Wittgenstein'" (LCAPRB, p. 53).

Thus there are at least four reasons, four obstacles, which
amply explain Wittgenstein's refusal to imply that his examples of alternative grammars and concepts convey a literal
understanding of them but without entailing the sort of position that Williams and Lear ascribe to him. As a purely
exegetical matter, it would therefore be a mistake to infer
from this refusal that he is committed to the Williams-Lear
position.

In light of the copious and clear positive evidence for his
commitment to the diversity thesis and for his intention to
illustrate it by means of his examples, together with this alternative explanation of his initially puzzling refusal to imply
that his examples convey literal understanding, one must instead conclude that his official position is exactly the one that
Stroud ascribes to him: an intention to persuade us by means
of his examples that alternative grammars and concepts are
possible (and thereby to combat Platonism) combined with a
concession that his examples perforce fall short of making
such alternatives literally intelligible to us.

However, if this settles the *narrowly exegetical* questions to the
disadvantage of the Williams-Lear interpretation of Wittgenstein's intentions and in favor of ascribing to him just the sort
of position that Stroud ascribes to him, the *philosophical* questions involved are still very far from settled—and this in a way
threatens to permit a reopening of the exegetical ones as well,
namely at the beneficent, if not always trustworthy, hands of
interpretive charity.

In particular, the combination of positions which Stroud
ascribes to Wittgenstein (quite correctly, as I have argued),
namely an ambition to show us by means of his examples that

alternative grammars are possible combined with an insistence that such alternatives cannot be literally understood by us, is surely at best a highly unstable one, philosophically speaking. For the awkward question naturally arises: If we cannot literally understand the alleged actual or possible alternative grammars, then how can we know that they really are such, that they are not instead merely noise or else confused versions of our own grammar?

This problem would not, indeed, arise in any very acute form if the denial of literal intelligibility were grounded solely in the *first three* reasons, or obstacles, among the four recently listed. For the first reason (that concerned merely with the convenience of an abbreviated presentation) would be compatible with Wittgenstein himself understanding the alternatives, and even with his making them literally intelligible to other people as well if only he filled out his descriptions a bit more. Similarly, the second reason (grammar's transcendence of description) would be compatible with Wittgenstein and other people understanding alternative grammars as well. In fact, it is not even entirely clear that grammar's transcendence of description would have to prevent his *examples* from effecting such an understanding in other people. For might they not achieve this by causing things in his readers which transcended a mere grasp of the descriptions which they contain? (After all, as he notes in another context, even "bashing [a man] may make him understand red," though "it is no explanation" [WLPP, p. 135].) But even if grammar's transcendence of description does prevent them from achieving this, that still leaves open the possibility of Wittgenstein and other people coming to understand alternative grammars by different means—for example, by "going native," participating in the practices of people who actually have them. A similar point applies to the third reason (the role of a social tradition), which even in its stronger and less plausible version would be compatible with Wittgenstein and other people gaining access to alternative grammars by coming to participate in other social traditions that actually have them, and which in its weaker and more plausible version would be consistent with their overcoming the causal and normative obstacles to understanding involved by means of a little hard imaginative or hermeneutical work. However, the *fourth* reason makes the problem an acute one.[17]

It does so in two ways, which can be distinguished as the (more obvious) *epistemic* way and the (less obvious) *conceptual* way. As I have stressed, Wittgenstein's examples are clearly intended to persuade us that alternative grammars and concepts are sometimes actual and always possible. Now the *epistemic* problem which the doctrine of exclusive commitment causes is of course the following (already mentioned, but now due for a little more elaboration): If, because of this doctrine, it is in principle impossible for anyone ever to understand an actual or possible alternative grammar, then how could anyone ever *know*, or even have justified belief, that any putative example presented to him really constituted an actual or possible alternative grammar (rather than either mere meaningless noise or else a confused version of his own)? And so how could anyone ever *know*, or even have justified belief, that alternatives are actual or possible?

At first sight, this might seem like a mere pseudo-problem, but I want to suggest that it is in fact serious. It might appear a pseudo-problem for this reason: On the face of things, it is quite possible for someone to arrive at a justified belief, and arguably even knowledge, that an alien people is using alternative concepts, despite the fact that he is himself unable to understand the concepts in question. Consider, for example, these three sorts of cases (the first real, the other two imaginary): (1) I have a justified belief, arguably even amounting to knowledge, that the Chinese employ certain concepts which are alternatives to my own, despite the fact that I am unable to understand them because I happen not to have learned Chinese. (2) I find myself shipwrecked on a previously "undiscovered" island whose native inhabitants seem to be using a strange language intertwined with practices which appear to me in some ways familiar and in some ways unfamiliar; my best efforts at interpretation fail; nonetheless, I arrive at a justified belief, arguably even amounting to knowledge, that they are employing concepts which are alternatives to my own. (3) A group of Martians descend to Earth performing what seem to be amazing technological feats and speaking what seems to be a language; despite our best efforts over many years, we humans find ourselves unable to interpret their language; nonetheless, we arrive at a justified belief, arguably even amounting to knowledge, that they possess concepts which are alternatives to ours, ones which we are simply not intelligent enough to understand. These all seem to be perfectly possible scenarios, and they might well encourage one to suppose that if the doctrine of exclusive commitment were true, then the obstacle to understanding alternative grammars and concepts that it would constitute would no more prevent one from arriving at justified belief, and arguably even knowledge, that such things existed than do the obstacles to understanding them which occur in these three scenarios.

However, I want to suggest that such an inference is a mistake. For one thing (and perhaps most importantly), it seems clear that in all three of these scenarios, if we excavate the implicit basis for a person's claim to have justified belief or even knowledge of the presence of alternative concepts, we find that it essentially includes either (a) *other people* having been in the position of understanding both the concepts which he uses and the alien ones, and having therefore been able to serve him as authorities concerning their comparative characters (this applies to the Chinese scenario) or (b) he himself or other people who serve him as authorities at least having understood alternative concepts in such a way in *analogous* cases, thus warranting his inference that they are present here too (this might apply to the Chinese scenario, but it seems essential to the shipwreck and Martian scenarios). However, *the doctrine of exclusive commitment would preclude both (a) and (b).*

For another thing, these three scenarios all in one way or another at least leave open a *possibility* of coming to verify one's belief in the presence of alternative concepts directly by achieving an understanding of them and comparing them to one's own concepts. This is even true of the Martian scenario, where, for all the example says, the future invention of some "smart drug" or some novel form of brain surgery for transplanting Martian grey matter into human grey matter or whatnot might eventually enable us to understand Martian concepts alongside our own. By contrast, the doctrine of exclusive commitment rules out any such direct verification as *impossible in principle*. Now it seems plausible to suggest that the notions of justified belief and knowledge involve a tacit implication that there is at least a *possibility* of arriving at direct verification (in this spirit, Wittgenstein writes at one point, "*If* it makes sense to say 'I know directly that he sees,' it makes sense to say 'I know indirectly that he sees'" [LSD, p. 300]). If so, then this constitutes a further reason why it would be a mistake to infer from the fact that justified belief and knowledge seem possible in these three scenarios that they would therefore also be possible if the doctrine of exclusive commitment were true.

Nor would it help the case for saying that the problem in question is a mere pseudo-problem to redirect attention away from others and towards ourselves, to note that we might ourselves give up (or have given up) one grammar in order to embrace another, alternative one. For, although that is true enough, our doing so (or having done so) would immediately put us in precisely the same epistemic blind spot concerning our own earlier grammar as we would otherwise be in with respect to other people's: we would now be unable to understand it, and so would be obliged to look back on it with exactly the same sort of skepticism as in the other-directed case (just as we often, in waking from a dream, look back with skepticism on what in all probability really were mere illusions of an unusual sense that occurred during the dream).[18]

It might possibly still be objected that, both in the other- and in the self-directed cases, a belief in alternative concepts could be justified, and perhaps even attain the level of knowledge, as an inference to the best explanation. However, such an objection is undercut by the fact that there would be other plausible explanations available: Refraining from imputing to others or to our past selves concepts which are alternatives to

ours would not necessarily force us to impute sheer meaninglessness to them; we might instead impute to them a confused grasp of our own present concepts. And in the case of
such examples as the Martians, it should also be kept in mind
that nature routinely "performs" all sorts of extremely "clever
feats" without entertaining concepts at all (think, for example,
of nature's construction of DNA, the human brain, and the
ecosystem).

Moreover (though less obviously), this epistemic problem
would arguably engender a *conceptual* problem as well. For it
seems that a forceful argument would lead from the position
that alternative grammars are unknowable in principle to the
conclusion that it does not even make sense to suppose that
they exist.

I shall develop this point, a little circuitously, in three
stages: First, I shall show that the later Wittgenstein at least
himself suspects that such an argument exists (so that he at
least faces this much of an internal problem here). Second, I
shall identify the argument which I take to be uppermost in
his mind, but also suggest that it is in fact a philosophically
dubious one. Then, third, I shall sketch a case that there is
nonetheless a much more compelling argument available
which can be, though not straightforwardly lifted, at least "reconstructed" from his texts.

To begin with the first (and easiest) point: One can already
see in an indirect way that Wittgenstein would probably believe that an argument of the general sort in question existed
from his reaction in his 1946–47 lectures to the relevantly similar case of Lytton Strachey's speculations concerning Queen
Victoria's final, unexpressed thoughts on her deathbed:[19] "Remember Lytton Strachey talking of the thoughts of Queen
Victoria on her deathbed. If he could not conceivably know,
what sense could this have? If no sense, then why say it?"
(WLPP, p. 229; cf. p. 99). But one need not rest content with
such indirect evidence, for there happens also to be a late
"smoking gun" passage in which Wittgenstein directly implies that there is such an argument and that his thesis of the

possibility of alternative grammars and concepts is therefore in danger of proving, not only unknowable, but also, and for that very reason, senseless. In a clear, albeit tantalizingly un-developed, passage from the late *Remarks on Color* (mainly 1950–51) he says: "If [people] really have a different concept than I do, this must be shown by the fact that I can't quite figure out their use of words. But I have kept on saying that it's conceivable for our concepts to be different than they are. Was that all nonsense?" (RC, III, #123–24).

What sort of argument does Wittgenstein have in mind here? The strictly exegetical answer to this question lies, I think, in what one might call the *verificationist impulse* in his thought.

As is by now well known,[20] there was a short period in the late 1920s and early 1930s when Wittgenstein adopted a rather strong and unqualified version of verificationism. For exam-ple, during this period he said things like the following: "The sense of a proposition is the way it is verified";[21] "A proposi-tion that cannot be verified in any way has no sense";[22] "How a proposition is verified is what it says . . . The verification is not *one* token of the truth, it is *the* sense of the proposition";[23] contrary to the conception that "I can never completely verify the proposition," "The . . . conception . . . I want to cham-pion says: No, if I can never verify the sense of the proposition completely, then I cannot have meant anything by the propo-sition either. Then the proposition doesn't mean anything at all either."[24]

Occasionally, something like this strong and unqualified verificationism at least seems to resurface in later work as well. An example is Wittgenstein's 1946–47 comments con-cerning Lytton Strachey on Queen Victoria. Thus, consider along with the passage on that subject already quoted the following passage from the same lectures (slightly spoiled for this point by Wittgenstein's denial here that Strachey's spec-ulations are outright nonsense, but recall that, as we saw, he elsewhere in the lectures implies that they are, and recall also that the later Wittgenstein standardly equates meaning with use and hence lack of use with lack of meaning): "Ask another question: What must Queen Victoria have been thinking when she died? Is it nonsense? No. What use can one make of this? As it stands there, it has no use. There is no verification" (WLPP, p. 152).

Clearly, if such a form of verificationism were applied to the case in which we are here interested, it would similarly lead directly from the position that alternative grammars and concepts are in principle unknowable by us to the conclusion that any supposition by us of their existence must therefore be senseless.

As is also well known, however, the later Wittgenstein's *official* position seems rather to be one of skepticism about any such strong and unqualified form of verificationism (even to the point of denying that he had ever advocated it!). For example, in later years he reportedly said the following to a meeting of the Moral Science Club at Cambridge: "I used at one time to say that, in order to get clear how a sentence is used, it was a good idea to ask oneself the question: 'How would one try to verify such an assertion?' But that's just one way among others of getting clear about the use of a word or sentence. For example, another question which is often very useful to ask oneself is: 'How is the word learned?' But some people have turned this suggestion about asking for the verification into a dogma—as if I'd been advancing a theory about meaning."[25] Similarly, in the *Philosophical Investigations* he writes, "Asking whether and how a proposition can be verified is only a particular way of asking 'How d'you mean?' The answer is a contribution to the grammar of a proposition" (PI, #353).

Moreover, there are good reasons for such skepticism; the sort of verificationism in question seems quite implausible. For example, it seems to conflict, not only with the apparent meaningfulness of speculations like Lytton Strachey's, but also with the still more evident meaningfulness of speculations about other minds *generally*—and taken together, such conflicts surely look like a much better argument against *it* than against the meaningfulness of these speculations.

During his verificationist period, Wittgenstein had in a way bitten not only the former but also the latter of these two bullets, holding, in light of his verificationism, that one could not meaningfully ascribe minds or mental conditions to other people in the same sense in which one could ascribe them to oneself (albeit while also stressing the alleged good news that one could and did ascribe them to other people meaningfully in a different sense which merely concerned other people's behavior) (PR, #64–65). But by the time he wrote the *Blue Book* (1933–34), he had come to recognize the implausibility of biting the latter bullet in this way; he had come to perceive that one can indeed meaningfully ascribe minds and mental conditions to others in just the same sense in which one can ascribe them to oneself, and that if a philosophical theory such as verificationism forces one to say otherwise, then that is so much the worse for the theory.[26]

However, the statements quoted above in which the later Wittgenstein distances himself from any strong or unqualified form of verificationism can also be misleading. For the considered position of his mature works still includes something that is clearly recognizable as a descendant of verificationism.[27] After verificationism comes son-of-verificationism (the suggestion being, of course, that, as in the horror movies, the latter may not in the end be a huge improvement over its more notorious parent).

That verificationism does not simply disappear without trace from the considered position of his mature work can be seen in connection with his philosophy of mind (the area of most relevance here), not only from his late treatment of such cases as the Strachey case, but also from his central thesis that the meaningfulness of psychological propositions depends on the possibility of verifying them by means of outward behavioral criteria: "An 'inner process' stands in need of outward criteria" (PI, #580).[28]

How, then, does son-of-verificationism differ from its superseded parent? A full account of this would be a complicated matter and is beyond both the scope and the needs of this essay. But, in connection with the philosophy of mind, I would especially emphasize the following modifications, all tending in the direction of a modest liberalization of verificationism aimed at making it more defensible:

(1) Concerning the mind, Wittgenstein now admits a striking class of exceptions, or at least apparent exceptions, to the verificationist requirement for meaningfulness, and, surprisingly enough, precisely where such an admission might have seemed least necessary and least helpful in order to serve the verificationist impulse. During his outright verificationist period, he had taken first-person psychological reports about one's own current mental condition to be the very paradigm of conclusively verifiable, and hence meaningful, statements (see, for example, PR, #62–63; WLC, pp. 17–18). One might therefore have expected that a verificationist impulse would have motivated him to sustain such a conception of them (and, say, try to extend it to further statements as well). However, in his mature work he instead argues that first-person psychological reports concerning the present do not (normally) admit of verification at all, but are nonetheless meaningful. This might seem to bespeak a renunciation of the verificationist impulse. But on closer inspection, it rather bespeaks the very opposite: Wittgenstein is merely throwing a battle in order to win the war. Contrary to initial appearances, the concession in question does not disregard or contradict the verificationist impulse, but instead preserves and serves it, for two reasons. First, since Wittgenstein now also claims that first-person psychological reports concerning the present are (normally) merely expressive rather than descriptive or fact-stating, the verificationist intuition is not hereby really violated, namely as an intuition about descriptive or fact-stating propositions. Second, this move promises a huge payoff for the verificationist impulse, in that *second-* and *third-*person psychological reports now no longer look like hopelessly poor competitors in the verification-stakes: now that certainly verifiable truth in the case of first-person psychological reports concerning the present has been dispelled as an illusion, it seems plausible to say that second- and third-person psychological reports often have a perfectly good claim to have been verified and to constitute knowledge. Such verifica-

tion and knowledge do indeed fall short of certain truth, infallibility, but then so, it now seems apparent, do *all* reports in
this subject area. Provided that we think of verification in
such a modestly and reasonably deflated way, as including
fallible verification, we can now reconcile a principle of verificationism with the evident meaningfulness of second- and
third-person psychological reports after all. We have won the
war on behalf of (a form of) verificationism! (For this whole
move, see, for example, PI, #244–46. Also Z, #472; RPP2,
#63: "Plan for the treatment of psychological concepts. Psy-
chological verbs characterized by the fact that the third person of the present is to be verified by observation, the first
person not. Sentences in the third person of the present: information. In the first person present: expression . . . The first
person of the present akin to an expression.")[29]

(2) Closely connected with this move of helping the verificationist impulse by allowing the *fallible* verifiability of sec-
ond- and third-person psychological reports to constitute genuine verifiability and hence to satisfy the demands of a
modestly modified verificationism, the mature Wittgenstein
also develops a *criterial*, or assertibility-condition, account of
the relation between such psychological reports and observ-
able behavior, and allows mere ascertainment of the satisfac-
tion of behavioral criteria or assertibility-conditions to count
as verification of the sort required for meaningfulness by his
modified verificationism. Both of these moves might seem to
involve substantial relaxations in the sort of verificationism
defended, and in a way they do. However, the latter move in
fact also takes back some of the apparent relaxation. For on
this criterial, or assertibility-condition, account, the strikingly
pervasive and indefinite openness of second- and third-person
psychological reports based on observed behavior to revision
in the light of further behavior is no longer seen as the result
of a cognitive shortfall from mental facts (a shortfall which
some more privileged epistemic vantage point—say, God's—
might at least in principle be able to overcome), but instead
simply as a consequence of the circumstance that psychological concepts relate to their entirely behavioral basis in an

open-ended, assertibility-condition, manner.[30] This is the
thrust of Wittgenstein's remark: "It looks like obscurantism to
say . . . that pain is not a form of behavior. But only because
people believe that one is asserting the existence of an intangible, i.e. a shadowy, object side by side with what we all can
grasp. Whereas we are only pointing to different modes of
employment of words" (RFM, III, #76). Consequently, sec-
ond- and third-person psychological reports can be verified
quite as conclusively as the very nature of the concepts involved could conceivably allow, so to speak; and this is all that
a verificationist impulse could reasonably require. (For this
whole line of thought, see, for example, PI, #304–8, #352–
56.)

(3) A further aspect of the later Wittgenstein's liberalization
of verificationism concerns the distinction between rule and
exception. Whereas a strict verificationism such as he had earlier advocated would say that one's utterance of a sentence
only makes sense if there is a way for one to verify it (because
that is what its sense consists in), his later variant of verificationism allows that a sentence which its utterer cannot verify
may nevertheless be meaningful, provided only that sentences
of the general *type* in question are *normally* verifiable. (For this
line of thought, see, for example, NFL, p. 233; LSD, p. 295; PI,
#344–45.)[31]

This modestly liberalized offspring of verificationism arguably has some significant advantages over its parent. In particular, it avoids the implausibility of entailing the meaninglessness (or at least, sharp difference in meaning) of reports
concerning other minds (not surprisingly, since this was the
main motive behind the liberalizing).

Yet it arguably still entails Wittgenstein's conclusions that
Strachey's speculations about Queen Victoria and speculations about alternative grammars and concepts are meaningless. In the Strachey case, the reason would be twofold. First,
like any version of behaviorism, the version of it which Wittgenstein introduces in (2) cannot allow that the notion of people being in mental states of which they give no behavioral
manifestation at all makes sense (cf. PI, #344: "Our criterion

for someone's saying something to himself is what he tells us and the rest of his behavior"). Second, it seems plausible to say that not only this particular speculation but also the *general type* of speculation to which it belongs is unverifiable, so that even the loosened verificationist standard indicated in (3) fails to be met here (see WLPP, p. 152).

In the case of speculations about alternative grammars and concepts, the reason would be of the latter sort only: there is no question here of a lack of behavioral manifestations, but we *do* arguably again confront an in-principle unverifiability of a whole type of judgments rather than merely an accidental unverifiability of particular tokens of a normally verifiable type, so that such speculations would fall short even of the loosened verificationist standard indicated in (3).

In terms of strict exegesis, therefore, I would suggest that this is the later Wittgenstein's considered argument for the skepticism that we saw him expressing about the very meaningfulness of speculations like Strachey's and speculations about alternative grammars and concepts, on the ground of their unknowability.

However, I would also suggest that even son-of-verificationism is a very philosophically dubious position in the end. A proper critical assessment of it would be beyond the scope or needs of this essay, but the following lines of criticism seem to me worth pursuing.

Concerning (1), Wittgenstein himself concedes that first-person psychological reports relating to the present are *sometimes* descriptive or fact-stating rather than merely expressive (PI, #585; cf. pp. 187–90). Moreover, it seems plausible to say that this is at least part of their function much more commonly than he allows.[32] Either way, do they not indeed in such cases enjoy something like the certain truth that was ascribed to them by traditional epistemology? And if so, does this not indeed leave second- and third-person psychological reports looking like epistemologically poor relatives after all?

Concerning (2), it seems clear that, like all other forms of behaviorism, criterial or assertibility-condition behaviorism cannot be right because it fails to account for the evident meaningfulness, and indeed frequent truth, of speculations like Strachey's, that is to say, speculations about mental conditions which happen not to be manifested in behavior at all. This is the great Achilles' heel of all forms of behaviorism, including Wittgenstein's. As we saw, Wittgenstein bites the bullet concerning such cases, denying them meaningfulness (and a fortiori truth)—but biting bullets is a good way to break one's teeth, and it seems plausible to say that that is what happens here.

In consequence, it also seems plausible to say, contra Wittgenstein, and in the spirit of traditional epistemology, that second- and third-person psychological reports do not in fact relate to behavioral evidence as to their criteria, or assertibility-conditions, but instead do concern facts which transcend behavioral evidence, and hence fall *far* short of the sort of conclusive verifiability that is (sometimes or even often) available from the first-person standpoint.

Concerning (3), two problems arise. First, a problem which affects both Wittgenstein's specific applications of (3) to the Strachey and alternative-grammar cases and its tenability as a general principle: As I noted, Wittgenstein seems to classify the two cases in question as belonging to general types which are in principle unverifiable. This does, I think, have some intuitive plausibility. However, on further reflection, a difficulty rears its head here due to the fact that any given speculation will belong to *multiple* types. If we choose to classify Strachey's speculation as a member of the type *speculations about unexpressed deathbed thoughts* (as Wittgenstein in effect does at WLPP, p. 152), then we will indeed get the result that it is a member of an in-principle unverifiable type. But what if we instead classify it as a member of the type *speculations about deathbed thoughts*? In that case, it will belong to a normally verifiable type, and so will satisfy condition (3). Similarly, if we choose to classify speculations about alternative grammars and concepts as members of the type *speculations about alternative grammars and concepts*, then certainly we will get the conclusion that they are members of an in-principle unverifiable type. But what if we instead classify them as members of the type *speculations about other people's grammars and concepts*? In that case, they will arguably belong to a normally verifiable type (other people often have grammars and concepts which one shares, and which one can therefore understand and know about), and therefore satisfy condition (3).

It might seem that there is an obvious solution to this problem: focus on the most *specific* of the types to which a speculation belongs. However, this seems unlikely to work, since for one thing it promises to lead to the "wrong" verdict for speculations which Wittgenstein wants to see as *satisfying* condition (3): if we were always to identify the type in as specific a way as possible, then that would guarantee that *any* unverifiable proposition became classified as belonging to an unverifiable type, and so failed to meet condition (3).

There may be some other way of saving Wittgenstein's principle (3), and his application of it to the Strachey and alternative-grammar cases, in the face of this problem. But if so, that way is at least not obvious.

Second, even if principle (3) could be saved from that problem, the points which were recently urged against Wittgenstein's way of understanding second- and third-person psychological reports and in favor of a more traditional epistemological understanding of them would arguably leave us with at least one whole type of statement which never can really be verified but whose members are nonetheless perfectly meaningful, namely these ones—in which case even the loosened verificationism represented by (3) would be refuted (much as its stricter ancestor was refuted by the nature of such reports before it).[33]

If such skepticism about son-of-verificationism is justified (whether for the above or for other reasons), then even Wittgenstein's more considered, son-of-verificationist, case for saying that the unknowability of alternative grammars and concepts would entail the senselessness of hypothesizing them will ultimately fail.

In sum, I suggest that one should in the end be very skeptical of both Wittgenstein's earlier verificationist and his later son-of-verificationist reasons for thinking that the unknow-

ability of alternative grammars and concepts would make the
very supposition that there were such things senseless.

However, I believe that it is possible to "reconstruct" from
ideas in Wittgenstein's texts a much better argument for
thinking so.

Recall from the last chapter Wittgenstein's point about the
vague or fluid state of such concepts as "language" and "concept," his implication that we therefore need to make a choice
between restrictive and liberal versions of these concepts, and
the prima facie case which I sketched for defining them in a
liberal rather than a restrictive way—especially the argument
from assessments of the comparative natures of our own and
other ages' and peoples' concepts made by such empirically
informed disciplines as classical scholarship and anthropology,
together with auxiliary arguments in terms of the undesirability of foreclosing our own future intellectual and practical
development, and the undesirability of interpreting cultural
others in insensitive and disrespectful ways (these additional
arguments implicitly resting on the first one).

Now if Wittgenstein's doctrine of exclusive commitment,
and its consequence that we are in principle prevented from
ever literally understanding alternative grammars and concepts, were correct, then this sort of case for liberalism would
be quite undercut. For it would then turn out that all of those
putative results from disciplines such as classical scholarship
and anthropology which seem to constitute the primary and
strongest argument for liberalism were in fact *illusory*: it would
be impossible in principle for a classicist or anthropologist
ever to have been in the sort of situation that they commonly
suppose themselves to be in of understanding an alien's concept, comparing it with the closest available concept of their
own, and finding the two to be discrepant. And since that
fundamental empirical argument also implicitly underpinned
the two auxiliary arguments, its demise in this fashion would
also entail theirs.

In addition to thus expelling the weightiest reasons from
the liberal pan of the balance of reasons, Wittgenstein's doctrine of exclusive commitment and its implication of the unin-

telligibility to us of alternative grammars and concepts would also throw a weighty reason into the restrictive pan. For, given that the doctrine and implication in question would make it in principle impossible for us ever to verify the propositions attributing, or claiming the availability of, alternative grammatical principles and concepts which a liberal mode of expression would render coherently expressible, what function would such a liberal mode of expression serve, except perhaps the undesirable one of promoting idle (that is, in principle unverifiable) speculation?[34]

Now if, for such reasons as these, our concepts of "language," "concept," and so forth were instead to be restricted by definition to our own grammatical principles and concepts, then the very idea of alternative grammatical principles and concepts would thereby become an incoherent one for us, so that their very possibility would be excluded. And in that case, Wittgenstein's putative examples of actual and possible alternative grammatical principles and concepts could in fact be nothing more than either mere noise or else confused attempts to express the only grammatical principles and concepts that there are or could be, namely ours.

In short, even without any appeal to verificationism or son-of-verificationism, Wittgenstein's doctrine of exclusive commitment would arguably lead to the conclusion that the very notion of alternative grammars and concepts, and hence also Wittgenstein's diversity thesis, were in fact senseless.

The moral to be drawn from this whole situation is that Wittgenstein probably needs to make a choice between his diversity thesis and his doctrine of exclusive commitment; he cannot plausibly sustain both.

Exegetically speaking, this shows that there is somewhat more to be said for the Williams-Lear interpretation of Wittgenstein's position than there initially seemed to be.

But which way should our final exegetical decision fall here? If we are to attribute to Wittgenstein a "considered" position (as is no doubt optional), which should it be? And which way should our final *philosophical* decision fall?

It seems to me that both decisions (both the exegetical and

the philosophical) should fall on the side of preferring the diversity thesis over the doctrine of exclusive commitment. Let me briefly sketch some reasons for this judgment which may already be evident from things I have said before, and then attempt to reinforce it by adding a further consideration in a little more detail.

Concerning the exegetical question first, it seems to me, in light of the sort of evidence presented in chapters 2 and 5, that the later Wittgenstein is even more deeply committed to the diversity thesis than he is to the doctrine of exclusive commitment, so that if he had to choose between them, it would be the former rather than the latter that would survive. (This is not to say that his commitment to the latter is by any means superficial either, however. In particular, if he were to abandon it, that would also entail abandoning a central part of his anti-skeptical case in *On Certainty*. The choice that he faces here would be a genuinely painful one for him.[35])

Philosophically speaking too: It seems to me that there are powerful arguments available in support of the diversity thesis—especially, the sort of argument from the results of actually interpreting historical and cultural aliens which I have cited as favoring a liberal rather than a restrictive definition of such concepts as "language" and "concept." By contrast, I can see no good argument for accepting the doctrine of exclusive commitment.

However, rather than elaborating further on those points, I would like now to try to reinforce them by showing that the rejection of the doctrine of exclusive commitment which they advocate both for exegesis and for philosophy is also attractive on plausible grounds, including plausible Wittgensteinian grounds, which are independent of the consideration that the doctrine conflicts with the diversity thesis and that the diversity thesis is more deeply grounded both exegetically and philosophically.

The doctrine that literally understanding a grammatical principle and the concepts for which it plays a constitutive role requires that one accept the principle in question with a firm commitment making impossible divergence from the use of terms which it prescribes is, it seems to me, a strange one for Wittgenstein to have embraced in the first place.

We commonly think of the understanding of a linguistic expression as consisting in a knowledge of its meaning. And so one would expect Wittgenstein, who normally equates the meaning of an expression with its use, to think of the understanding of an expression as a knowledge of its use, or, perhaps better, a knowledge of how to use it. And indeed, this is exactly how he does characterize understanding in several places. For example, in the *Philosophical Grammar* he writes: "Do I understand the word 'perhaps'?—And how do I judge whether I do? Well, something like this: I know how it's used, I can explain its use to somebody, say by describing it in made-up cases. I can describe the occasion of its use, its position in sentences, the intonation it has in speech.—Of course this only means that 'I understand the word "perhaps"' comes to the same as: 'I know how it is used etc.'" (PG, I, #28); "'Understanding a word' may mean: *knowing* how it is used; *being able to* apply it" (PG, I, #10; cf. WLC, pp. 48, 78–79; NPL, p. 456; BT, pp. 27, 105).[36]

Now, the question that one should ask oneself here, I think, is this: If a linguistic expression's meaning *is* its use—and this certainly seems an extremely helpful proposal, despite the fact that I have raised doubts about some of the specificity which Wittgenstein builds into it, in particular at levels (3), (4), and (5), suggesting that it should be pruned back towards the minimalist version of levels (1) and (2) (see chapter 4);[37] and despite the fact that it arguably remains an undesirably vague proposal which leaves some important questions open[38]—so that understanding a linguistic expression *does* consist in knowing its use, or in knowing how to use it, then does any exegetically or philosophically plausible interpretation of this definition leave room for the idea that understanding an expression requires the sort of certain commitment to the rules of use for the expression, making impossible its use in ways that deviate from those prescribed by the rules, which the doctrine of exclusive commitment says it requires? I would suggest that the answer is pretty clearly "No."

To exploit Wittgenstein's own analogy between language-games and games like chess (with which this essay began): A person may know the use of the chess pieces perfectly—in particular, he may possess the ability to engage in their correct use and to communicate the rules for their correct use to other people (in strict analogy with the abilities described in the passages recently quoted from the *Philosophical Grammar*)—and he may therefore understand the game of chess perfectly too, and yet he may have nothing resembling the sort of firm commitment to these rules, and consequent inability to deviate from the use that they prescribe, which the Wittgensteinian doctrine of exclusive commitment implies. On the contrary, he might think (for whatever reasons or none) that the rules of chess are silly or boring, and spend most of his time, when not called upon to demonstrate his understanding of chess, instead playing some close variant of the game which involves systematic deviations from what the rules of chess would permit. Why should not the knowledge of the use of a linguistic expression which constitutes a person's understanding of it allow him the same kind of freedom?[39]

Indeed, Wittgenstein's analogy with games aside, is it not clear that it does? Is it not clear, for example, that a clever classical mathematician who believes that intuitionism is a misguided position may nonetheless be able to do mathematics in the intuitionists' mode with perfect competence upon demand (disregarding the law of excluded middle and so on with the best of them), and hence demonstrate that he understands the intuitionists' non-classical meanings for the truth-functions just as well as they do themselves, even though he has no inclination at all to adopt this alternative grammar and these alternative concepts seriously, let alone a commitment to doing so to the exclusion of all competitors (in particular, his beloved classical ones)?

Or to raise another objection against the doctrine of exclusive commitment: How can this doctrine be reconciled with the fact that we quite commonly seem to be in situations of just the sort that it denies to be possible—that is, situations of simultaneously grasping subtly opposed grammars and hence meanings of words—with respect to single words *within our own everyday languages*? Think, for example, of the subtle ambiguities in the everyday words "man" and "lady" which make cutting remarks like "He's a man but not a man" and "She's a lady but not a lady" immediately intelligible to any native speaker of English as something other than self-contradictions; or of the subtle ambiguity in the everyday word "impressed" which makes the response to the observation "I hear you were impressed by him" "Negatively impressed!" readily intelligible to any native speaker of English as dissent rather than assent. Wittgenstein himself occasionally discusses similar cases; for example, in the *Blue Book* he discusses subtle ambiguities in our words "proof" and "kind" (BB, pp. 28–29).

In short, there seem to be good reasons, including good Wittgensteinian ones, for being skeptical about the doctrine of exclusive commitment anyway.[40] And this reinforces the primary case recently sketched for saying that in the conflict between the diversity thesis and this doctrine, it is the former which should be preferred over the latter both exegetically and philosophically.

One final observation. The philosophical problem which I have discussed in this chapter arises quite frequently in one variant or another, and the philosophical moral at which I have been driving generalizes to other cases. For example, Gadamer sometimes seems to want to argue *both* that human language and mentality have changed in profound ways over the course of history *and* that each of us is locked into a historically specific form of "pre-understanding" which precludes undistorted access to the language and mentality of historical others. But to the extent that he does want to argue in this way, he surely courts epistemic and conceptual difficulties precisely analogous to those which we have found Wittgenstein running into. And analogously again, I would suggest that the proper solution here is to retain the thesis of historical change (which seems amply justified), and to recognize that the mistake instead lies in the thesis that we are doomed to a distorted understanding of historical others by our confinement to a specific "pre-understanding."

In this case, I would argue that the mistake should be located, more specifically, not in the doctrine of "pre-understanding" itself—however much this doctrine seems to be, and probably really is, at odds with Wittgenstein's anti-psychologism, or conviction that mental processes are inessential to understanding and that understanding instead consists solely in linguistic competence[41]—but rather in a neglect of the power of the imagination, in particular a neglect of its power to reproduce historical others' "pre-understandings" in a way which, while more than merely a propositional description of them, is also less than the sort of committed "pre-understanding" that underlies our use of our own concepts.

However, this is a subject for another place. My purpose in mentioning it here is simply to make a little more vivid the suggestion that Wittgenstein's problem as it has been described in this chapter also arises in other forms, and that when it does, it requires solutions analogous to the one that I have proposed here too.

Appendix

The *Philosophical Investigations*

IT MAY BE appropriate to conclude by appending a few brief comments about the *Philosophical Investigations* and its relation to the topics considered in this essay.

As I mentioned at the beginning of the essay, the *Philosophical Investigations* is not as obviously concerned with the question of grammar and its arbitrariness as some of Wittgenstein's other late texts. Moreover, as we have now seen, when it *does* touch on the latter topic, it often seems to stress *non-*arbitrariness (examples of this are #185, p. 230, and #520, which stress various aspects of the non-arbitrariness discussed in chapter 3) and to undercut the idea of arbitrariness in other ways (see, for example, the implication at #136 that classical logic is internal to propositionality [discussed in chapter 5], and the implication at #206–8 that there are narrow limits to the "linguistic" [discussed in chapter 6]).

I suspect that these features of the *Philosophical Investigations* largely explain the confidence with which some advocates of the Williams-Lear reading of Wittgenstein's position have recommended it; they have been misled by focusing too exclusively on the *Philosophical Investigations* to the neglect of other late texts.

A champion of the Williams-Lear reading might, however, try to turn this weakness into a strength by arguing that, since the *Philosophical Investigations* was the only late work actually prepared for publication by Wittgenstein himself, it can claim an official and final status which the other texts lack, so that its one-sidedness on this question should be seen as a faithful reflection of Wittgenstein's considered position.

The instinct to make this sort of move when interpreting a

philosopher—to look for an "official and final" statement of his position which eliminates all the tensions (and favors one's own philosophical preferences)—is almost always misguided, in my experience. But in this particular case there are at least two more specific considerations which would make such a move inappropriate.

First, on closer inspection the apparent bias in the *Philosophical Investigations* mentioned above is in fact almost entirely illusory. Thus, the arbitrariness thesis is fully represented there if one looks for it. Not only is the claim of grammar's arbitrariness itself present (#372, #497), but so too are all of the main components of this thesis distinguished in chapter 2: grammatical principles and concepts, including those of formal logic and mathematics, have alternatives (#554–55, pp. 226–27, p. 230); grammar cannot be justified by appeal to truth-in-virtue-of-meaning (p. 147), or by appeal to facts (#497, p. 230), or by appeal to the fulfillment of purposes (#496–97); particular grammars are neither correct nor incorrect vis-à-vis alternatives (p. 147, note b); nor do some grammars make possible factual truths but others not (p. 230), or make for greater accuracy in factual statements than others (p. 225).

In addition, the several aspects of grammar's non-arbitrariness mentioned at #185, p. 230, and #520 are fully consistent with the arbitrariness thesis, as this essay has shown.

So in the end, it could really only be the passages at #136 concerning classical logic's internality to propositions and at #206–8 concerning the narrow bounds of the linguistic that might be thought to show some sort of bias in favor of pruning back the arbitrariness thesis in the direction of the Williams-Lear position. However, the former of these passages is consistent with Wittgenstein's most prominent strategy for preventing the putative internality of classical logic to propositions and so forth from undercutting arbitrariness (the "If not propositions, then why not schmpropositions?" strategy discussed in chapter 5); moreover, that strategy is invoked within the *Philosophical Investigations* itself (at pp. 226–27, in a mathematical version). And, as we saw in chapter 6, paragraphs #206–8 are both vague and significantly less radical than the (A) passages from the *Philosophical Grammar* and elsewhere in the extent to which they might require a pruning back of the arbitrariness thesis.

Second, the idea that the *Philosophical Investigations* represents Wittgenstein's official and final position to the exclusion of the ideas found in other late works will not stand up to scrutiny. For one thing, Wittgenstein for a long time intended to include in the work the sort of material on mathematics and formal logic which is found in the *Remarks on the Foundations of Mathematics* and which emphasizes arbitrariness, only deciding against doing so quite late, and due to despair at bringing the project to a satisfactory conclusion rather than to design;[1] and the published *Philosophical Investigations* itself points towards this material prominently in its final paragraph (p. 232). For another thing, Wittgenstein's very last work, *On Certainty*, is one of the richest sources for his thesis of grammar's arbitrariness.

In short, any attempt to mount a challenge to the sort of interpretation which has been offered in this essay on the grounds that the *Philosophical Investigations* adopts a contrary position and that this is Wittgenstein's official and final position would involve both a dubious reading of the *Philosophical Investigations* itself and an unjustified gerrymandering of the available textual evidence.

Notes

NOTES TO THE INTRODUCTION

1. A classic essay by Davidson on these subjects is "On the Very Idea of a Conceptual Scheme," in D. Davidson, *Inquiries into Truth and Interpretation* (Oxford: Clarendon Press, 1991). For a critical discussion of Davidson's views, see my "On the Very Idea of Denying the Existence of Radically Different Conceptual Schemes," in *Inquiry*, vol. 41, no. 2 (1998).

2. Noteworthy exceptions to this rule are the very helpful discussions in P.M.S. Hacker, *Insight and Illusion* (Oxford: Oxford University Press, 1972), ch. 6, and G. P. Baker and P.M.S. Hacker, *Wittgenstein: Rules, Grammar, and Necessity* (Oxford: Basil Blackwell, 2000), chs. 3, 6.

3. The *Philosophical Investigations* is indeed somewhat atypical in the impression it tends to give of Wittgenstein's positions on these subjects. I shall address this point in an appendix at the end of the essay.

4. Aversion to such positions is also largely responsible for an important, but I think ultimately misguided, reading of the later Wittgenstein's views in this area originally invented by B. Williams in his essay "Wittgenstein and Idealism" (in *Understanding Wittgenstein*, ed. G. Vesey, Ithaca, NY: Cornell University Press, 1976) and subsequently developed in a less qualified but more elegant version by J. Lear in "Leaving the World Alone" (*Journal of Philosophy*, vol. 79, no. 7 [1982]) and "The Disappearing 'We'" (*Proceedings of the Aristotelian Society*, supplementary vol. 58 [1984]). This reading will serve as a sort of foil for the interpretation developed in the present work.

5. I am of course alluding here to a fairly widespread tendency in the secondary literature to base interpretation of Wittgenstein on an assumption, or strong presumption, that he must be, if not indeed simply correct on all essential points, then at least self-consistent, at the very least within a given phase of his work.

An approach of this sort is sometimes advocated by philosophers as essential to sound interpretation generally (see, e.g., Davidson's "principle of charity"), and is widely practiced by historians of philosophy more particularly. However, it is sadly misguided as a principle of interpretation generally (for some helpful discussion of this large and difficult topic, see Q. Skinner, "Meaning and Understanding in the History of Ideas," in *Meaning and Context*, ed. J. Tully [Princeton, NJ: Princeton Unversity Press, 1988]). And it is rarely appropriate or fruitful in the interpretation of philosophical texts in particular (though there are occasional exceptions).

An extreme example of this sort of interpretive approach to Wittgenstein is provided by recent proponents of a "resolute" reading of the *Tractatus* and a "new Wittgenstein," who, having implausibly read the *Tractatus* as holding a certain consistent position (for a devastating critique of this reading, see P.M.S. Hacker, "Was He Trying to Whistle It?" in *The New Wittgenstein*, ed. A. Crary and R. Read [London and New York: Routledge, 2000]; perhaps "resolute" really means "resolute in the face of overwhelming contrary textual evidence"?), implausibly find the same position consistently sustained in the later writings as well (the added implausibility here is twofold, lying both in the assertion of a basic consistency across the two periods and in the assertion of consistency within the later period itself). Nor does it help that the strand of Wittgenstein's writings which gets exalted to play the role of the true center of his philosophy in this dubious interpretive enterprise is their "purely-therapeutic" strand, with its conceptual and theoretical quietism (i.e., refusal to effect any conceptual change or to make any claims beyond those of common sense). This methodological strand is indeed amply present in the texts, but Wittgenstein also constantly contradicts it with his philosophical practice (note that one does not avoid making substantive claims merely by expressing them in the form of rhetorical questions, comments set in quotation marks, unstated implications of concrete examples, and so on!), and in its unrestricted form it is among the least philosophically defensible and interesting strands to be found there. (It is not part of the purpose of the present essay to argue for this view, though some of the specific claims that I shall be making could be seen as contributions towards such an argument—for example, my attribution to Wittgenstein of a theoretically loaded concept[ion] of use and hence of meaning, which is incompatible with conceptual quietism [chapters 3 and 4]; my attribution to him of a quasi-Kantian idealism and a doctrine of grammar's antecedence to truth, both of which are incompatible with theoretical quietism [chapters 1 and 2]; and my claim that embracing the vagueness or fluidity of everyday concepts, as conceptual quietism would require, entails unacceptable consequences [chapter 6].) The present essay will not have much more to say about the "new Wittgenstein." Instead, it will focus less fashionably on the old one, the one who died in 1951.

A more commonly fruitful interpretive approach in connection with philosophical texts is the contrary one recently exemplified by M. Burnyeat in his work on the *Theaetetus* and D. Henrich in his work on Kant's transcendental deduction of the categories: an approach which acknowledges tensions and even inconsistencies in a philosopher's thought where necessary, and sets about investigating these and adjudicating between them. As a rule, such an approach is *hermeneutically* superior, not only in the (obvious) sense that it avoids the grotesque interpretive falsifications which tend to result from the alternative approach but also in the (less obvious) sense that it is often precisely in the region of a philosopher's tensions and inconsistencies that one can see his deepest philosophical assumptions and motives most clearly revealed. It is also *philosophically* superior, in that it is often precisely in the area of a major philosopher's tensions and inconsistencies that one finds unusually difficult and important philosophical questions which deserve to be considered and tackled. Wittgenstein's texts, which, especially in his later period, are highly exploratory, ambiguous, and even inconsistent in character, are no exception to this general rule. They will accordingly be interpreted here very much in this Burnyeat-Henrich mode.

6. Although the essay will touch on a fairly broad range of issues in Wittgenstein's later philosophy, its real focus is thus quite narrow.

7. Due to Wittgenstein's slightly idiosyncratic system of divisions in the *Philosophical Investigations* and the *Philosophical Grammar*, I shall be referring to earlier passages by paragraph numbers but to later ones by page numbers, as here.

Notes to Chapter One
Grammar

1. I shall use these two words more or less interchangeably in this essay, although it should be noted that Wittgenstein occasionally draws a distinction between them, treating concepts as a subset of meanings, namely as meanings which have a descriptive content (see, e.g., RFM, VII, #71).

2. As time went on, the later Wittgenstein certainly became increasingly wary of this conception of *rules* governing our linguistic practices and thereby constituting our concepts (for some discussion of this, see D. G. Stern, *Wittgenstein on Mind and Language* [Oxford: Oxford University Press, 1995]). However, his wariness never drove him to give it up. Instead, he increasingly qualified it in various ways (e.g., by conceding an essential role to empirical application, embeddedness in "forms of life," vagueness, and non-explicitness or even non-explicitability). S. Cavell's well-known depiction of the later Wittgenstein as repudiating the notion that language is rule-governed—"The Availability of Wittgenstein's Later Philosophy," in *Wittgenstein*, ed. G. Pitcher (London: Macmillan, 1968), pp. 154–61—therefore contains a grain of truth, but one outweighed by a larger nugget of falsehood.

3. This analogy is a major part of the force of Wittgenstein's notion of a "language-game." There are also a number of others, however, including: the ideas that linguistic practices, like games, are very diverse and relate to each other in a "family-resemblance" manner (PI, #65–67); that linguistic practices, like games, are interwoven with actions and forms of life (PI, #7, #23); and that linguistic practices, like games, serve no single external purpose (BT, p. 166).

4. Thus Wittgenstein says: "What does it mean to use language according to grammatical rules? . . . There must be rules, for language must be

systematic. Compare games: if there are no rules there is no game, and chess, for example, is like a language in this sense" (LC, p. 48).

5. Thus Wittgenstein says that grammatical

"rules do not *follow* from the idea . . . ; *they constitute it* . . . What idea do we have of the king of chess, and what is its relation to the rules of chess? The chess player has an idea of what the king will do. But what the king can do is laid down by the rules. Do these rules follow from the idea? Can I deduce the rules once I get hold of the idea in the chess player's mind? No. The rules are not something contained in the idea . . . and got by analyzing it. They constitute it" (WLC, p. 86; cf. PI, #136).

6. Thus Wittgenstein notes concerning grammatical rules: "The general rule is the standard in terms of which we judge what we are doing" (LC, pp. 40–41).

7. Wittgenstein is acutely aware of a danger of, and concerned to avert, some possible misunderstandings here, however. For example, contrary to a temptation to infer that grammar is therefore a trivial or dispensable matter, he insists on "the *deep* need for the convention" (RFM, I, #74). And contrary to a temptation to infer that grammar is therefore not only social—which he usually implies that it is—but also the product of an explicit social decision, he repudiates any such conclusion (WLC, pp. 156–57). His characterization of grammar as consisting in "conventions" has also led to certain further misunderstandings of his position in the secondary literature, especially in a well-known essay by M. Dummett, "Wittgenstein's Philosophy of Mathematics" (in *Wittgenstein*, ed. Pitcher), and it will be part of the task of the present work to dispel these by in effect explaining more exactly some senses in which grammar is, and some senses in which it is not, for Wittgenstein a matter of conventions.

8. This seems to be denied by Baker and Hacker, who write that for the later Wittgenstein "there can be no hidden rules awaiting discovery, which we cannot yet formulate, but which we tacitly know and follow" (*Wittgenstein: Rules, Grammar, and Necessity*, p. 36). However, Wittgenstein's contrary position is clear. For example, already in *Wittgenstein's Lectures: Cambridge 1930–1932* he tells us that "correct use does not imply the ability to make the rules explicit" (LC, p. 53; cf. pp. 54, 84; WWK, pp. 77–78). And in *On Certainty* (1950–51) he says of certain fundamental empirical-seeming propositions which he is inclined to regard as in fact grammatical (or "logical") that "their role is like that of rules of a game; and the game can be learned purely practically, without learning any explicit rules" (OC, #95); that although they are ones which "I do not explicitly learn," nevertheless "I can *discover* them subsequently like the axis around which a body rotates" (OC, #152).

Indeed, as time went on the later Wittgenstein came increasingly to believe that certain aspects of grammar were resistant to explicit linguistic formulation *altogether*. Hence, for example, in the late *On Certainty* he writes (deliberately echoing the old saying/showing distinction of the *Tractatus*): "Am I not getting closer and closer to saying that in the end logic [i.e., grammar] cannot be described? You must look at the practice of language, then you will see it" (OC, #501; cf. WLPP, pp. 5–7; RPP1, #654, #944; RPP2, #167, #200, #202, #206). Consequently, my "may" in "may subsequently achieve explicit formulation" strictly means "may *in some cases*."

Wittgenstein's reasons for thinking that certain aspects of grammar resist explicit linguistic formulation altogether will be discussed in more detail later (chapter 7), but they seem to fall under four main headings: (1) the *family-resemblance* character of certain concepts resists explicit linguistic formulation; (2) both the individual identification and the exhaustive specification of the *criteria* for concepts such as psychological concepts resist explicit linguistic formulation; (3) *linguistic holism* presents a further obstacle to explicit linguistic formulation (especially when combined with (1) and (2)); (4) there is for Wittgenstein an essential *non-cognitive*, "animal" component to grammar which resists explicit linguistic formulation.

This raises some important questions bearing on our subject, which can perhaps be briefly addressed here via consideration of a recent dispute between S. Affeldt (following S. Cavell) and S. Mulhall concerning the nature of Wittgenstein's position, conducted in the *European Journal of Philosophy*, vol. 6, no. 1 (April 1998). Their dispute largely addresses the issue of whether or not it is correct to think of Wittgensteinian grammar as consisting in rules. Mulhall's position is that it *is*, and that what is exegetically controversial is rather the exact *sense* of the word "rules" that is in question for Wittgenstein, whereas Affeldt (following Cavell) is skeptical about the appropriateness of the concept of a rule for capturing Wittgenstein's position in this area. The account of Wittgenstein's conception of grammar which I am developing here, according to which for him grammar both literally consists of rules and is analogous to the rules of games—as well as several other fundamental features of his position (e.g., his famous *rule*-following argument, which is predicated on an assumption that meaning is constituted by grammatical rules)—suggests that the former view must be correct. However, the points just made about certain aspects of grammar being for Wittgenstein not only linguistically unformulated but also linguistically unformulable suggest that there is also something to Affeldt's (and Cavell's) skepticism about the appropriateness of the concept of a rule for capturing Wittgenstein's position. For, while the idea of a linguistically unformul*ated* rule seems unproblematic enough, that of an unformul*able* rule is surely counterintuitive to the point of near-unintelligibility.

I think that it was largely a recognition of this fact and of the consequent need for a more illuminating way of characterizing such features of grammar that motivated the later Wittgenstein's deep interest in the phenomenon of *recognizing aspects*, or as one might more fully describe this phenomenon in order to bring out the connection: recognizing aspects and the directions of assimilation and contrast that are internal to them (PI, p. 212: "What I perceive in the dawning of an aspect is not a property of the object, but an internal relation between it and other objects") in ways which transcend any linguistic explicitation or interpretation of those directions (PI, p. 211: "Is being struck looking plus thinking? No"). Thus, in the *Philosophical Investigations* Wittgenstein's extended discussion of recognizing aspects is preceded by some points concerning limitations to the idea that understanding (language-)games consists of grasping rules (PI, #567) which he concludes with the cryptic remark, "Meaning is a physiognomy" (PI, #568); and he repeatedly stresses the kinship between recognizing aspects and grasping meanings in the course of that discussion itself: "I can see [an arbitrary cipher] in various aspects according to the fiction I surround it with. And here there is a close kinship with 'experiencing the meaning of a word'" (PI, p. 210), "The importance of this concept [of aspect-blindness] lies in the connection between the concepts of 'seeing an aspect' and 'experiencing the meaning of a word'" (PI, p. 214). In this spirit, he says in the *Remarks on the Philosophy of Psychology* that it would be difficult to give rules for words like "this," "that," "these," etc., but that it is nonetheless possible to understand their use, which "gets to be felt as if each had a single physiognomy" (RPP1, #654; cf. #944).

However, I do not think that any of this in the end shows that Wittgenstein came to see, or should have come to see, either his literal equation of grammar with rules or his analogy between grammatical rules and the rules of games as really errors. Rather, it shows that in the literal equation, as Mulhall implies may be the case, we are dealing with a slightly unusual concept of "rules" (namely, one modified so as to drop the usual implication of full linguistic explicitability and to incorporate such things as a supra-linguistic recognition of aspects and their directions of assimilation and contrast), and that in the analogy—as indeed in all analogies—our attention is being drawn to similarities which at a certain point give way to significant differences.

9. This remains the case despite the fact that Wittgenstein does perhaps more than any other major philosopher before him to alert us to the many uses of language, and indeed whole language-games, which are *not* concerned with stating truths (see, e.g., PI, #23-24).

10. Strictly speaking, one should perhaps qualify this a little. This at least seems to be the case when what is in question is the grammar of "true-false" language-games, and—anticipating a point to be discussed later in this chapter, namely Wittgenstein's somewhat surprising official assimilation of his sense of "grammar" to the traditional one, and hence inclusion of traditional grammar under "grammar" in his sense—more specifically those aspects of it which especially concern the philosopher. However, one might possibly argue that for Wittgenstein a certain (broader) sort of necessity extends even to the grammar of non-"true-false" language-games and to the rules of traditional grammar.

11. The later Wittgenstein sometimes uses the word "logic" to mean formal logic, sometimes to mean the much broader category of grammar.

12. The addition of this class of apparently-empirical propositions to grammar—already foreshadowed in the *Philosophical Investigations* (PI, #251: "something whose form makes it look like an empirical proposition, but which is really a grammatical one")—is the most important constructive innovation which Wittgenstein makes in his last work, *On Certainty*, where it also forms the basis of the work's main strategy for combatting skepticism.

13. This heavily qualified, rather cagey way of putting the point is designed to avoid begging some nice questions, much debated in the literature, concerning the exact character of Wittgenstein's conception of the criteria of psychological states, which we need not go into here.

14. In saying this I am to some extent disagreeing with J. A. Coffa, who in his excellent book *The Semantic Tradition from Kant to Carnap: To the Vienna Station* (Cambridge: Cambridge University Press, 1991) tends to depict the later Wittgenstein as (along with Carnap) the culmination of a "semantic tradition" that, rather, *freed itself from Kant's errors*—in particular, from Kant's appeal to pure intuition and from Kant's conception of analyticity. Putting things in this way seems to me a case of overlooking the forest for the trees—that is, failing to notice the forest of their shared explanation of the necessity of certain principles in terms of mind-imposition for the trees of some admittedly significant differences in the extent to which and the detailed ways in which they think this explanation applies.

I also find significantly more echoes of Kant at the level of the details of Wittgenstein's theory than Coffa does (e.g., Wittgenstein's development of a naturalistic counterpart and substitute for Kant's conception that the human mind is somehow constrained by its nature to impose the synthetic a priori principles it does, and Wittgenstein's commitment to a form of idealism, on both of which subjects more anon).

Aside from these interpretive disagreements, there are many points on which I would agree with Coffa's very illuminating account, however (e.g., concerning Wittgenstein's rejection of Kant's pure intuition and Kant's conception of analyticity, and Wittgenstein's substitution for the latter of a [relatively] novel conception of a priori principles as constituting rather than deriving from concepts).

15. For this vitally important assumption behind Kant's position, see especially the revealing precritical essay *The Only Possible Proof of God's Existence* (1763), in which this assumption motivates a conclusion that we need to posit God as the ground of all possibilities.

16. *Critique of Pure Reason* (1781/1787), A 52/B 76: formal logic "contains the absolutely necessary rules of thought without which there can be no employment whatever of the understanding." Kant evidently overlooks the fact that this explanation itself includes a modal claim: "*can* be no."

17. This was in fact Kant's earliest argument for transcendental idealism, already being central to his first case for such a position, in the *Inaugural*

Dissertation of 1770. He later added to it (and also tended to run together with it) a second argument for transcendental idealism motivated by the puzzle of how we can *know in advance of experience* that experience and its objects will conform to synthetic a priori propositions (this again being, by contrast, quite unpuzzling in his view in the case of logical and analytic propositions); and also a third argument motivated by a puzzle, first adumbrated in his famous 1772 letter to Herz, concerning how a priori concepts (such as cause and substance) can refer, given that reference requires causal dependence in one direction or the other between concept and referent, and that, unlike empirical concepts, which are causally dependent on their referents, a priori concepts are not.

18. This is why, whereas Kant saw fundamental differences between several different kinds of necessary propositions, as contrasted with empirical ones—namely, logical necessities, (other) analytic necessities, and synthetic a priori necessities—for Wittgenstein all (more than merely causal) necessities are fundamentally similar, and the distinction between necessary principles and empirical ones is fundamentally just a *two*-term distinction: *grammar* versus the empirical.

For this reason, it seems to me quite misleading of Baker and Hacker to lead off their list of "leitmotivs" in Wittgenstein's account of necessity with the observation that for him "necessary truths are heterogeneous" (*Wittgenstein: Rules, Grammar, and Necessity*, p. 264). It is, of course, true that he identifies significant differences among necessary or grammatical principles (see, e.g., RFM, IV, #39), as he almost *always* does when treating *any* class of language-uses (recall his envisaged motto for the *Philosophical Investigations*: "I'll teach you differences"). But what is much more striking and noteworthy in this case is his *denial* of the sorts of fundamental differences between them that had been alleged by philosophical predecessors such as Kant and Frege (who even in his logicist phase acknowledged synthetic a priori necessities in geometry as well as the necessities of formal logic/arithmetic).

In this respect, Wittgenstein's later work is remarkably continuous in spirit with the *Tractatus*, which had likewise sought to subvert that philosophical tradition by arguing that all necessities were of a single sort, namely for the *Tractatus* necessities of formal logic (T, 6.37: "The only necessity that exists is *logical* necessity").

19. For a discussion of the early history of the "linguistic turn" in philosophy, see my essays "Herder's Philosophy of Language, Interpretation, and Translation: Three Fundamental Principles," in *The Review of Metaphysics*, vol. 56, no. 2 (2002); "Gods, Animals, and Artists: Some Problem Cases in Herder's Philosophy of Language," in *Inquiry*, vol. 46, no. 1 (2003); and "Language," forthcoming in the *Cambridge History of Philosophy in the Nineteenth Century*, ed. A. Wood (Cambridge: Cambridge University Press, 2004).

20. Cf. Coffa, *The Semantic Tradition*, esp. ch. 14. Coffa plausibly argues that the development of this conception by Wittgenstein, Carnap, and some of their predecessors was a huge philosophical advance.

21. It is one of the main virtues of Dummett's essay "Wittgenstein's Philosophy of Mathematics" to have clearly recognized that the later Wittgenstein's conception of (mathematical) grammar as consisting in rules imposed by us is motivated by a puzzle concerning the source of necessity (see especially pp. 424 ff.). However, Dummett overlooks the Kantian background to this line of thought, the way in which Wittgenstein generalizes Kant's problem and solution, and (an especially serious shortcoming) this whole second limb of Wittgenstein's explanation, Wittgenstein's claim that, and explanation how, we are *constrained* to impose the necessary principles that we do.

22. In a somewhat exaggerated statement of this aspect of his account, Wittgenstein writes, "The mathematical Must is only another expression of the fact that mathematics forms concepts" (RFM, VII, #67). As will become clear in chapter 2, this feature of his explanation of the nature of necessity is greatly deflated in comparison to more traditional versions of it because (a) he sees necessary principles as constituting meanings or concepts rather than meanings or concepts as constraining necessary principles and (b) he believes there to be a variety of alternative meanings or concepts available in each area of discourse. Nonetheless, as can be seen from the passage just quoted, the modest sort of internality of necessary principles to concepts which these two qualifications leave intact still constitutes *part* of his explanation of the nature of necessity.

23. It is only superficially inconsistent with this assessment that the later Wittgenstein himself speaks of "idealism" in very critical terms (see, e.g., WL, pp. 102–3; PI, #402). For the sort of "idealism" that is in question in these critical remarks is quite different from the sort of "idealism" that I am attributing to him here: to put it in terms of a distinction of Kant's, it is (roughly) empirical idealism rather than transcendental idealism. See, e.g., BT, pp. 334–35; WL, pp. 102–3.

24. Note that because Kant and Wittgenstein hold such a view, the metaphor of the human mind's "imposing" necessary principles can be a dangerous one to use in explicating their position, unless it is kept clearly in view that the imposition in question is for them as much a *constitution* of facts as a structuring or ordering of them.

25. G.E.M. Anscombe, "The Question of Linguistic Idealism," in G.E.M. Anscombe, *From Parmenides to Wittgenstein* (Minneapolis: University of Minnesota Press, 1981); D. Bloor, "The Question of Linguistic Idealism Revisited," in *The Cambridge Companion to Wittgenstein*, ed. H. Sluga and D. G. Stern (Cambridge: Cambridge University Press, 1999). Cf. N. Garver ("Philosophy as Grammar," in the same volume), who claims that for the later Wittgenstein modality is imposed by us on a world of independent facts (p. 161); also Coffa, *The Semantic Tradition*, p. 263.

26. The motivation behind the later Wittgenstein's conception of the grammar of "true-false games" which has been explained, and this idealist consequence thereof, show that there is an important sense in which his

later philosophy is genuinely Kantian in *character*. It is also here largely Kantian in *inspiration*. Note, for example, besides passages explicitly referring to Kant like the one just quoted, also such facts as the following: (1) Already as a schoolboy Wittgenstein had been exposed to relevant Kantian ideas through such authors as Boltzmann and Hertz and had found them sympathetic (see R. Monk, *Ludwig Wittgenstein: The Duty of Genius* [New York: Penguin, 1991], p. 26). (2) The early Wittgenstein was in particular attracted to Kant's (and Schopenhauer's) doctrine of the transcendental ideality of time and space (see P.M.S. Hacker, *Insight and Illusion*, revised edition [Bristol: Thoemmes, 1997], pp. 99–100). (3) Frege, who strongly influenced both the early and the late Wittgenstein, although he was an anti-Kantian about arithmetic, was a Kantian in conceiving geometry as synthetic a priori and in holding a transcendental idealist theory of space. (4) Logical positivism, which heavily influenced Wittgenstein in the transition between his early and later periods, began as a form of neo-Kantianism (see Coffa, *The Semantic Tradition*, p. 189), logical positivists such as Reichenbach and Schlick adopting even Kant's idealist conception of the mind's constitution of objects (ibid., pp. 191–92, 201).

This thesis of the later Wittgenstein's Kantianism should be sharply distinguished, however, from certain other allegations of his Kantianism to be found in the secondary literature. For example, Lear claims that Wittgenstein's later philosophy is Kantian by virtue of denying that there are or could be alternative grammars ("Leaving the World Alone," p. 392). Such a claim seems to me quite mistaken. For, while Kant certainly issued a form of such a denial (concerning human intelligence for many necessary principles, concerning all intelligence for the necessary principles of formal logic), the later Wittgenstein does not. It is indeed one of the main differences between their respective ways of developing their explanations of necessity that, whereas Kant is a unitarian (at least where human intelligence is concerned), Wittgenstein is a committed pluralist (see esp. ch. 2). In a later paper, "The Disappearing 'We,'" Lear in a way makes his misinterpretation still more extreme by pointing out, quite correctly, that Kant's unitarianism is (largely) restricted to human intelligence—or more precisely, to discursive intelligence with spatiotemporal intuitions—but then claiming that in contrast Wittgenstein's unitarianism is even more radical because unrestricted.

In chapter 5 we shall encounter another allegation of the later Wittgenstein's Kantianism which turns out to be basically false, this time an allegation of his Kantianism concerning the nature of formal logic made by H. Putnam and J. Conant.

27. Wittgenstein took this position in an exchange with G. E. Moore. See LC, pp. 97–98; WL, p. 69. R. Monk, *Wittgenstein: The Duty of Genius* gives an account of this at pp. 322–23. Cf. Wittgenstein's distinction in the *Philosophical Investigations* between "surface grammar" and "depth grammar" (PI, #664).

28. See, for example, P, p. 17: "We could say that we are calling something else grammar than [the philologist] is" (cf. WLC, p. 31).

29. The latter point addresses a criticism of Wittgenstein's assimilation of his sense of "grammar" to the ordinary sense of "grammar" leveled by N. Garver at "Philosophy as Grammar," p. 150.

30. Wittgenstein's interest in this descriptive sort of grammar derives mainly from the fact that it promises to serve the diagnosis and cure of philosophical errors, which in his view arise from confusions about ordinary language's grammar (in the primary sense)—for example, from assuming that substantives like "number" or "meaning" must refer to things, or from mistaking grammatical rules for superstrong empirical facts (as, for instance, when a philosopher misconstrues the exclusion of doubt and error about one's own current mental states by a grammatical rule as a fact of incorrigible self-knowledge through introspection). PI, #90: "Our investigation is therefore a grammatical one. Such an investigation sheds light on our problem by clearing misunderstandings away. Misunderstandings concerning the use of words, caused, among other things, by certain analogies between the forms of expression in different regions of language."

31. See, e.g., Moore at WL, pp. 62–63; Hacker, *Insight and Illusion*, p. 151; R. Harris, *Language, Saussure, and Wittgenstein* (London: Routledge, 1988), p. 69; N. Garver, "Philosophy as Grammar," p. 157.

32. Note that this interpretation runs contrary to numerous claims to be found in the secondary literature that for Wittgenstein grammar (in the secondary sense) is purely descriptive, non-normative: for example, R. Harris, *Language, Saussure, and Wittgenstein*, pp. 62–64, 68; N. Garver, "Philosophy as Grammar," p. 148. It may seem that this interpretation cannot be right and that the contrary claims just mentioned must be, because Wittgenstein himself repeatedly characterizes the relevant sort of grammar as merely descriptive—for example, at PI, #109, #496 and OC, #189, #628. However, this appearance is illusory. For, as can be seen from a closer examination of the passages in question, the contrast at which Wittgenstein is aiming in calling the relevant sort of grammar merely descriptive is a contrast with an activity that involves setting up an *ideal language* and measuring ordinary language against it, or *explaining* ordinary language, not with an activity that involves any sort of normativity at all.

NOTES TO CHAPTER TWO
GRAMMAR'S ARBITRARINESS

1. Wittgenstein's picture is that they are both different enough and similar enough to be real *alternatives*, or rivals: If they were at bottom merely notational variants of each other, then their alternativeness or rivalry would be undermined by insufficient difference. But equally, if they were too different—like, say, arithmetic versus color attribution, or the taxonomy of

mammals versus that of fish—then they would again fail to be alternatives, or rivals, in the sense that Wittgenstein has in mind.

Just what this sense is is a rather tricky question. Since for Wittgenstein such grammatical rivalry always involves conceptual incommensurability, there can be no question for him of there being a literal contradiction or other logical incompatibility between rival grammars. Instead, his idea is that there is a different sort of rivalry which can still occur even when the rivals are separated by conceptual incommensurability. This idea seems intuitively plausible. How it might be defined or explained more precisely is a difficult question, though, and Wittgenstein gives few clues. Here is one possibility: Two grammatical principles A and B are rivals in this sense if they are such that, although they are not logically incompatible, satisfying the behavioral criteria for conviction in A is incompatible with at the same time satisfying those for conviction in B.

Given his focus on rivalries which exhibit a measure of similarity, Wittgenstein largely ignores the—in a sense, more radical—question of whether there might not be grammatical or conceptual schemes that are more or less *wholly* different from ours, perhaps ones grounded in quite different perceptual organs from ours, for instance (an important question with which T. Nagel has been much concerned, for example in his *The View from Nowhere* [New York and Oxford: Oxford University Press, 1989]). This important further question is therefore left aside in the following discussion. It is, though, indirectly addressed in this modest sense: As we shall see in chapters 5, 6, and 7, there are certain strands in Wittgenstein's texts which threaten to undercut even the relatively mild pluralism of his diversity thesis, and which would certainly undercut this more radical sort of pluralism as well—so, in dissolving those strands, both exegetically and philosophically, as I shall attempt to do, I shall (among other things) in effect be removing some obstacles to thinking of this more radical pluralism as one that he could countenance and that might be genuinely viable.

2. For the moment, I shall not bother with certain subtleties of formulation that would be required in order to describe these examples with complete accuracy. Concerning such subtleties, see chapter 7.

3. I shall not here challenge this interpretation of the *Tractatus*, though aspects of it might possibly be challenged.

4. See B. Stroud, "Wittgenstein and Logical Necessity," in *Wittgenstein*, ed. Pitcher, esp. p. 489. Stroud takes Wittgenstein's examples of alternative grammars and concepts to be aimed against the "Platonism" of Frege and the early Russell (ibid., p. 479). "Platonism" can be a confusing term in this connection, however. Plato had himself held at least two positions which might be relevant here: (1) that meanings are *sparse*, so to speak, that there is just one concept of Virtue, one concept of Justice, and so on; (2) that meanings are eternal objects ontologically independent of human beings. These two doctrines are logically autonomous of each other: one could coherently be a Platonist in sense (1) without being a Platonist in sense (2),

or vice versa. Like Plato, Frege had in fact held versions of both of these doctrines, however (his commitment to a version of (2) is obvious, though sometimes questioned; concerning his commitment to a version of (1), recall, for example, his notorious judgment that even "and" and "but" are identical in sense). Now in interpreting Wittgenstein's appeal to examples of alternative grammars and concepts as aimed against "Platonism," Stroud is apparently thinking primarily of versions of doctrine (1), and it is clear, indeed trivially so, that exhibiting such alternatives would indeed refute Platonism in *this* sense. Wittgenstein is also, and equally, opposed to versions of doctrine (2). But it is much less clear whether, or if so how, his appeal to examples of alternative grammars and concepts is meant to defeat Platonism in *this* sense. Indeed, one might plausibly argue that, on the contrary, his main case against *this* doctrine is quite different in character, and his examples of alternative grammars and concepts *presuppose* that case rather than *constituting* it (since as long as Platonism (2) seems a viable position, it will be open to someone confronted with the linguistic practices which allegedly represent the alternatives to question whether they really do so, to suggest that they may instead simply be different, perhaps more or less adequate, reflections of a single concept, i.e., a single eternal object).

5. Cf. PI, #420. Incidentally, interpreters who follow the current orthodoxy in the secondary literature that Wittgenstein was in no sense a behaviorist or even tempted to adopt a form of behaviorism should reflect carefully on this example. Of course, he often seems to deny that he is a behaviorist explicitly, and such interpreters tend to seize gratefully on these apparent denials. But they are highly ambiguous and need to be read very carefully. What they are often really saying, I think, is not that there is anything more to the mental than behavior, but rather that mental talk relates to what Wittgenstein is indeed inclined to take to be its entirely behavioral basis in a distinctively open-ended "criterial," or assertibility-condition, manner, so that it is a mistake simply to *identify* mental conditions with behavioral processes, to suppose that if such and such a behavioral process occurs, then it *simply constitutes* a corresponding mental condition (since whatever behavioral process occurs, the ascription of the mental predicate in question, unlike that of the behavioral process predicate, can still be overturned in the light of further behavior which might occur). For this reason, *standard* conceptions of behaviorism are in Wittgenstein's view no, or at least little, better than other philosophies of mind—for example, dualism or mind-brain identity theories—which similarly misunderstand the distinctive feature of the grammar of mental talk in question and, on the basis of this misunderstanding, equate mental conditions with *non*-behavioral processes, states, or objects of some sort. It is in this spirit, I suggest, that one should read such ambiguous denials of behaviorism as the following: "It looks like obscurantism to say . . . that pain is not a form of behavior. But only because people believe that one is asserting the existence of an intangible, i.e. a shadowy, object side by side with what we all can

grasp. Whereas we are only pointing to different modes of employment of words" (RFM, III, #76); "'Are you not really a behaviorist in disguise? Aren't you at bottom really saying that everything except human behavior is a fiction?'—If I do speak of a fiction [note that Wittgenstein does not deny that he does!], then it is of a *grammatical* fiction" (PI, #307; cf. #304–8).

A subtler objection to a behaviorist reading might go like this:

> Wittgenstein's account of rule-following, meaning, understanding, intending, and similar phenomena can helpfully be seen as a sort of naturalistic transcription of Frege's anti-psychologism about sense, a sort of displacement of Frege's "third realm" from a non-natural Platonist plane to the natural plane of human behavior: in addition to such mental states and processes as having sensations and images, and in addition to physical objects, states, and processes, there are also these behaviorally based but criterial, or assertibility-conditioned, phenomena. But (1) this move involves still seeing *other* psychological phenomena, such as having sensations and images, as *non*-behavioral, and moreover (2) its presence in the texts suggests that the behaviorist reading arises through a hasty generalization from Wittgenstein's genuinely behaviorist analysis of rule-following, meaning, understanding, intending, etc. to a false imputation to him of such an analysis of *all* psychological phenomena.

Now the constructive proposal here concerning how to read Wittgenstein in light of Frege seems to me roughly correct (and also important). However, the alleged negative consequences for a behaviorist interpretation do not follow. For, ad (2), as Wittgenstein's "soulless tribe" example illustrates, it is by no means the case that the only evidence for his attraction to a global behaviorism lies in his behaviorist treatment of rule-following, meaning, understanding, intending, etc.; and ad (1), it may well be that the contrast between these phenomena and such phenomena as having sensations and images is ultimately, for Wittgenstein, a contrast, not between concepts which are criterially based entirely in behavior and concepts which are not, but instead between concepts so based in *one* specific way and concepts so based in *another*.

6. Closely related to these examples, though, are Wittgenstein's attempts to unmask the nonsensicality of philosophical positions more generally (cf. PI, #464: "My aim is: to teach you to pass from a piece of disguised nonsense to something that is patent nonsense") and his attempts in the *Blue Book* to show that philosophical positions such as idealism, solipsism, and sense-datum theories, which seem to represent exciting alternatives to the outlook of common sense, are in fact only *notationally* different from it (see BB, pp. 29–30, 57–60, 70, 73).

7. N. Malcolm, "Wittgenstein and Idealism," in *Idealism Past and Present*, ed. G. Vesey (Cambridge: Cambridge University Press, 1982).

8. "The Disappearing 'We,'" p. 233, n. 37.

9. In (a sort of) fairness to Williams, he is acutely aware of evidence like that cited earlier and of its prima facie conflict with his reading ("Wittgenstein and Idealism," pp. 87–89), and he is accordingly extremely hesitant about claiming that Wittgenstein really holds the view which he attributes to him (p. 85: "In fact I am not going to claim anything as strong as that he held it; it seems to me that both the nature of the view, and the nature of the later Wittgenstein material, make it hard to substantiate any unqualified claim of that kind"). With exegetical enemies like that, who needs friends? By contrast, Lear pays hardly any attention at all to such contrary evidence, and presents the reading simply as an accurate interpretation of Wittgenstein.

10. Certain of Wittgenstein's own actual examples constitute small steps in this direction. For some interesting further steps—though ones which are no more motivated by the reason of principle that I have just sketched than his own—see Baker and Hacker, *Wittgenstein: Rules, Grammar, and Necessity*, pp. 318 ff. Their discussions of older Japanese concepts of time and of the introduction of negative integers into mathematics are especially suggestive.

11. Concerning this picture, see, for example, LFM, pp. 180, 184, 190.

12. This is a good example of a type of stunning reversal of perspective in which the later Wittgenstein specializes. We will see another example in chapter 7 in connection with his philosophy of mind. These reversals of perspective are sometimes successful and sometimes not. The present one arguably is, the one in chapter 7 arguably not.

13. To be a bit more precise, the two parties *share* the trousers. The reason why the metaphor of *sharing* the trousers is really the more apt one here is that for the later Wittgenstein (in sharp contrast to the middle Wittgenstein, for whom logical or grammatical principles were still strictly speaking meaningless—see, e.g., LC—and moreover independent of any extra-logical applications—see, e.g., WWK) grammatical principles are themselves essentially meaningful and, as we shall see in chapter 3, the meanings or concepts which articulate them must also have factual or empirical applications (must also appear "in *mufti*," as he puts it), so that grammatical principles cannot *by themselves* constitute the meanings or concepts which effect their own articulation.

14. A possible response to this point, which as far as I know Wittgenstein nowhere considers, might be as follows: Even if there is a modicum of conceptual incommensurability between the facts appealed to and the grammatical principle which is supposed to be justified or refuted in light of them, can there not still be a *sort* of agreement or conflict between the two, and hence a *sort* of justification or refutation? Indeed, is Wittgenstein not himself implicitly committed to such a possibility? For, on the one hand, he himself often speaks of such grammatical principles as those of mathematics as resulting from a hardening of an empirical regularity into a grammatical rule (see, for instance, RFM, VI, #22-23)—the idea being roughly

that, for example, people first observe that putting together two sets of two things always yields four things (except in a reasonably well defined class of exceptional cases—chemical reactions, and so forth), and then harden this regularity into the grammatical rule $2 + 2 = 4$—which, since on his theory of grammar such a grammatical rule is always internal to its concepts, commits him to allowing that the concepts which articulated the prior regularity were not quite the same as those which articulate the resulting grammatical rule (and henceforth also the empirical claims connected with it), so that he is here committed to conceding that there is a kind of *agreement* and support between factual propositions and grammatical rules which crosses a modest conceptual divide. And on the other hand, as we have seen, he believes that there is always a kind of rivalry between alternative grammatical principles in a subject area (the diversity thesis), despite the fact that it is a consequence of his conception of the internality of grammatical principles to concepts that in such cases the rivals are never articulated in quite the same concepts, so that he is thereby committed to allowing that there can also be a kind of *conflict* which crosses a modest conceptual divide.

15. The texts also contain a few further arguments against the possibility of justifying grammar by appeal to facts, but they seem to me less significant. For example, *Wittgenstein's Lectures: Cambridge 1930–1932* contains the following two arguments: (i) Any justification of grammar would have to employ grammar itself and so would be viciously circular (LC, p. 44). (ii) Any attempt to describe features of reality which conform with grammar in order to justify grammar (e.g., "There really are four primary colors") would be nonsensical because in order for a proposition to have a sense its negation must have a sense as well, but the negation of the putative description in question would be excluded by grammar and hence would not have a sense, so that the putative description in question would not have a sense either (LC, pp. 47, 49; cf. BT, p. 167).

Argument (i) sounds fallacious at first hearing, and would be if it were meant to thwart the sort of justification of grammar with which we have been concerned here, namely a justification of particular grammatical principles (over against possible alternatives), since in that case it would be sufficient to point out in reply to the argument that the grammar used in the justification could be different from that to be justified, so that vicious circularity would be avoided. However, the argument is perhaps instead aimed against a different sort of justification of grammar from that with which we have been concerned, namely a justification of using grammar *at all*. In that case, the argument avoids being fallacious, but it does so by simply not bearing on the question with which we have been concerned, that of justifying particular grammatical principles (over against possible alternatives).

Argument (ii) seems vulnerable to a serious objection. Note, to begin with, that the doctrine to which this argument appeals, "Meaningful claim, meaningful negation," is one which Wittgenstein later qualified in a certain way. At this date, i.e., in the early 1930s, he still thought of grammatical principles as meaningless (as he had thought of formal logical principles in the *Tractatus*). But he later came to accord them a sense, and in doing so created a class of exceptions to the doctrine mentioned: grammatical principles do have a meaning even though their negations do not (albeit that things which *look* very much like their negations, and which, while not logically inconsistent with them, are genuinely incompatible with them in another way, *may*). However, the doctrine still held for *factual* claims. And so this change of position would not itself have precluded use of the argument, which precisely depends on an application of the doctrine to factual claims. The real objection here is, rather, that it is by no means clear that every description of reality that might serve to justify a grammatical principle would have to be *required* by that grammatical principle, in the way that "There really are four primary colors" perhaps *is* required by the similar-sounding grammatical principle which it might be called on to justify; the description might instead conform with the grammatical principle, and hence arguably support it, in a way which nonetheless left the description's negation consistent with the principle, and so meaningful. For example, someone might attempt to justify the grammatical principle "Every event has a cause" by noting that every event which we have investigated so far has been found to have an identifiable cause.

16. Passages suggesting that Wittgenstein may sometimes be tempted to commit this fallacy include the one recently quoted in which he argues for the arbitrariness of grammatical rules on the ground that, unlike cookery, which is defined by an independent end, "'speaking' is not," and also the following: "For the rules of grammar there is no justification. The language in which we might try to justify the rules of grammar of our language would have to have a grammar itself" (LC, p. 44).

17. Wittgenstein could probably have chosen a better example here.

18. Presumably, in the latter case—since the elasticity that Wittgenstein has in mind is one of extension rather than compression, and better business is a matter of greater profit—the grocers would have to be exploiting their strength when buying their produce wholesale, not when selling it retail!

19. I am grateful to Paul Horwich for encouraging me to address this subject.

20. For example, he already writes in 1914: "If we say one *logical* proposition *follows* logically from another, this means something quite different from saying that a *real* proposition follows logically from *another*" (N, p. 109).

21. In the *Tractatus* he writes: "All propositions of logic are of equal status: it is not the case that some of them are essentially primitive propositions and others essentially derived propositions" (T, 6.127).

22. As might be expected given his official quietude, Wittgenstein does

on occasion imply that they can constitute justifications in *some* sense, however (see, e.g., RFM, VI, #3, #4, #9).

23. Wittgenstein's considered conception of proofs of necessary principles is that they in fact involve both scenarios in a certain order, moving from the latter one to the former one (RFM, VI, #10, #22).

24. It is worth noting that, as it stands, this argument seems inadequate for establishing the conclusion that the rules of grammar cannot be correct or incorrect, because it leaves open the possibility that their correctness might consist in their constitution of meanings which make possible the articulation of true, or at least *more* adequate, factual claims, and their incorrectness in their constitution of meanings which fail to make this possible. However, as we shall see when we turn to Wittgenstein's stance concerning factual claims themselves, he would reject this suggestion, thereby plugging this lacuna in the argument.

25. Concerning the method-of-measurement analogy used here, cf. PG, I, #133 for an application of it to grammar generally again, RFM, I, #156 (as quoted shortly) for an application of it to formal logic specifically, and RFM, III, #75 for an application of it to mathematics specifically.

See PI, p. 225 for some remarks designed to block the following inference which someone might be tempted to draw from this analogy: since methods of measurement come with different degrees of accuracy, some bringing us closer, and some less close, to the objects measured, a similar situation will hold for grammars.

26. One should not too hastily assume that Wittgenstein's references here to a "correspondence" to truth or reality function to restrict his target to the idea that logical inferences have a *certain sort* of truth. As we shall see later, he does on occasion restrict his target in such a way, and this may well be *one* of the things that is in his mind here (cf. RFM, I, #8). But he sometimes in his later work uses the notion of correspondence to reality in a deflated sense in which it simply *means* true—for example, in the following passage: "If we . . . translate the words 'It is true . . .' by 'A reality corresponds to . . .'—then to say a reality corresponds to [some mathematical propositions] would say only that we affirm some mathematical propositions and deny others" (LFM, p. 239). And this is probably at least part of what is happening here too. Thus note that in this passage he goes on to say that logical inferences are antecedent to "correctness or incorrectness," i.e., to something that certainly includes, and is indeed even more generic than, truth (or falsehood) in general. The bottom line is that this passage is probably ambiguous between the two positions in question.

27. Concerning the doctrine of antecedence to truth and falsehood as it applies to the logical and mathematical parts of grammar specifically, cf. C. Wright, *Wittgenstein on the Foundations of Mathematics* (Cambridge, MA: Harvard University Press, 1980), passim. H. Glock well stresses Wittgenstein's application of the doctrine to grammar more generally in his "Necessity and Normativity," in *The Cambridge Companion to Wittgenstein*. Un-

characteristically for him, but like many other commentators, Hacker seems initially to have overlooked this rather fundamental aspect of Wittgenstein's position concerning grammar, since he repeatedly applies the concept of truth to grammatical principles in *Insight and Illusion* (see, e.g., pp. 154–55, 162). This has since been somewhat corrected in Baker and Hacker, *Wittgenstein: Rules, Grammar, and Necessity* (see, e.g., p. 54), but only with a lot of vacillation on the matter (see, e.g., pp. 276 ff., 343). Similarly in Hacker, *Insight and Illusion*, revised edition (see, e.g., pp. 185, 192–93, 198, 201, 207–8), but again with much vacillation (see, e.g., pp. 204, 207 n. 21). As we shall find, Wittgenstein is himself guilty of vacillation in this area—but the doctrine of antecedence to truth and falsehood does seem to be his considered position.

28. Along with his positive characterization of grammatical principles as (like) rules, conventions, commands, commandments, or categorical imperatives, and his—thereby implied—negative characterization of them as not really statements or assertions, Wittgenstein, especially in *On Certainty*, also offers a number of further positive and negative characterizations of them. To begin with some negative ones: Since they cannot be correct or incorrect, true or false, and are rules rather than assertions, he not surprisingly also denies that they can really be *known* (though this is not the only reason for the denial). Thus in *On Certainty* he notes that "'I know' relates to a possibility of demonstrating the truth" (OC, #243), and elsewhere he writes concerning the grammatical principles of mathematics in particular: "If you know a mathematical proposition, that's not to say you yet know *anything*. I.e., the mathematical proposition is only supposed to supply a framework for a description" (RFM, VII, #2). For similar reasons, *On Certainty* sharply contrasts the attitude of accepting grammatical principles with believing (*glauben*), suspecting (*vermuten*), and seeing (*sehen*). Accordingly, concerning the grammatical principles of mathematics specifically, Wittgenstein suggests that, like chess rules, they play a role which precludes believing them (RFM, I, #111). Again for similar reasons, he also denies that coming to accept a grammatical principle in mathematics is ever a matter of discovery (suggesting, as a positive alternative, that we should instead see it as a matter of invention) (RFM, I, #168; I, appendix II, #2). On the positive side, *On Certainty* characterizes the attitude of accepting grammatical principles as instead a kind of standing fast of the principles for one (*feststehen*), being certain of them (*gewiß/sicher sein*), or having faith in them (again, but now in a different sense, *glauben*—the distinction between the two senses of this word is a commonplace in everyday German, and is explicitly noted by Wittgenstein at OC, #459). And the work also argues that this standing fast, certainty, or faith which constitutes the acceptance of grammatical principles has less in common with such attitudes as knowing, believing, suspecting, and seeing than with *actions*: "The end is not certain propositions' striking us immediately as true, i.e. it is not a kind of *seeing* on our part; but it is our *acting*, which lies at the bottom of the language-game" (OC, #204;

cf. #510-11, #534). Accordingly, Wittgenstein assimilates the grammatical principles of mathematics in particular to forms of action (RFM, IV, #32; VII, #21). *On Certainty* adds that this attitude should be regarded "not as something akin to hastiness or superficiality, but as a form of life" (OC, #358), "as it were, as something animal" (OC, #359).

29. I am heavily indebted to Gideon Rosen for the first four objections which follow.

30. One could also put this by saying, more simply, *declarative sentence*— so long as one understands by this expression, not a sentence *actually* declared or asserted, but a sentence *apt* for declaration or assertion.

31. P. Winch makes use of an idea somewhat similar to this in his essay "Understanding a Primitive Society" (in *Rationality*, ed. B. R. Wilson [New York: Harper and Row, 1971]), written in conscious exploitation of Wittgenstein's views. He writes there: "What [God's] reality amounts to can only be seen from the religious tradition in which the concept of God is used, and this use is very unlike the use of scientific concepts, say of theoretical entities. The point is that it is *within* the religious use of language that the conception of God's reality has its place . . . Reality is not what gives language its sense. What is real and what is unreal shows itself *in* the sense that language has" (pp. 81-82).

32. Note that a question analogous to the one that has been discussed here could also be raised concerning transitions between different "language-games" *of our own*—for example, between the language-games of enumerating objects, ascribing colors to them, attributing mental processes to people, morally assessing them, and so on (cf. the preceding note on Winch)—and that a similar range of answers would in principle be available in reply (i.e., successful claims in all of these domains are simply true; they are "true" only in different senses of "true" [cf. Winch]; or they are sometimes "true" in the same sense, sometimes in different senses). I shall not pursue this point any further, however.

NOTES TO CHAPTER THREE
GRAMMAR'S NON-ARBITRARINESS

1. Dummett writes, for example: "[Wittgenstein] appears to hold that it is up to us to decide to regard any statement we happen to pick on as holding necessarily, if we choose to do so" (pp. 433-34).

2. The explanation of Wittgenstein's talk of choices or decisions in passages such as those just cited is in fact complex. Occasionally, it probably *does* reflect a passing attraction to the view which Dummett attributes to him but which I am denying to be his considered view. At other times, it may express the somewhat similar but also significantly different thought that we are *sometimes* in a position to choose between alternative grammatical principles (a less radical thought which will play a role later in this essay,

in chapter 6). More commonly, though, Wittgenstein's talk of choices or decisions is intended to convey one or more of a variety of more technical philosophical points none of which implies that the adoption of a grammatical principle is a matter of choice or decision in any normal sense of the words: for example, that accepting a grammatical principle is more akin to embracing an imperative or to performing an act than to having an opinion; that it is always an adoption of a grammatical principle to the exclusion of possible alternatives; that it always lacks any justification; and that when we adopt a new grammatical principle, even as the result of a logical or mathematical proof, we are in a certain sense never *bound* to do so by the grammatical principles which we have adopted in the past, so that our transition from the latter to our new conclusion always in a certain sense involves a "decision."

3. Wittgenstein is reluctant, though, to fix the line between what is natural in human behavior and what is acquired through social practices and traditions (the next constraint) too precisely or confidently. In his view, this is really an empirical question whose exact settlement is not essential for his purposes. See, for example, WLPP, p. 163.

4. Note that this last passage shows with special clarity that Wittgenstein does indeed intend the—here, social—constraints which he is invoking to function as part of his explanation of the nature of necessity.

5. The nature of the rule-following argument and of its conclusion are of course deeply controversial questions. I shall say a little more about them in what follows.

6. "Wittgenstein's Philosophy of Mathematics," pp. 434-36.

7. It is worth noting that this strategy of argument would not yet have been available to Wittgenstein in the very early 1930s because at that time he still believed that it was part of the *nature* of grammatical principles to be meaningless, just as he had previously believed this of principles of formal logic in the *Tractatus* (see, for example, LC, passim).

8. It may be worth briefly addressing some common and tempting misunderstandings of this famous passage. First, it should not be assumed that "for a large class of cases—though not for all" implies any very dramatic qualification of the doctrine here. For by the time Wittgenstein writes this passage, he is in all likelihood merely thinking of such obvious exceptions as, for example, one which he discusses later in the *Philosophical Investigations*, namely the fact that sometimes when we ask about the "meaning" of what someone has said, we mean by this not the semantic content of his remarks but rather something more like their *point*, their real thrust or weight: "But when one says 'I hope he'll come'—doesn't the feeling give the word 'hope' its meaning [*Bedeutung*]? . . . If the feeling gives the word its meaning, then here 'meaning' means *point* [*worauf es ankommt*]" (PI, #545; cf. #676-77; also Z, #3, #397; another example of the sort of thing that Wittgenstein means to exclude might be what Grice calls *natural* meaning, as in "Dark clouds mean rain").

(However, it is interesting, and quite instructive for what follows, to note that when Wittgenstein *first* developed his doctrine of meaning-as-use, he was much more inclined than later to acknowledge more significant exceptions, such as that in ordinary usage "meaning" does in fact sometimes signify the sorts of mental accompaniments, for instance images, which his mature position teaches us to distinguish from it so sharply [see, e.g., WL, p. 51; WLC, p. 121], and that he was accordingly much more inclined than later to present his doctrine rather as a proposal for simplifying and improving ordinary usage than as a simple reflection of it [see, e.g., WLC, p. 48].)

Second, nor would it be correct to argue—as I recently heard a Wittgenstein scholar argue at a conference—that finding a doctrine of meaning as use in this passage depends on a mistranslation by Anscombe of *erklären* as "define" when it really just means "explain." For one thing, even if the word *did* merely mean "explain" here (as it indeed usually does in everyday German), this interpretive argument would still need to confront the awkward fact that Wittgenstein goes on to say that "the meaning of a word *is* its use in the language." For another thing, this argument is itself the product of a sort of linguistic error. For, while *erklären* does indeed usually mean "explain" in everyday German, there has also been a more technical use of the word in circulation among philosophers and mathematicians since at least Kant—including, besides Kant himself, also Hilbert, for example—in which it does mean "define" (concerning this technical use, see Coffa, *The Semantic Tradition*, esp. p. 10 on Kant, and p. 129 on Hilbert). Wittgenstein was certainly familiar with this more technical use. Indeed, in *The Big Typescript* he himself sometimes uses *erklären* in the sense of defining, or giving a statement of meaning (see, e.g., pp. 21, 23), moreover in several places switching back and forth between *erklären* and *definieren* as though they are virtual synonyms (see, e.g., pp. 22, 42, 57, 127).

9. Levels (4) and (5) of the sense that the word "use" comes to bear in Wittgenstein's equation of meaning with use are incorporated by him into the meaning of the word on the strength of his view that the conditions which they specify are shown to be necessary for rule-following, and hence for meaning, by his famous rule-following argument.

In ascribing to Wittgenstein the view that meaning requires a social practice, I am in agreement with a long line of interpreters, notably including S. A. Kripke, *Wittgenstein on Rules and Private Language* (Cambridge, MA: Harvard University Press, 1982), and N. Malcolm, "Wittgenstein on Language and Rules," in his *Wittgensteinian Themes: Essays 1978–1989* (Ithaca and London: Cornell University Press, 1995), the latter of whom helpfully cites much additional textual evidence.

It is sometimes argued in the literature that Wittgenstein does *not* believe that meaning requires society, that in his view a one-man enduring practice could suffice—for example, by Baker and Hacker, in *Wittgenstein: Rules, Grammar, and Necessity* and in "Malcolm on Language and Rules," in P.M.S. Hacker, *Wittgenstein: Connections and Controversies* (Oxford: Clarendon Press,

2001); C. McGinn, *Wittgenstein on Meaning* (Oxford: Oxford University Press, 1984); and J. Lear, "The Disappearing 'We.'" As Malcolm suggests, this line of interpretation often seems to stem less from scrupulous exegesis of the texts than from philosophical aversion to the sociality doctrine. However, it is by no means entirely without textual support. Note, for example, the caginess of Wittgenstein's expression of the sociality doctrine at PI, #199 and in many passages of RFM (e.g., III, #67; VI, #21, #32), which contrasts quite strikingly with the greater confidence of his commitments there to the need for an enduring practice *simpliciter* (though note that he occasionally even seems doubtful about this, e.g., at RFM, VI, #34). And consider also MS 124, an early draft of PI, #243 quoted and discussed by Baker and Hacker in "Malcolm on Language and Rules" (perhaps the star exhibit for this line of interpretation).

A very interesting and plausible compromise interpretation has been suggested by A. MacIntyre, in his "Color, Culture, and Practices," in *Midwest Studies in Philosophy*, vol. 17, ed. P. A. French, T. E. Uehling, Jr., and H. K. Wettstein (Notre Dame, IN: University of Notre Dame Press, 1992), who argues that the question of whether there could be a solitary user of language may be one which does not have a determinate answer in Wittgenstein's view, one concerning which he therefore remains torn *on principle*. In support of this suggestion, note Wittgenstein's general remark, "Our use of the words 'rule' and 'game' is a fluctuating one (blurred at the edges)" (PG, I, #55; cf. RFM, VI, #48). (I will have something more to say about such principled vacillations in Wittgenstein later, in chapter 6.)

I shall go into this whole thorny topic a little further in the next chapter. To anticipate, my basic view is that Wittgenstein is committed to both the enduring practice and the sociality doctrines, albeit with moments of doubt or even retraction, and probably with the sort of principled uncertainty or vacillation suggested by MacIntyre. However, I am very skeptical of the doctrines themselves, and of Wittgenstein's attempt to establish them with the rule-following argument. Note, though, that abandoning the argument and these doctrines would by no means entail altogether abandoning Wittgenstein's notion of a limit to arbitrariness deriving from social practices and traditions, for he could still appeal to the merely *causal and normative* constraints which these impose.

10. This example naturally tends to sound dubious and problematic to us post–Apollo 11. I shall refrain from discussing whether or not it can be defended, except to suggest that the general direction in which to look for a defense would be the variability of a sentence's meaning(fulness) in different *contexts* of use.

11. This prompts the difficult question of whether or not Wittgenstein *really is* a revisionist in mathematics. As far as I can see, he is torn: often committing himself emphatically to non-revisionism, but on the other hand also making some very revisionist-sounding statements, especially against Cantor's transfinite mathematics (one memorable example from BT, p. 426:

"Philosophical clarity will have the same influence on the growth of mathematics as sunlight on the growth of potato tubers. (In a dark cellar they grow meters long.)"). Insofar as he has a way of reconciling these two tendencies, it is, I think, one suggested by the conditions on the meaningfulness of grammatical principles which we are considering here: namely, that the shortcomings which he sees in a position like Cantor's show that it is *not really meaningful, and so not really a position at all.* This, I take it, is part of the underlying force of his remark that he has no wish to expel mathematicians from Cantor's "paradise," but merely to show them that it is not a paradise, only a mirage in a waterless desert, so that they will leave of their own accord (R. Rhees, *Discussions of Wittgenstein* [London: Routledge and Kegan Paul, 1970], p. 46; LFM, p. 103). However, this solution does not *fully* resolve the tension between the two tendencies in Wittgenstein, because his commitment to non-revisionism in mathematics often seems to be stronger than a mere commitment not to revise mathematicians' *meaningful* principles, to be in addition a commitment not to revise their practice at all (see, for example, PI, #124: "[Philosophy] leaves everything as it is. It also leaves mathematics as it is").

It is perhaps worth noting here that the question of Wittgenstein's revisionism is not connected with the question of whether the Williams-Lear reading of his position or a contrary one such as that advocated in this essay is correct in the way that Lear implies in "Leaving the World Alone." Lear takes Wittgenstein to be a non-revisionist, and he may well be right about that. He also indicates that the Williams-Lear reading makes Wittgenstein a non-revisionist, and that seems right as well. But in addition, he gives the strong impression that a contrary reading of Wittgenstein as committed to the genuine possibility of alternative grammars (rather than to their ultimate incoherence) would automatically commit Wittgenstein to revisionism as well, and that seems clearly untrue. Indeed, when Wittgenstein's commitment to the possibility of alternative grammars is conjoined with the further aspects of his thesis that grammar is in a sense arbitrary which were discussed in chapter 2—in particular, with his denial of the possibility of justifying or refuting grammars, and his denial that they are ever correct or incorrect, true or false—and with his thesis that grammar is in a sense non-arbitrary, as this thesis is being explicated in the present chapter, it if anything itself implies a form of non-revisionism.

12. It is perhaps worth mentioning in this connection that Wittgenstein occasionally in the *Remarks on the Foundations of Mathematics* uses the whole notion of "application" in relation to mathematical principles in a much looser way than the one that I am in the process of spelling out here, and that to the extent that he does so, he courts additional problems of excessive liberality over and above the ones that I am about to describe.

13. Note that this would not rule out the possibility of concepts in grammatical principles which failed to have real instances. It would only require that they be analyzable into component concepts which had them.

Notes to Chapter Four
Some Modest Criticisms

1. Cf. OC, #239: "Catholics believe . . . that in certain circumstances a wafer completely changes its nature, and at the same time that all evidence proves the contrary."

2. Cf. RFM, III, #80: "I should like to ask something like this: 'Is it usefulness that you are out for in your calculus?—In that case you do not get any contradiction. And if you aren't out for usefulness—then it doesn't matter if you do get one.'"

3. This alternative position is somewhat in the spirit of R. Carnap, *Logical Foundations of Probability* (Chicago: University of Chicago Press, 1950), ch. 1. Carnap discusses, for example, the compelling justification that led zoologists to reclassify whales as mammals rather than fishes in defiance of preexisting linguistic intuitions.

4. It might perhaps be objected that, even if, as they seem to, these proposals escape the "vicious circularity or incommensurability" dilemma which we saw Wittgenstein urging against attempts to justify grammar in terms of facts in chapter 2, they still face his "wrong epistemic asymmetry" objection. However, as we shall see in chapter 7, the assumptions on which the plausibility of this objection rests, namely that any understanding of a grammatical principle requires certain commitment to it, and that at least any acceptance of a grammatical principle does so, are in fact dubious ones.

5. The argument sketched in the last two sections for a sense in which, pace Wittgenstein's arbitrariness thesis (as explained in chapter 2), one grammar might be justifiable (or refutable) in its competition with another, and precisely in light of empirical facts and usefulness, may require one further qualification: It is not clear that such justification (or refutation) could work in *all* areas of grammar, and in particular it is not clear that it could work in the area of *formal logic*. For does not any appeal to degree of smoothness in the regulation of factual claims essentially involve an implicit assumption of the ideal of *consistency*, or non-contradiction? And does not any appeal to justification in terms of fulfillment of purposes essentially involve an implicit appeal to certain principles of logical inference? In other words, would not any attempt to justify classical logic in this way be in danger of proving viciously circular? However, it is perhaps enough just to mention this thorny issue here without exploring it any further. For the point of my suggestion in the last two sections is that Wittgenstein's official *blanket* denial of the justifiability (or refutability) of one grammatical principle over against another, especially in terms of the facts or usefulness, is questionable—and this could remain correct even if there were *one area* of grammar in which that denial was true.

6. There are certainly *other* ways in which someone might attempt to uncover a commitment to enduring social practice buried in our everyday concept of meaning as well. A noteworthy example is an argument devel-

oped by T. Burge in his "Individualism and the Mental" (in *Midwest Studies in Philosophy*, vol. 4, ed. P. A. French, T. E. Uehling, Jr., and H. K. Wettstein, Minneapolis: University of Minnesota Press, 1979). The points which I am about to make against seeing the rule-following argument as a revelation of such a buried commitment therefore fall short of showing that *no* argument could reveal one. For what it is worth, however, I am no more convinced by the other arguments of this sort with which I am familiar, such as Burge's, than by Wittgenstein's.

7. For interpretations along roughly these lines, see J. H. McDowell, "Wittgenstein on Following a Rule" (in J. H. McDowell, *Mind, Value, and Reality*, Cambridge, MA: Harvard University Press, 1998), and B. Stroud, "Mind, Meaning, and Practice" (in *The Cambridge Companion to Wittgenstein*).

The interpretation offered in G. P. Baker and P.M.S. Hacker, *Scepticism, Rules, and Language* (Oxford: Basil Blackwell, 1984) is similar, except for seeing only enduring practice (not enduring social practice) as the issue.

These interpretations all explicitly define themselves in opposition to Kripke's famous interpretation of the rule-following argument in his *Wittgenstein on Rules and Private Language*. The gist of my case here will be that, while they are indeed more faithful to Wittgenstein's intentions in strictly exegetical terms, they (unwittingly) reveal a serious philosophical weakness in Wittgenstein's argument which Kripke has in effect quietly remedied, so that Kripke's reading should in the end be seen less as a misinterpretation of Wittgenstein's argument than as a charitable reinterpretation of it.

8. For the corresponding objection to the Baker/Hacker variant of the interpretation in question, simply substitute for each occurrence of "enduring social practice" in this sentence "enduring practice."

9. See Kripke, *Wittgenstein on Rules and Private Language*.

10. The preceding discussion of Wittgenstein's vulnerability to a number of internal criticisms in connection with his doctrine of meaning as use illustrates a more general weakness in his later philosophy which may be worth briefly describing and further illustrating from other areas: He officially professes conceptual and theoretical quietism, i.e., faithfulness to ordinary language's concepts and to common sense, but he in fact deviates rather radically from both, and masks this discrepancy by faulty hermeneutics, i.e., by implausible judgments about what ordinary language or common sense means, and in particular about what it means as compared to what he himself means.

A few further examples of this dubious pattern: (i) Wittgenstein normally implies that the sort of quasi-Kantian account of necessary principles which we have seen him develop, according to which they are not assertions about necessary truths or facts, but instead something more like commands which we issue to ourselves regulating our factual judgments, is compatible with commonsense conceptions concerning necessary principles. But this seems pretty clearly false. For example, common sense is surely committed to the view that in affirming that $2 + 2 = 4$ we are *asserting* a necessary *truth*, a necessary *fact*. (As we saw earlier, Wittgenstein indeed himself sometimes virtually concedes as much, for example at RFM, VII, #6.)

(ii) Wittgenstein is attracted to a form of behaviorism; but the most plausible candidates to serve as the alleged behavioral constituents of a person's mental states or processes are often his later verbal reports of them (and his later behavior more generally); so Wittgenstein wants to allow that such later performances are indeed such constituents. However, this theory seems to fly in the face of a commonsense conception that if, for example, I was thinking X at time t, then that thinking was something wholly constituted by what happened by or at time t. So how does Wittgenstein propose to save his quietism in the face of this apparent conflict? His solution is, in effect, to interpret common sense's attribution of mental states and processes to particular (past) times as merely a sort of *façon de parler*, not really meant in the way that it seems to be, and in particular not in a way that is incompatible with Wittgenstein's theory. This, I take it, is the force of such passages as the following: "'You said, "It'll stop soon."'—Were you thinking of the noise or of your pain?' If he answers 'I was thinking of the piano-tuning'—is he observing that the connection existed, or is he making it by means of these words?—Can't I say *both*? If what he said was true, didn't the connection exist?—and is he not for all that making one which did not exist?" (PI, #682). But such an interpretation of what common sense means is surely very implausible. Surely, what common sense means when, for example, it assigns my having thought X to time t is *not* consistent with that thinking's (total or partial) constitution by later occurrences, but instead implies that whatever happened or might have happened after time t is simply *irrelevant* to the fact of my having thought X at time t if I did so (so that if it really was the case that I thought X at time t, then eliminating my subsequent report of it, or for that matter altering my future behavior in any way at all, could not have affected that fact one whit).

(iii) A final example: Wittgenstein draws a sharp distinction between, on the one hand, philosophers, who are misled by the grammar of their language and are consequently the victims of confusion, and on the other hand, ordinary language and common sense, which are quite innocent of such confusion (see, for example, PI, #194: "When we do philosophy we are like savages, primitive people, who hear the expressions of civilized men, put a false interpretation on them, and then draw the queerest conclusions from it"; LSD, p. 367: "A philosopher has temptations which an ordinary person does not have. You *could* say he knows better what a word means than others do. But in fact philosophers generally know *less*. Because ordinary persons have no temptations to misunderstand language"; cf. RFM, V, #53). But this is surely extremely implausible as an interpretation of what ordinary language and common sense are like. Are they not, on the contrary, largely constituted by *réchauffé* philosophy from yesteryear? Think, for example, of the widespread presence in ordinary language and common sense of dualist conceptions of the mind and the body which originally had their source in philosophers such as Pythagoras, Socrates, and Plato, and were subsequently popularized by Christianity, and which would certainly for Wittgenstein be paradigmatic examples of philosophical confusion.

11. For a criticism of Kripke's case along these lines, see especially P. A. Boghossian's excellent article "The Rule-Following Considerations," in *Mind* vol. 98, no. 392 (1989). McDowell too finds more merit in the *sui generis* suggestion than Kripke allows, and indeed takes a version of it to be Wittgenstein's own position (see McDowell, "Intentionality and Interiority in Wittgenstein," in his *Mind, Value, and Reality*, p. 298). See also C. Wright, *Rails to Infinity* (Cambridge, MA: Harvard University Press, 2001), pp. 111–14.

12. This realist assumption about dispositions may well only be one that Wittgenstein means to impute to someone who is tempted to offer the theory of knowing the ABC in question here, rather than one that he makes himself. That is to say, his own considered concept of a disposition may well be more anti-realist in character.

13. Since Wittgenstein emphatically divorces knowledge from certainty, he could hardly object to this suggestion that one could not have knowledge of such a state because its existence would not be certain.

14. Kripke, *Wittgenstein on Rules and Private Language*, esp. pp. 23–24, 28–30, 37.

15. For a similar point, elaborated in more detail, see G. Forbes, "Scepticism and Semantic Knowledge," in *Proceedings of the Aristotelian Society*, vol. 84 (1983–84).

16. Actually, the situation is even a little more complicated: within the category of behaviors consistent with a disposition one needs to distinguish not only typical ones (e.g., the salt's dissolving when put in water) and atypical ones (e.g., its failing to do so due to an explanatory-excusing condition obtaining, such as its being coated with the plastic film) but also merely *non*-typical ones (e.g., its remaining out of water and not dissolving).

17. Kripke, *Wittgenstein on Rules and Private Language*, esp. pp. 26–27.

18. Cf. RFM, VI, #23: "Can one make infinite predictions?—Well why should one not for example call the law of inertia one? . . . In a certain sense of course the infinity of the prediction is not taken very seriously."

19. Kripke has a few further objections to the dispositional theory which may be worth briefly mentioning and addressing as well: (1) If understanding were a disposition, then how could one ever *know* that one (had) understood a term in a certain way rather than in any number of possible alternative ways equally consistent with one's performances hitherto (*Wittgenstein on Rules and Private Language*, p. 23)?—However, it is perhaps a sufficient answer to this rhetorical question to point out that knowledge of our own mental dispositions is evidently something of which we are *routinely* capable. For example, one might equally well ask how I can ever know that I have (or had) a disposition to find this gender attractive rather than that (all my past experiences have been consistent with my being disposed to find this gender attractive in all the places in which I have actually lived, but the

other one elsewhere . . .). This is not to say that such knowledge is infallible (in either case). Nor is it to deny that our ability to have (even fallible) knowledge of our own mental dispositions is a mystery. The point is simply that since it is pretty clear that we *do* have (fallible) knowledge of our own mental dispositions in many other cases, the fact that the dispositional theory of understanding would be committed to saying the same can hardly count against it.

(2) Kripke raises a more technical objection based on the fact that Church has proved there to be many functions which can be defined but which cannot be computed by any algorithm (ibid., pp. 26, 36). (Kripke might also have pointed out that Wittgenstein is committed to saying something similar about family-resemblance concepts, whose defining feature is that they apply in virtue of facts of some other sort but in such a way that it is impossible to specify necessary and sufficient conditions for their application in terms of those facts.)—However, it seems arguable that this sort of objection misses the point of a dispositional theory of understanding, which is simply to identify understanding with a disposition to a certain pattern of responses, *and need not involve commitment to any particular account of how that pattern of responses is or could be arrived at.*

(3) Kripke implies that a dispositional account would force us to classify any old causally determined set of verbal responses as understanding (ibid., p. 24).—However, this seems incorrect, for a reason related to the previous one: it is not just any old set of causally determined responses that can constitute a disposition, but only, at best (since actually even this is not sufficient, due to the essential role of a *typical* behavior/merely *consistent* behavior distinction in the concept of a disposition, as discussed earlier), a *pattern* of such responses; and it is by no means the case that every causally determined set of responses exhibits a pattern (in the relevant sense).

20. For some suggestive criticism along these lines, see S. Blackburn, "The Individual Strikes Back," in *Synthese,* vol. 58, no. 3 (1984).

NOTES TO CHAPTER FIVE
THE CASE OF FORMAL LOGIC

1. I use the term "classical logic" to refer to the sort of logic that was developed by Frege in his *Begriffsschrift* and Russell and Whitehead in their *Principia Mathematica,* and any earlier logical principles which it subsumes, such as Aristotle's laws of contradiction and excluded middle and rules of syllogistic inference.

2. Cf. Coffa, *The Semantic Tradition,* pp. 164–66; Hacker, *Insight and Illusion,* revised edition, pp. 52–53.

3. For this whole line of argument, cf. LFM, pp. 213–14, 231–32. Note that this line of argument does not imply either of two things which it might mistakenly be thought to imply: (1) It might be thought to imply that

classical logical laws and rules of inference are *contained in the meanings of the truth-functions and derivable from them by analysis*. However, as we saw in chapter 2, Wittgenstein would reject this as at best a misleading picture; for, in his view, while they are indeed *in a sense* internal to those meanings, it is not a matter of the meanings existing in some prior or independent way and the laws and rules of inference then being derivable from them, but rather, conversely, of the laws and rules of inference constituting the meanings. This is the force of his reservation about saying "It looks as if it followed from the nature of negation that a double negative is an affirmative": "It looks as if it followed from the nature of negation that a double negative is an affirmative. (And there is something right about this . . .)" (PI, p. 147). Thus just a couple of lines earlier in the text he had written: " 'The fact that three negatives yield a negative again must already be contained in the single negative that I am using now.' (The temptation to invent a myth of 'meaning.')" (ibid.). (2) An opposite mistake would be to assume that the internality of classical logical laws and rules of inference to the meanings of the truth-functions, when construed in the correct, "constitutive" way, entails that the meanings of the truth-functions are *entirely* constituted by the laws and rules of inference in question. In this spirit, other philosophers sometimes seem to imply that if logical laws and rules of inference constitute the meanings of the truth-functions, then they must be *all* that does so (e.g., W. V. Quine, *Philosophy of Logic* [Englewood Cliffs, NJ: Prentice Hall, 1970], p. 81). Such a position involves a non sequitur, and moreover one to an implausible conclusion. The later Wittgenstein does not commit himself to any such simplistic view. That he avoids doing so can be seen from a thesis of his already noted previously: concepts which occur in grammatical principles, including those of formal logic, must also occur in factual ones ("in *mufti*"), for example the "v" of "p v ~p" must also occur in propositions like "He went to the movies *or* he stayed at home."

4. See Baker and Hacker, *Frege: Logical Excavations* (New York: Oxford University Press, 1984), pp. 44–45, and *Wittgenstein: Rules, Grammar, and Necessity*, pp. 306 ff. (though in the latter work they do belatedly enter a much-needed qualification on p. 318); Hacker, *Insight and Illusion*, revised edition, pp. 331–32; J. Conant, "The Search for Logically Alien Thought: Descartes, Kant, Frege, and the *Tractatus*," *Philosophical Topics*, vol. 20, no. 1 (1991), pp. 176–77, nn. 108–9; D. R. Cerbone, "How to Do Things with Wood: Wittgenstein, Frege, and the Problem of Illogical Thought," in *The New Wittgenstein*.

These authors tend to focus on the later Wittgenstein's flat statements of the internality of classical logic to propositions, language, and thought, rather than on his argument for that internality just explained, so I have if anything added a little extra grist to their exegetical mills here.

5. Cerbone, "How to Do Things with Wood."

6. Ibid.

7. H. Putnam, "Rethinking Mathematical Necessity," in Putnam, *Words*

and Life, ed. J. Conant (Cambridge, MA: Harvard University Press, 1996); Conant, "The Search for Logically Alien Thought," p. 123; Cerbone ("How to Do Things with Wood") is silent on the question, but since he largely follows the preceding two authors, his silence presumably implies agreement with them.

8. Baker and Hacker seem to imply that Wittgenstein was its inventor at *Frege: Logical Excavations,* pp. 44–45.

9. Pace Putnam, Conant, and Cerbone, who all imply that a strand of the mature Frege's thinking about the status of logic was along these lines as well, the mature Frege does not belong to this group. The early Frege of the *Begriffsschrift,* who was still under very heavy influence from Kant, arguably did (for some relevant discussion, see H. Sluga, *Gottlob Frege* [London: Routledge and Kegan Paul, 1980], p. 108). But by the time Frege wrote *The Basic Laws of Arithmetic* (1893), and ever henceforth, he unequivocally rejected the position in question, instead unambiguously holding a conception of logical laws as "laws of truth," i.e., something like the most general laws of nature. Some relevant features of the case to note: (1) Putnam neither quotes nor cites any textual evidence in support of his apparent implication that even the mature Frege was half-committed to the position in question ("Rethinking Mathematical Necessity," pp. 247–48). Conant tries to supply this deficiency, citing a passage from *The Basic Laws of Arithmetic* which, if taken out of context (as he takes it), can indeed sound like an expression of this position at first blush: "the most general laws of thought . . . [which] prescribe universally the way in which one ought to think if one is to think at all" (Conant, "The Search for Logically Alien Thought," p. 134). But when put back in its context, this passage can be seen to be instead part of an *attack* on any such position, in favor of the contrary conception of logical laws as merely the most general laws of nature: "In one sense a law asserts what is; in the other it prescribes what ought to be. Only in the latter sense can the laws of logic be called 'laws of thought': so far as they stipulate the way in which one ought to think. Any law asserting what is, can be conceived as prescribing that one ought to think in conformity with it, and is thus in that sense a law of thought. This holds for laws of geometry and physics no less than for laws of logic. The latter have a special title to the name 'laws of thought' only if we mean to assert that they are the most general laws, which prescribe universally the way in which one ought to think if one is to think at all" (*The Basic Laws of Arithmetic,* ed. M. Furth [Berkeley and Los Angeles: University of California Press, 1967], p. 12). Cerbone's textual evidence for this reading of the mature Frege is even flimsier ("How to Do Things with Wood," pp. 297–98). (2) Frege's sharp rejection of the position in question in *The Basic Laws of Arithmetic* is also visible from his firm assumption there that it is quite possible for thought to contravene logical laws: "The laws of truth are not psychological laws: they are boundary stones set in an eternal foundation, *which our thought can overflow,* but never displace" (p. 13; emphasis added). (3) It is also visible from

the fact that the work's attack on "psychologism" in logic, far from being directed exclusively against the idea that logical laws are merely laws describing how we happen to think, in order by contrast to favor the idea that they are laws conformity to which is constitutive of the very nature of thinking (as in Kant's attack on "psychologism"), is clearly intended as an attack on *both* ideas. (In other words, Fregean anti-psychologism is not the same as Kantian anti-psychologism; it subsumes it, but in addition includes an attack on Kant's own position.) (4) The same stances are sustained by Frege in all of his subsequent works concerned with the nature of logic as well, notably in the two sketches entitled "Logic" in his *Posthumous Writings* (Chicago: University of Chicago Press, 1979), esp. pp. 4, 145–49, and in the late *Logical Investigations*, in his *Collected Papers on Mathematics, Logic, and Philosophy* (London: Basil Blackwell, 1984), esp. pp. 351, 405. Incidentally, Wittgenstein himself understood Frege's mature views on this matter perfectly: "Next time I hope to start with the statement: 'The laws of logic are laws of thought.' The question is whether we should say we cannot think except according to them, that is, whether they are psychological laws—or, as Frege thought, laws of nature. He compared them with laws of natural science (physics), which we must obey in order to think correctly" (LFM, p. 230; cf. p. 214).

10. The commentators just discussed have thus (to borrow a nice metaphor from one of them, Conant) mistaken the bait for the hook.

11. A minor puzzle, though one which does not affect my point: Wittgenstein's way of putting his thought here, namely by implying that propositionality would survive beyond the contradiction itself, is a bit puzzling, since in light of the argument concerning the internal connection of classical logical laws to the truth-functions and to propositionality which we earlier saw him suggesting, one would have expected him to see the acceptance of a contradiction as undermining not only its own propositionality but also that of other sentences. His reason for implying the contrary here may possibly be that he is assuming an idea which he sometimes sketches elsewhere, that (so to speak) in order to minimize the damage that would be done by accepting a contradiction, one might quarantine it by debarring inferences from it (LFM, pp. 209, 220, 230; RFM, III, #80). On the other hand, he goes on to add here, "Might one not even begin logic with this contradiction? And as it were descend from it to propositions" (RFM, IV, #59)—which, unless the "descent" in question is supposed to be a noninferential one, sounds incompatible with this idea of quarantining. So the puzzle remains.

12. I of course choose these examples in part because they are all cases of rather *disciplined* rejections of and deviations from the law (so to speak). But these are the right sorts of cases to look at. It is easy enough to make cases of merely *random* rejections and deviations look like examples of nonthought. But then, merely random utterances of *any* kind tend to look like

examples of non-thought, whether they violate classical logical principles or not.

13. "Rethinking Mathematical Necessity," p. 257.

14. This is a complex and much-discussed subject which can only be treated rather cursorily here. Some helpful secondary literature: J. Barnes, "The Law of Contradiction," *Philosophical Quarterly*, vol. 19, no. 77 (1969); R. M. Dancy, *Sense and Contradiction: A Study in Aristotle* (Dordrecht: Reidel, 1975); T. Irwin, *Aristotle's First Principles* (Oxford: Clarendon Press, 1988), pp. 181–88; J. Lear, *Aristotle: The Desire to Understand* (Cambridge: Cambridge University Press, 1999), pp. 249–64; J. Lukasiewicz, "Aristotle on the Law of Contradiction," in *Articles on Aristotle*, ed. J. Barnes, M. Schofield, and R. Sorabji (London: Duckworth, 1975–79), vol. 3.

15. For such a charge, see, e.g., Barnes, "The Law of Contradiction," pp. 308–9.

16. Barnes embraces this line of argument, and elaborates on it at great length. But he too begs the original question, namely in assuming that belief and disbelief are contraries, so that it is necessarily true that, as he puts it, $(x) ((xD{:}(P)) \supset (\sim xB{:}(P)))$, i.e., if anyone disbelieves ("D") a proposition P, then he does not believe ("B") proposition P (ibid., p. 304).

17. One can imagine fuller elaborations of such a position. For example, Kant could have argued that the internality of the concept of classical logical principles to the concept of thought held in virtue of a Kantian version of the sort of situation that we saw both the early and the later Wittgenstein suggesting at the beginning of this chapter: If one analyzes the concept of a thought, one finds that of a proposition (or for Kant, a "judgment"), but if one analyzes this in turn, one finds that of the applicability of the truth-functions, but then if one analyzes this in its turn, one gets that of conformity to classical logical principles, and so implicitly the concept of thought contains that of conformity to classical logical principles. (What would make this a distinctively *Kantian* version is the picture of the nature of meanings or concepts and of conceptual analysis which it assumes.)

18. There might be a temptation to respond to this point that the necessity in question here is not supposed to be, as it were, *metaphysical*, in any of the three ways just canvased, but instead purely *normative*, more like the necessity of morals. Such a response contains a grain of truth, but misses the mark. For, while Kant does indeed recognize such a normative necessity here, he takes this to be *grounded in a metaphysical necessity*, as can be seen from the sentence quoted near the start of the present paragraph from the *Critique of Pure Reason*.

19. It might reasonably be doubted that this step is true *without limitation* (though Wittgenstein's conception of the grammatical, and hence concept-forming, nature of all logical principles would not allow *him* such a doubt). For example, someone might concede that a failure to acknowledge the law of double-negation elimination by treating double negations as meaning-

less—as in Wittgenstein's own example—would undermine the usual meaning of "not," but reasonably doubt that the same would be true if the failure only set in at, say, the "law" of *ten-thousandfold*-negation elimination (cf. LFM, p. 273). However, even if the step in question did need limitation for this sort of reason, it would probably still remain true in a sufficiently strong form for a version of the argument to go through.

20. W. V. Quine has offered a related but simpler argument, based only on a version of Wittgenstein's second step, for the conclusion that (except in complex cases where people become corrigibly confused) we must find other people conforming to and believing in the logical laws of the sentential calculus, such as the law of contradiction (*Word and Object* [Cambridge, MA: MIT Press, 1996], pp. 57–60; *Philosophy of Logic*, ch. 6). However, Quine's experiment in flying Wittgenstein's (already doomed) aircraft on one wing breaks down over precisely the feature just pointed out. Quine argues, plausibly, that a person's understanding of the truth-functions is constituted by patterns of assent and dissent to sentences of a sort that would be subverted by his failure to conform to, or attempt to deny, a law of the sentential calculus (except in complex cases where he becomes corrigibly confused), so that this could not in fact constitute a disagreement about the law in question, but only a failure to understand, or an assignment of different meanings to, the truth-functions. But this argument could only show (1) that people cannot be found violating or denying laws of the sentential calculus, not (2) that they must be found conforming to and believing them—since, for all that the argument could show, a person might quite well fail to conform to or believe them and instead conform to and believe a set of deviant logical laws involving a correspondingly deviant construal of the truth-functions. (Quine tends to slide illicitly from (1) to (2), despite the fact that in his more careful moods he himself acknowledges this possibility.)

Alternatively, Quine sometimes implies that the first part of this simpler argument rules out the possibility of logical deviancy merely by establishing (1), i.e., merely by showing that any putative denial of a law of the sentential calculus could only (at best) involve a different understanding of the truth-functions, and therefore not really be such a denial at all (*Philosophy of Logic*, pp. 81, 83). This alternative argument rests on an assumption that real logical deviancy or rivalry would have to involve logical contradiction of, and hence conceptual commensurability with, classical logic. However, Wittgenstein would of course reject such an assumption, and plausibly so. For in Wittgenstein's view it is a fundamental feature of grammatical diversity in *any* area—not only in the area of formal logic—that it *always* involves conceptual incommensurability, and hence an absence of any strict logical inconsistency, between alternative grammatical principles, and that the alternativeness or rivalry in question therefore *always* consists, not in outright logical inconsistency, but in something else. What exactly this "something else" is is no doubt a good and difficult question (in an earlier note I hazarded a suggestion in terms of incompatibilities between the behavioral criteria for conviction in two principles, and hence between convictions in them). But Wittgenstein's assumption of it in the case of formal logic is at least anything but ad hoc (he assumes it equally for all areas of grammar). And that there is such a form of alternativeness or rivalry not involving outright logical inconsistency seems highly plausible.

A final argument of Quine's against the possibility of our finding logical deviancy is even weaker than the two just considered, and may be dealt with more briefly: He argues that (1) in interpretation we must attribute to others an acknowledgment of "obvious" claims, and (2) the laws of the sentential calculus are "obvious," so that (3) in interpretation we must find those whom we interpret acknowledging these laws (*Philosophy of Logic*, pp. 82-83; cf. *Word and Object*, p. 59, where, though, the version of (1) invoked is weaker, only proscribing attributions of obvious falsehoods, and would therefore not generate the desired conclusion). However, if "obvious" here means obvious *to us*, then (1) is surely a sadly misguided principle of interpretation, while if it means obvious *to us and anyone whom we might want to interpret*, then (2) simply begs the crucial question.

21. For example, unlike Latin, which has *vel* as well as *aut*, ordinary English does not typically use "or" or any other word with the meaning of the classical logician's "v"; nor does ordinary language normally use any word—in particular not the words "if . . . then"—with the meaning of the classical logician's material conditional "⊃"; and dialects of English sometimes seem to use a variant of negation which is unlike the classical logician's "~," for instance in failing to respect the law of double-negation elimination (rather as in Wittgenstein's own example)—hence in dialect "He ain't no fool" means that he is not a fool, not that he is one (cf. LFM, p. 179: "In some languages, a double negation is a negation"; RFM, I, appendix I, #1).

22. This final point is admittedly less clear as a matter of exegesis (recall Wittgenstein's reluctance even to classify "It's raining" as an expression of a thought [PI, #501]). However, even if he *does* not infer that a sort of thought is involved here, it is surely arguable that he *should*.

23. It may perhaps be worth briefly drawing together the several main criticisms which I have leveled against the Putnam-Conant-Cerbone account of the later Wittgenstein's position on logical laws and related matters (I disregard some variations between their views, especially some finer points in Putnam's interpretation and assessment of the later Wittgenstein's position): (1) Contrary to their account, the doctrine of classical logic's internality to thought was not new with Kant, but was originally due to Aristotle, of whom Kant was in this area merely a careless epigone. (2) Contrary to their account, the mature Frege was not half-committed to this doctrine, but was instead unequivocally opposed to it. (3) Contrary to their account, the later Wittgenstein does not embrace this doctrine as his bottom line and consequently reject the notion of logical deviancy as implicitly

incoherent, but instead develops a powerful case deflating the doctrine and thereby defends the possibility of logical deviancy. (4) Moreover, contrary to their account, it is not the former of these two positions which is philosophically plausible but the latter.

24. My adjustment from Kant's notion of the containment of a predicate-concept in a subject-concept to a more generic notion of truth-in-virtue-of-meaning is motivated by charity (not malice!), in particular by the need to accommodate analytic sentences which are not subject-predicate in form, e.g., "If someone is a bachelor, then he is unmarried."

25. I suggested earlier that if Kant had thought harder about his explanation of the necessity of classical logical principles, he might have found himself driven to see that necessity as constituted by truth-in-virtue-of-meaning—i.e., roughly, by the subject-concept "thought" containing the predicate-concept "conforms to classical logical principles." And I noted that he might have developed such an explanation further in something like the following way: the concept of a "thought" contains that of a proposition (or "judgment"), the latter in turn contains that of subjection to the classical truth-functions, and the latter in its turn contains that of conformity to classical logical principles. We can now see that, and why, Wittgenstein would reject any such explanation of logical necessity. Indeed, in the passages just quoted and cited in which he is unmasking the illusoriness of the idea of truth-in-virtue-of-meaning (WLC, pp. 4, 86, etc.) he is deploying his insight into that illusoriness against a similar sort of explanation of logical necessity (namely, a simpler explanation of it in terms of logical principles being true in virtue of the meanings of the truth-functions).

NOTES TO CHAPTER SIX
THE LIMITS OF LANGUAGE

1. This rhetorical question can be difficult to interpret. It is tempting at first reading to understand it as offering a deliberately absurd suggestion, since in German *Regelmäßigkeit* seems to bear the etymological meaning "accordance with a rule" on its face, so to speak, and to propose to define "rule" in terms of "accordance with a rule" seems absurd. However, one can see from some passages at RFM, VI, #41 in which Wittgenstein clearly envisages the possibility of regularity occurring without rules, and as a mere preliminary step towards following rules, that his suggestion here is not in fact meant to be absurd after all. The etymological meaning is dead, as it were (like a dead metaphor). It is possible, however, that Wittgenstein means to tease us with a sense of paradox on the way to this realization.

2. Cf. RFM, III, #70.

3. There are the following differences between the two cases: (1) The behavior whose regularity was in question in the passage from the *Philosophical Investigations* had a verbal character, whereas that is not stipulated

of the behavior in this passage. (2) The reason for a temptation to postulate a linguistic regularity in the former case was the confusion into which people's actions fell when they were prevented from engaging in their verbal behavior, whereas the reason for a temptation to postulate a behavioral regularity in this case is the apparent occurrence of learning and instruction. However, these differences seem inessential.

4. Concerning some similar contradictions in Wittgenstein's middle period, see Coffa, *The Semantic Tradition*, pp. 270–71.

5. Some further passages of relevance for Wittgenstein's conflation of vagueness or fluidity with family-resemblance: BT, pp. 174–75; BB, p. 19.

6. Consider in this connection, for example, Wittgenstein's discussion of the disappearing and reappearing chair at PI, #80; his discussion of "plant" at PG, I, #73; and his discussion of "'blurred' intervals" at PG, I, appendix 8.

7. Consider in this connection especially Wittgenstein's frequent choice of such words as "fluid [*fließend*]" and "fluctuating [*schwankend*]" to characterize the use of terms from this family. Inconsistency is in fact also implied by his employment of the words "vagueness" or "indeterminacy" to characterize their use, as can be seen, for example, from his analogy between the use of elastic rulers or measuring by pacing and the admission of a contradiction to mathematics (RFM, VII, #15).

8. Now that these two central components of the vagueness or fluidity that Wittgenstein has in mind have been isolated, one can see more clearly that both "family-resemblance" and the sort of technical indeterminacy of all concepts in relation to new applications which the rule-following argument implies need to be distinguished from them: It seems that it would at least in principle be possible for a concept to be a "family-resemblance" concept in Wittgenstein's sense, i.e., to be such that it applies in virtue of facts of some other sort but in such a way that we are unable to specify necessary and sufficient conditions for its application in terms of those other facts (even elaborate disjunctive ones), as in the case of the concept "game" for example, and yet also to be such that competent users of the concept were always entirely decided and consistent as to whether or not the concept applied in concrete cases. Again, since the indeterminacy (and inconsistency) in question here pertains only to some applications of a concept *but not others* and only to some concepts *but not others*, it is clearly different from the sort of technical indeterminacy implied by the rule-following argument, which by contrast pertains to *all* applications of *all* concepts.

9. Wittgenstein tends to assess this question in *social* terms—our *collective* considered judgments using these concepts exhibit indeterminacies and inconsistencies—due to his social conception of the nature of meaning. But his thesis would arguably survive a transition to an individualistic conception of the nature of meaning: individuals' considered judgments in this area exhibit indeterminacies and inconsistencies as well.

10. See, for example, the following two pioneering empirical studies concerning our ordinary intuitions about synonymy and about analyticity-syn-

theticity (respectively): A. Naess, *Interpretation and Preciseness* (Oslo: Dybwad, 1953); L. Apostel, W. Mays, A. Morf, and J. Piaget, *Les liaisons analytiques et synthétiques dans les comportements du sujet* (Paris: Presses Universitaires de France, 1957).

11. Wittgenstein's thesis of the vagueness or fluidity of our semantic concepts in their ordinary use does not, of course, provide an a priori guarantee that Kripke's and Putnam's method must fail; in principle, they might be fortunate enough to be dealing with areas in which our ordinary language intuitions happen *not* to be at bottom indeterminate or inconsistent (in contrast to other areas in which they are). My suggestion is not that because Wittgenstein's thesis is true such a method *must* fail, but rather that because his thesis is true it *does*. Of course, actually proving this would require a detailed consideration of Kripke's and Putnam's arguments and a detailed confrontation of them with empirical data about people's ordinary language intuitions, a project which could not even be begun here.

12. I would suggest that in the end this position should be regarded as an overreaction against the sort of (equally dubious) extreme disparagement of ordinary language in favor of an ideal language which the later Wittgenstein found in Frege, Russell, and a strand of his own earlier work (see, e.g., T, 3.325, 4.0031).

13. It is not at all obvious that this consequence which afflicts the Wittgensteinian philosopher also afflicts the non-philosophical competent speaker whom he is attempting to emulate. For whereas the Wittgensteinian philosopher is aware that his shrugs are not merely expressions of epistemological agnosticism but concern the absence of a fact of the matter, the non-philosophical competent speaker may well be shrugging in a spirit of mere epistemological agnosticism, or at least in a spirit that is ambiguous or undecided between merely expressing epistemological agnosticism and denying that there is a fact of the matter. It's a little like the Garden of Eden: before you eat of the tree of philosophical knowledge, you can maybe wander around naked without sin, but afterwards not.

14. Z, #351 and #366–67 make a complementary point concerning transitions in the opposite direction, namely *from* sharpness *to* vagueness or fluidity: in such cases, too, the concept would be changed.

15. This whole problem afflicts Wittgenstein (and also some of his commentators) in several further areas relevant to the present study as well. For example, as I pointed out earlier, alongside the Wittgenstein who tells us that grammatical principles are not assertions but imperatives, and that they are neither true nor false, there is another Wittgenstein who tells us that they are indeed assertions rather than imperatives, and that they are indeed true or false. (Baker and Hacker accordingly vacillate in their interpretation of Wittgenstein on this issue in precisely analogous ways, and to this extent in faithful imitation of the master.) Or to give another example, as I noted earlier, Wittgenstein sometimes implies that rule-following and hence meaning essentially require society, but at other times that they do not. These positions run into just the same sort of dilemma as I have

sketched here: *Either* such vacillations indeed stay faithful to ordinary language, but in that case they involve self-contradiction, and so are unacceptable both in fact and by Wittgenstein's own considered lights; *or* they avoid real self-contradiction by carefully underlaying the verbal appearance of self-contradiction with a saving distinction between two (or more) different uses or meanings of key words—but in that case (1) the faithfulness to ordinary language is only *apparent*, not real, and moreover, (2) it produces unnecessary confusion, and amounts to an evasion of our intellectual responsibility to make a decision concerning the encountered disputes, and all for no reason, since the underlying motive of staying faithful to ordinary language has been violated anyway.

16. It should be noted, however, that remarks like this one are often equivocal between the idea in which I am interested here, that some of the essential concepts in terms of which the philosopher *states his own philosophical position* should be more precise than their correlates in ordinary language, and the very different idea which Wittgenstein the conceptual quietist can and often does express, that the philosopher should generate concepts which are more precise in this way *for particular therapeutic purposes, though not for the statement of his own position.* The latter idea is often expressed in the *Blue Book*, for example, where Wittgenstein writes, for instance: "Ordinary language is all right. Whenever we make up 'ideal languages' it is not in order to replace our ordinary language by them; but just to remove some trouble caused in someone's mind by thinking that he has got hold of the exact use of a common word" (BB, p. 28; cf. p. 59). The passage which I quote here from PG, I, #35 seems to me equivocal in just this way—the subsequent discussion at PG, I, #36 indeed tending to focus more on the latter of the two ideas just distinguished than on the former one in which I am interested.

17. This second Wittgenstein has something in common with Carnap, who in his *Logical Foundations of Probability*, ch. 1 argues that (in preparation for formalization) vague terms should be replaced by precise ones, normally (though not always, since more radical revisions are sometimes justified) in such a way that the precise ones agree with the vague ones which they replace with respect to all of the negative and positive cases which were already definite for the latter, but in addition either apply or do not apply definitely in all of the cases which were not definite for the latter.

18. In light of this, the remarks about reasons and utility quoted in the previous paragraph, which might initially have struck one as rather platitudinous, instead take on an appearance of some unorthodoxy and daring.

NOTES TO CHAPTER SEVEN
THE PROBLEM OF ACCESS

1. See, for example, Baker and Hacker, *Wittgenstein: Rules, Grammar, and Necessity*, p. 327.

2. "Wittgenstein's Philosophy of Mathematics," p. 430.

3. "Wittgenstein and Logical Necessity," p. 489. I believe that Stroud has in fact here captured the nature of Wittgenstein's official position quite precisely. However, this is by no means exegetically obvious, and so in what remains of the present section and the next I shall in effect attempt to make a somewhat fuller case for Stroud's reading than he himself does.

4. Cf. Stroud, "Wittgenstein and Logical Necessity," p. 493.

5. One of the most striking of these examples occurs in *On Certainty*, where Wittgenstein says, concerning two competing principles of the sort that he is there inclined to classify as apparently-empirical principles of grammar, "*Very* intelligent and well-educated people believe in the story of creation in the bible, while others hold that it is proven false, and the grounds of the latter are well-known to the former" (OC, #336), which seems to imply the literal intelligibility of the alternative grammatical principles in question to both sides. However, this is rough material (recall Wittgenstein's complaint at OC, #532 that he is now doing philosophy "like an old woman"). And contrast with this passage Wittgenstein's very different description elsewhere of a precisely analogous case: "Suppose someone were a believer and said: 'I believe in a Last Judgment,' and I said: 'Well, I'm not so sure. Possibly.' . . . It isn't a question of my being anywhere near him, but on an entirely different plane, which you could express by saying: 'You mean something altogether different, Wittgenstein'" (LCAPRB, p. 53).

6. "Wittgenstein and Logical Necessity," pp. 487-88.

7. This backs up Stroud's suspicion that his point would apply to "most, if not all, of Wittgenstein's examples" ("Wittgenstein and Logical Necessity," p. 488).

8. For example, in one of his many concessive remarks, Williams writes that for Wittgenstein, "other ways of seeing the world are not imaginatively inaccessible to us; on the contrary, it is one of Wittgenstein's aims to encourage such imagination" ("Wittgenstein and Idealism," p. 87).

9. Cerbone, "How to Do Things with Wood."

10. Wittgenstein's notion of family-resemblance concepts has often, rightly, been contrasted with a Platonic-Socratic assumption that any meaningful general term must be definable by giving informative (i.e., non-trivial) necessary and sufficient conditions for its application. It is less well known, but can I think be shown from writings belonging to the period in which he first developed the notion, that he also developed it in conscious and deliberate opposition to this Platonic-Socratic assumption (see, e.g., BT, pp. 58-59).

11. There are some nice questions in the secondary literature concerning the precise nature of the behavioral criteria of psychological concepts and of their relation to their context for Wittgenstein. For example, is a criterion's identity *exclusive* of the context in which it warrants applying a psychological concept, so that it is only the criterion *plus* the context that is in some sense sufficient for applying the concept, and a change of context

might leave the criterion in existence but override its authorization of the application (Baker et al.), or is a criterion's identity instead *inclusive* of the context in which it warrants applying a psychological concept, so that it is in some sense by itself sufficient for applying the concept, and any subverting change of context would not so much override the criterion as show it to have been illusory (McDowell) or else eliminate it (a perhaps more plausible variation on and alternative to McDowell's suggestion)? (Concerning the first two of these interpretations, see J. H. McDowell, "Criteria, Defeasibility, and Knowledge," in *Proceedings of the British Academy*, vol. 78 [1982].) However, it is not, I think, necessary to decide such issues as this in order to see the force of the worries here. For on *any* plausible view of Wittgenstein's position, it will be the criterion with the context—whether the "with" is one of addition or one of inclusion—which warrants the application of the concept in a particular case, and which is therefore part of the grammar of the concept, and there will be a numerous and diverse set of such combinations relating to each other in a family-resemblance manner which together constitute the full grammar of the concept.

12. These Wittgensteinian forms of holism are extensions of Frege's famous "context principle" from the *Foundations of Arithmetic* (1884), i.e., Frege's principle that a word has meaning only in the context of a sentence. Wittgenstein had already committed himself to that principle in the *Tractatus* (T, 3.3, 3.314; cf., in his middle period, LC, pp. 2, 66, 113–14; BT, p. 15). By 1929 he extended the relevant context to a grammatical system (see WWK, pp. 63–64; cf. PR, #15, #82; the passages from WL and LC already cited; also BT, pp. 53, 73, 139). The main motive behind this shift seems initially to have been his discovery in 1929 of the color problem afflicting the *Tractatus*'s conception of the logical independence of atomic propositions (see WWK, pp. 63–64; SRLF, pp. 32–33). However, it is worth noting that Frege had himself already developed his context principle in the same direction, especially in his essay "On the Principle of Inertia" (1891). Finally, in *The Big Typescript* (1932–33) at latest, Wittgenstein tentatively extended the relevant context still further to encompass a whole language (BT, p. 73; cf. BB, p. 5).

13. This final indecision can also be seen from the fact that even in late writings Wittgenstein sometimes stops short of the second, more radical form of holism. For example, in one late passage (1949–51) he says: "Sometimes it happens that we later introduce a new concept that is more practical for us.—But that will only happen in very definite and small areas, and it presupposes that *most concepts remain unaltered*" (LWPP2, p. 43; emphasis added).

14. Note that a doctrine that some sort of commitment is necessary in order to mean or understand anything by words could take weaker or stronger forms: In a weaker form it might merely say that in order to mean or understand a word in a particular sense, one must associate a corresponding general rule for its use with it and be capable of following this rule (which, note, would be consistent with simultaneously associating with it

and being capable of following other, incompatible rules for its use as well). In a stronger form such a doctrine might instead say that in order to mean or understand a word in a particular sense, one must be, so to speak, *locked into* following the corresponding general rule for its use (which would *not* be consistent with simultaneously being locked into—or even capable of—following other, incompatible rules for its use). It seems clear from the dire, Kierkegaardian tone of Wittgenstein's remarks here that it is the latter, stronger sort of commitment that he has in mind as necessary for meaning and understanding. However, it may well be that only the former, weaker sort of commitment is really necessary. And it is tempting to suspect that Wittgenstein may have been seduced into his stronger doctrine in part by a failure to distinguish between these two possible claims.

15. Stroud aptly cites this passage in support of his interpretation ("Wittgenstein and Logical Necessity," p. 486).

16. Note that the Paul-Anscombe translation is misleading here and has been corrected.

17. It is in fact a version of this fourth reason, or obstacle, that Stroud has in view as his explanation of Wittgenstein's refusal to claim that his examples are literally intelligible ("Wittgenstein and Logical Necessity," p. 486). Hence Stroud's interpretation runs into philosophical trouble here in a very direct manner.

18. Cf. Z, #197: "I tell myself 'Of course that's a . . .' and give myself a nonsensical explanation, which at the moment seems to me to make sense. (Like in a dream.)"

19. L. Strachey, *Queen Victoria* (New York: Harcourt, Brace, and Co., 1921), pp. 423–24:

> "She herself, as she lay blind and silent, seemed to those who watched her to be divested of all thinking—to have glided already, unawares, into oblivion. Yet, perhaps, in the secret chambers of consciousness, she had her thoughts, too. Perhaps her fading mind called up once more the shadows of the past to float before it, and retraced, for the last time, the vanished visions of that long history—passing back and back, through the cloud of years, to older and ever older memories—to the spring woods at Osborne, so full of primroses for Lord Beaconsfield—to Lord Palmerston's queer clothes and high demeanor, and Albert's face under the green lamp . . ."

20. See especially Hacker, *Insight and Illusion*, revised edition, pp. 134 ff.; Coffa, *The Semantic Tradition*, pp. 257, 360, 406–7; Monk, *Ludwig Wittgenstein*, pp. 286–88.

21. WWK, p. 244.

22. WWK, p. 245.

23. Quoted by Monk, *Ludwig Wittgenstein*, p. 288.

24. WWK, p. 47. Some further texts from around this period which contain remarks in the spirit of verificationism are PR, LC, WL, and BT.

25. *Ludwig Wittgenstein: The Man and His Philosophy*, ed. K. T. Fann (New York: Dell, 1967), p. 54.

26. BB, p. 46: "There is a temptation for me to say that only my own experience is real: 'I know that *I* see, hear, feel pains, etc., but not that anyone else does. I can't know this, because I am I and they are they.' On the other hand I feel ashamed to say to anyone that my experience is the only real one; and I know that he will reply that he could say exactly the same about his experience . . . Also I am told: 'If you pity someone for having pains, surely you must at least *believe* that he has pains?' But how can I even *believe* this? How can these words make sense to me? How could I even have come by the idea of another's experience if there is no possibility of any evidence for it? But wasn't this a queer question to ask? *Can't* I believe that someone else has pains? Is it not quite easy to believe this?—Is it an answer to say that things are as they appear to common sense?—Again, needless to say, we don't feel these difficulties in ordinary life. Nor is it true to say that we feel them when we scrutinize our experiences by introspection, or make scientific investigations about them. But somehow, when we look at them in a certain way, our expression is liable to get into a tangle" (cf. BB, p. 48).

27. This is commonly overlooked, for example by Hacker in *Insight and Illusion*, revised edition.

28. Cf. the strand in Wittgenstein's later philosophy of mathematics which argues that the meaningfulness of at least an important class of mathematical principles depends on the availability of a proof-procedure for them (see, for example, PI, #352–56; WLC, pp. 195–99; PR, #162). It would certainly be a distortion of his later position to say that mathematical proof was for him simply another species of verification, and this doctrine simply another application of verificationism—in particular because, as we saw earlier, his considered view is that mathematical principles are not strictly speaking true (and hence not strictly speaking verifiable) at all. Thus in one passage he goes as far as to say: "Nothing is more fatal to philosophical understanding than the notion of proof and experience as two different but comparable methods of verification" (PG, II, p. 361; BT, p. 410). However, it remains the case that something strikingly analogous to verificationism holds true of at least an important class of mathematical principles for the later Wittgenstein. Indeed, when he had first developed a doctrine of this general sort concerning mathematics, in WWK, he had himself spoken unabashedly of verification in connection with it. (This note is in mild disagreement with Hacker, *Insight and Illusion*, revised edition, pp. 142–43.)

29. This whole move exemplifies a broader strategy in the later Wittgenstein which similarly aims to make a modestly revised version of verificationism defensible. The broader strategy can be characterized as follows: Traditional epistemology held there to be particular classes of claims which were unusual in being certain truths, conclusively verifiable, real knowledge—especially, first-person psychological reports concerning the present,

and the necessary truths of logic, mathematics, analyticity, and so on—and in comparison with these saw the great bulk of our claims as uncertain, not really verifiable, not really known. This made the latter claims look epistemologically suspect, and in addition made verificationism look implausible, since there seemed to be this great mass of counterexamples to it, this great mass of claims which were meaningful but not verifiable, not knowable. Solution: First, dispel as an illusion the appearance that the special classes of claims in question really do constitute certain truths, something conclusively verifiable, real knowledge—first-person psychological reports concerning the present, in the manner just described; logical, mathematical, analytic, and other necessities, by showing them not to be truths or knowledge at all but instead grammatical imperatives (as discussed in chapters 1 and 2). This move is cost-free for verificationism, namely insofar as verificationism is strictly a principle concerning the meaningfulness of descriptive, fact-stating claims. Second, now that the great mass of propositions no longer look epistemologically second-rate through an invidious comparison with those ones, raise (some of) them to the status of—admittedly, fallible—verifiability and knowability. (Note, for example, that *On Certainty* firmly disassociates knowledge from infallibility and on the contrary associates it with *fallibility*.) In this way, a modestly and reasonably revised form of verificationism—namely, one which ties the meaningfulness of descriptive, fact-stating propositions to their *fallible* verifiability—now becomes defensible, free of obvious counterexamples.

30. In order to perceive that this is the force of the later Wittgenstein's conception of "criteria," it helps to realize—with Hacker, *Insight and Illusion*, revised edition, pp. 142, 145, 307 ff.—this conception's descent from the middle Wittgenstein's conception of an "hypothesis." Cf. WWK, pp. 100, 210-11, 255, 259-60.

31. This position also plays an important epistemological role for the later Wittgenstein, blocking versions of the argument from illusion, i.e., roughly, arguments which infer that because one *sometimes* cannot tell whether propositions of a certain sort are true, therefore one can *never* tell whether they are true (the best known version of the argument from illusion concerns perceptual illusions). To put Wittgenstein's thought a little facetiously: It is a condition of the very meaningfulness of propositions of a certain sort that, while you may be able to fool some of the people some of the time, you cannot fool all of the people all of the time.

32. I refrain from rehearsing a familiar set of arguments against Wittgenstein's theory that first-person psychological reports are normally merely expressive, not descriptive (e.g., concerning their logical relations with other, clearly descriptive reports). Two points are perhaps worth making, however: (a) Note that his old problem of implausibly positing a discrepancy of *sense* between first-person and third-person psychological reports in a way resurfaces in this new theory as the arguably no more tolerable problem of implausibly positing a discrepancy of illocutionary *force* between them (first-

person reports are normally mere expressions, third-person reports descriptions). (b) It is easy enough to seduce oneself into finding this plausible by dwelling on how the first-person cases "feel," as it were. But observe that (1) it is far from clear that introspective feeling is the proper criterion to use here (a very Wittgensteinian point!), and (2) for every visceral, non-detached "I'm in pain," there is also a visceral, non-detached "He's in pain."

33. Similarly, where the mathematical analogue of son-of-verificationism is concerned, there is surely great plausibility in the contrary position that such propositions as, for example, that there are four consecutive 7s in the decimal expansion of pi do have a perfectly definite sense (and truth value) even though they are in principle "unverifiable" by means of any proof-procedure (pace WLC, pp. 195–99; PI, #516; RFM, V, #9–20, #42).

34. Note that this point does not rest on any version or variant of verificationism (as it might superficially seem to). It would be quite consistent, for example, with allowing that in other subject areas where our linguistic intuitions are not vague or fluid as they are here, claims which are in principle unverifiable are nonetheless perfectly meaningful.

35. Perhaps not for people like myself who are more sympathetic to skepticism, however.

36. Strictly speaking, one should say that this is Wittgenstein's conception of understanding *in a central sense of the word.* For, just as he acknowledges that there are other senses of the word "meaning" than the one which he defines in terms of use (PI, #43), so he is aware of a variety of senses of the word "understand" (see BT, pp. 17 ff.).

37. For a philosophically subtle recent defense of a theory of meaning as use in such a minimalist spirit, see P. Horwich, *Meaning* (Oxford: Clarendon Press, 1999).

38. Wittgenstein would probably have been the first to acknowledge that his proposal leaves some important questions open. A good example is the question of how one should *identify*, or *count*, uses in the relevant sense, and hence meanings. He raises this question repeatedly throughout his later works—see, for example, BT, p. 118; BB, p. 58; BrB, pp. 139–40; RFM, I, appendix I, #17–26; VII, #36; LWPP1, #272–307.

He sometimes treats this question as though it were merely a secondary one following in the train of the establishment of the doctrine of meaning as use. But there is also lurking in the background at least some level of awareness of a danger that if no principled way of counting uses can be found which squares with and explains our existing intuitions concerning the counting of meanings, then this calls into doubt the very equation of meaning with use.

His attempts to answer this question sometimes seem too cavalier: beyond a core of clearcut cases in which we can, for example, say with confidence that we are dealing with two uses and hence meanings of a word rather than one, we simply confront a lot of vagueness and choices.

However, in his late work he begins to develop a more intriguing line of response which exploits his general late invocation of the phenomenon of *recognizing aspects* in order to throw light on the way in which language is guided by unformulated, and sometimes indeed unformulable, rules. He hints that the recognition of different uses and hence meanings of a word or words is like the switch of aspects which we experience with visual objects such as the duck-rabbit or the two-dimensional drawing of a Necker cube: "The sudden change of aspect in the picture of a cube and the impossibility of seeing 'lion' and 'class' as comparable concepts" (RFM, VII, #36; cf. PI, p. 214).

39. Occasionally, Wittgenstein indeed himself makes remarks in this spirit. For example, he writes at one point: "Why do I always speak of being compelled by a rule; why not of the fact that I can *choose* to follow it? For that is equally important. But I don't want to say either that the rule compels me to act like this; but that it makes it possible for me to hold by it and let it compel me. And if e.g. you play a game, you keep to its rules. And it is an interesting fact that people set up rules for the fun of it, and then keep to them" (RFM, VII, #66).

40. Note that the preceding objections collectively undermine both the *exclusiveness* and the *firm commitment* aspects of the doctrine of exclusive commitment. To say a little more about *firm commitment*: In arguing that we have to adopt such an attitude towards grammatical principles, Wittgenstein relies heavily on this doctrine, with its implication that such commitment is required for any understanding of grammatical principles or concepts (see, for example, OC, #114-15; RFM, VI, #28; VII, #67). But he sometimes seems, rather, to rest his case on a simpler claim that it is just a brute fact about us that we adopt such an attitude towards grammatical principles: "Whence this certainty? But why do I ask that question? Is it not enough that this certainty exists? Why should I look for a source for it? (And I can indeed give *causes* of it.)" (RFM, VI, #47; cf. VII, #6, #67). So, even if he is indeed wrong that understanding requires such an attitude, he might still say that it is just a brute fact about human beings that when they seriously adopt grammatical principles, they inevitably do so in this firm way. But would even this be right? No doubt people usually do adopt their grammatical principles in such a way. But is it not also possible for them to live with an attitude that includes a measure of tentativeness and openness to revision towards all of their convictions, including their grammatical ones? Think, for instance, of the attitude both recommended and apparently adopted by the Quine of "Two Dogmas of Empiricism." Indeed, Wittgenstein himself occasionally seems to move in this direction, as for example when he says that recalcitrant experience might make us reject even a mathematical axiom such as the parallel postulate (RFM, IV, #4). These points are important, among other reasons, because they promise to take the wind out of the sails of Wittgenstein's "wrong epistemic asymmetry" argument against the possibility of any sort of justification of grammatical principles in terms of empirical facts or success in realizing purposes.

41. For a little discussion and criticism of Wittgenstein's anti-psychologism, see my "Herder's Philosophy of Language, Interpretation, and Translation: Three Fundamental Principles."

NOTE TO THE APPENDIX
THE *PHILOSOPHICAL INVESTIGATIONS*

1. For a good account of this, see Monk, *Ludwig Wittgenstein.*

Index

Affeldt, S., 197n.8
aliens (logical, conceptual), 29, 111, 135, 169–72, 184
analyticity, 11f., 31f., 122, 127f., 199n.14, 200nn.17–18, 228nn.24–25, 229n.10, 236n.29
Anscombe, G.E.M., 16, 201n.25, 214n.8, 234n.16
anthropology, 29f., 130, 150, 182
Apostel, L., 230n.10
arbitrariness. See grammar, as arbitrary
Aristotle, 113, 119f., 221n.1, 227n.23
aspects, seeing/recognizing, 197n.8, 238n.38

Baker, G., 109, 193n.2, 196n.8, 200n.18, 207n.10, 211n.27, 214n.9, 218nn.7–8, 222n.4, 223n.8, 230n.15, 231n.1, 233n.11
Barnes, J., 225nn.14–16
behaviorism, 26, 177–80, 205n.5, 219n.10
bivalence. See excluded middle, law of
Blackburn, S., 221n.20
Bloor, D., 16, 201n.25
Boghossian, P. A., 220n.11
Boltzmann, L., 202n.26
Burge, T., 218n.6
Burnyeat, M., 194n.5

Cantor, G., 76, 215n.11
Carnap, R., 199n.14, 200n.20, 217n.3, 231n.17

Cavell, S., 195n.2, 197n.8
Cerbone, D., 109f., 159, 222nn.4–5, 223nn.7,9, 227n.23, 232n.9. See also "new Wittgenstein"
certainty, 165f., 176f., 179f., 211n.28, 220n.13, 235n.29, 238n.40. See also knowledge; skepticism
chess, 8, 19, 62, 82, 141, 157, 186, 195n.4, 196n.5
Church, A., 221n.19
classical scholarship, 150, 164, 182
Coffa, J. A., 199n.14, 200n.20, 201n.25, 202n.26, 214n.8, 221n.2, 229n.4, 234n.20
color system, 2, 11, 12, 15, 23, 33f., 74, 79, 81, 86, 89, 93, 135, 162, 233n.12
common sense, 19, 53, 194n.5, 206n.6, 218n.10. See also quietism
Conant, J., 109, 202n.26, 222n.4, 223nn.7,9, 224n.10, 227n.23. See also "new Wittgenstein"
concept, 195n.1. See also grammar; meaning
context principle, 233n.12
contradiction, law of, 12, 22, 108–9, 113–14, 118f., 128, 143, 221n.1, 224n.11, 226n.20
conventions. See grammar, as convention
cookery, 40, 47–49, 62, 209n.16
criteria, 11f., 161, 163, 177f., 197n.8, 199n.13, 204n.1, 205n.5, 232n.11, 236n.30. See also psychological propositions

custom. *See* grammar, and enduring social practice; meaning, and
  enduring/social practice

Dancy, R. M., 225n.14
Davidson, D., 1, 162, 193nn.1,5
deduction, as distinguished from
  justification, 43–46. *See also*
  proof; validity
definitions, ostensive, 11–12, 23, 37,
  162
dispositions, 96–102, 220nn.12,16,19,
  221n.19
diversity thesis, 3, 21–30, 58, 65, 107–
  88. *See also* grammar, alternative
Dummett, M., 66, 68, 154, 196n.7,
  201n.21, 212nn.1–2, 232n.2

Engels, F., 118
erklären, 71, 131, 214n.8
Euclid, 63, 89
excluded middle, law of, 113, 116,
  118, 124f., 142, 186, 221n.1
exclusive commitment, doctrine of,
  19, 38, 60, 165–67, 169–87,
  233n.14, 238n.40

family-resemblance, 138f., 143, 161,
  163, 195n.3, 197n.8, 221n.19,
  229nn.5,8, 232n.10, 233n.11
Forbes, G., 220n.15
Forster, M. N., 193n.1, 200n.19,
  239n.41
Frazer, J. G., 30, 130
Frege, G., 83, 200n.18, 202n.26,
  204n.4, 206n.5, 221n.1, 223n.9,
  227n.23, 230n.12, 233n.12

Gadamer, H. G., 187f.
Garver, N., 201n.25, 203nn.29,31,32
Gebrauch, 71–72
Glock, H., 210n.27
Gödel, K., 78
grammar, 1f., chapter 1 passim; as
  action, 211n.28; as antecedent to

truth, 48–58, 65, 194n.5, 210n.27,
  218n.10, 230n.15; as arbitrary, 1f.,
  chapter 2 passim, 66, 88f., 189f.;
  as "channel," 10, 12, 35, 75f.; as
  commands, 8, 49, 51, 55f., 211n.28,
  218n.10, 230n.15; as "concept-
  formation," 10, 14, 21–22; as constitutive of meaning, 7, 196n.5; as
  convention, 9, 33, 39, 49, 196n.7,
  211n.28; as generic, 9, 18; as implicit, 9, 196n.8; as indescribable,
  160–63, 168, 197n.8; as meaningful, 57, 150, 207n.13, 209n.15,
  213n.7, 235n.28; as non-arbitrary,
  2, 14, chapter 3 passim, 82–88,
  94–103, 189f.; as non-cognitive,
  163, 197n.8, 211n.28; as primary
  vs. secondary, 18f.; as regulating
  empirical propositions, 8f., 17,
  35f., 75f., 84f., 150f.; as rules, 7f.,
  49, 55f., 195n.2, 197n.8, 211n.28; as
  surface vs. depth, 50, 202n.27; as
  Wittgensteinian vs. ordinary, 7,
  17f., 202n.27, 203nn.28–29; and
  application, 69f., 74f., 84f.,
  216n.12; and choice, 66f., 148f.,
  212nn.1–2; and commitment, 19,
  31, 38, 60, 165f., 169–87, 233n.14,
  238n.40; and enduring social
  practice, 67–69, 72–74, 94–103,
  163f., 214n.9; and human nature,
  14–15, 67f., 73, 122, 126f., 199n.14,
  213n.3; and usefulness (employment, application), 69–81, 83–94,
  149–52
grammar, alternative, 21f., 81, 143,
  203n.1, 216n.11; and access (intelligibility), 60, chapter 7 passim;
  and conceivability, 21, 153; imaginary vs. actual, 28–30, 207n.10.
  See also diversity thesis
grammar, justification of, 30–46, 65,
  79–81, 88–94, 148f., 209n.16,
  213n.2, 217nn.4–5, 238n.40; by appeal to truth-in-virtue-of-

meaning, 31–32; by appeal to facts, 33–39, 80, 88–92, 207n.14, 208n.15, 217n.5, 238n.40; by appeal to its success, 39–43, 80, 88–94, 238n.40; by appeal to more fundamental principles, 43–46

Grice, G. P., 213n.8

Hacker, P.M.S., 109, 193n.2, 194n.5, 196n.8, 200n.18, 202n.26, 203n.31, 207n.10, 211n.27, 214n.9, 218nn.7–8, 221n.2, 222n.4, 223n.8, 230n.15, 231n.1, 233n.11, 234n.20, 235nn.27–28, 236n.30

Harris, R., 203nn.31–32

Henrich, D., 194n.5

Heraclitus, 118

Herder, J. G., 14, 200n.19

Hertz, H., 202n.26

Hilbert, D., 214n.8

holism, linguistic, 41, 161f., 197n.8, 233nn.12–13

Horwich, P., 209n.19, 237n.37

idealism, 13, 15f., 194n.5, 199nn.14,17, 201nn.23,26, 206n.6. See also mind-imposition

incommensurability, 1, 36, 45, 62, 80, 91f., 203n.1, 207n.14, 217n.4, 226n.20

inconsistency in concepts, 138f.

indeterminacy in concepts, 138f.

intuitionism, 186

Irwin, T., 225n.14

Kant, I., 12–17, 67, 113, 121f., 126f., 194n.5, 199nn.14–17, 200n.18, 201nn.21,23–24, 202n.26, 214n.8, 223n.9, 225nn.17–18, 227n.23, 228nn.24–25

Kierkegaard, S., 234n.14

knowledge, 97f., 166, 168–82, 185, 203n.30, 211n.28, 220nn.13,19, 235n.29. See also certainty; skepticism

Kripke, S. A., 95f., 99–102, 139, 214n.9, 218n.7, 220nn.11,14,17,19, 230n.11

language, concept of, 28f., 108f., 113–25, chapter 6 passim, 182–83, 190. See also grammar; meaning; propositionality

language-games, 8f., 195n.3, 212n.32; primitive forms of, 25, 160; "true-false" forms of, 9f., 18, 21–22, 47, 58f., 74–75, 81, 107, 198n.10, 201n.26

Lear, J., 24–28, 107, 134, 137, 159, 167, 183, 189f., 193n.4, 202n.26, 207n.9, 215n.9, 216n.11, 225n.14

linguistic intuitions. See ordinary language

"linguistic turn," 14, 200n.19

logic, 10–11, 22, 31, 43, 48, 55–58, 68, 75–76, 78, 87, chapter 5 passim, 189f., 199nn.11,16, 200n.18, 202n.26, 209nn.20–21, 210n.25, 217n.5, 221–28, 236n.29; as constitutive of (internal to) thought, 13, 108f., 113f., 117f., 121, 123f., 223n.9, 227n.23

Lukasiewicz, J., 225n.14

MacIntyre, A., 215n.9

Malcolm, N., 23, 26, 118, 206n.7, 214n.9

mathematics, 7, 9, 11–12, 15f., 19, 22, 33–36, 42f., 50, 55–57, 67, 73–79, 89–90, 110f., 114, 190f., 200n.18, 201nn.21–22, 207n.14, 210n.25, 211n.28, 215n.11, 229n.7, 235n.28, 236n.29, 237n.33

Mays, W., 230n.10

McDowell, J. H., 218n.7, 220n.11, 233n.11

McGinn, C., 215n.9

meaning, 7f., 71f., 82f., 138, 185; and achievement of purposes, 72f., 81, 83f.; and enduring practice,

meaning (*cont.*)
72, 94f., 215n.9, 217n.6, 218nn.7–8;
and normativity, 99f.; and rules,
7f., 31f., 34f., 47, 71f., 195n.2,
197n.8; as sense vs. reference, 83,
87–88; and social practice, 72f.,
94–103, 164, 214n.9, 217n.6,
218n.7, 229n.9, 230n.15; and use,
70–73, 82f., 124, 145, 185, 194n.5,
213n.8, 214n.9, 237nn.37–38; and
usefulness (employment, application), 69f., 81, 83f.
mental states. *See* psychological
propositions
mind-imposition, 13f., 126, 128,
199n.14, 201n.24. *See also* idealism
Monk, R., 202nn.26–27, 234nn.20,23,
239n.1
Moore, G. E., 11, 58, 165, 202n.27,
203n.31
Morf, A., 230n.10
morphology, 18, 203n.29
Mulhall, S., 197n.8

Naess, A., 230n.10
Nagel, T., 204n.1
naturalism (empirical vs. noumenal), 14f., 24, 26f., 67f.
necessity, 10f., 49f., 67f., 121f., 126f.,
198–201, 213n.4, 225n.18, 228n.25
negation ("not"), 22, 31f., 47, 108f.,
112f., 128, 156f., 160, 209n.15,
222n.3, 225n.19, 227n.21. *See also*
logic; truth-functions
Newton, I., 102
"new Wittgenstein," 194n.5. *See also*
D. Cerbone; J. Conant
normativity, 68, 99f., 103, 203n.32,
225n.18

ordinary language, 17, 57, 82f., 87,
92, 95–96, 103, 123, 139, 141f.,
203n.30, 217n.3, 218n.10, 229n.10,
230nn.11–13, 231nn.15–16, 237n.38;
revision of, 144f. (*see also* quietism)

Paul, D., 234n.16
Piaget, J., 230n.10
Plato, 118f., 220n.10, 232n.10
Platonism, 25, 71, 154, 158, 167,
204n.4, 206n.5, 232n.10
pluralism, 1f., 14, 193n.4, 202n.26,
204n.1. *See also* diversity thesis
pre-understanding, 187–88
principles, analytic. *See* analyticity
principles, grammatical. *See*
grammar
proof, of necessary principles, 43–
46, 210n.23. *See also* grammar,
justification of
propositionality, 55, 71, 108f., 124,
129f., 145, 189f., 224n.11,
225n.17
propositions, apparently-empirical,
11–12, 23, 63, 68, 76, 79, 165–66,
196n.8, 199n.12, 232n.5
propositions, empirical/factual, 10,
12, 16–17, 35f., 58, 66, 69, 74–75,
77, 89, 208n.14
"propositions," grammatical, 55.
See also grammar
psychological propositions, 1, 12,
16, 98, 161, 163, 174–81, 197n.8,
199n.13, 205n.5, 232n.11,
235nn.26,29, 236n.32. *See also* behaviorism; criteria
psychologism, 122, 188, 206n.5,
224n.9, 239n.41
purposes (ends), of grammar/
language, 39–42, 62, 80–81, 91f.,
148f., 195n.3, 209n.16
Putnam, H., 118f., 139, 202n.26,
222n.7, 223n.9, 225n.13, 227n.23,
230n.11
Pythagoras, 220n.10

quietism, 17, 19, 57, 82, 86f., 141–
44, 146, 148, 194n.5, 209n.22,
218n.10, 231n.16
Quine, W. V., 222n.3, 226n.20,
238n.40

Regelmäßigkeit, 131, 228n.1
regularity, 79, 131f., 135, 208n.14,
 228nn.1,3, 229n.3
Reichenbach, H., 202n.26
relativism, 2, 61–64, 193n.4
religion. *See* theology
revisionism in mathematics, 76f.,
 215n.11
Rhees, R., 216n.11
Rosen, G., 212n.29
rule-following, 1, 68, 72, 94–103,
 135f., 138, 197n.8, 206n.5, 214n.9,
 218n.6, 228n.1, 229n.8, 230n.15,
 233n.14
rules, 7f., 19, 55f., 72, 94f., 178f.,
 195n.2, 197n.8, 214n.9, 228n.1,
 238n.39. *See also* grammar, as
 rules; meaning, and rules
Russell, B., 22, 62–63, 114, 204n.4,
 221n.1, 230n.12

Schlick, M., 202n.26
Schopenhauer, A., 202n.26
skepticism, 165f., 171, 184, 199n.12,
 235n.29, 236n.31, 237n.35. *See also*
 certainty; knowledge
Skinner, Q., 193n.5
Sluga, H., 223n.9
Socrates, 220n.10, 232n.10
solipsism, 24, 206n.6
Stern, D. G., 195n.2
Strachey, L., 172f., 178f., 234n.19
Stroud, B., 25, 154–58, 163, 167,
 204n.4, 218n.7, 232nn.3,4,6,7,
 234nn.15,17
synthetic a priori, 12f., 122, 124,
 200nn.17–18, 202n.26

theology, 84f., 91f., 167, 212n.31,
 217n.1, 232n.5
therapy, philosophy as, 194n.5,
 203n.30, 231n.16
truth: correspondence theory of,
 57, 210n.26; of empirical propositions, 9, 58f.; of grammatical

principles, 47–58, 65, 210nn.26–
 27; as internal to language-
 games, 61f., 212n.32; and necessity, 53; redundancy theory of,
 50f., 56–57, 60f., 63f.; and validity, 53–55
truth-functions, 108f., 122f., 222n.3,
 224n.11, 226n.20, 227n.21,
 228n.25. *See also* logic; negation
truth-in-virtue-of-meaning, 12–13,
 31f., 49, 122, 128, 190, 228nn.24–
 25. *See also* analyticity

understanding, 96–102, 184–86,
 220n.19, 233n.14, 237n.36, 238n.40.
 See also meaning
usefulness/utility of grammar/
 language, 39–43, 69–81, 83–94,
 124, 148–52, 217n.2, 231n.18. *See
 also* grammar, and usefulness;
 meaning, and achievement of
 purposes, etc.

vagueness/fluidity of concepts,
 28f., 58, 123, 141, 144, 137–48, 182,
 194n.5, 215n.9, 229nn.5–10,
 230n.14, 231n.17
validity, logical, 53–55
verificationism, 173–81, 234–37
Voltaire, F.-M., 85

Whitehead, A. N., 221n.1
Williams, B., 24–28, 107, 134, 137,
 159, 167, 183, 189f., 193n.4, 207n.9,
 216n.11, 232n.8
willkürlich, 66
Winch, P., 212nn.31–32
Wittgenstein, L. (works): *Blue Book*
 (BB), 11, 71–72, 82, 141–43, 147,
 175, 187, 206n.6, 229n.5, 231n.16,
 235n.27; *Brown Book* (BrB), 25,
 138, 160, 237n.38; *Big Typescript*
 (BT), 1, 7, 32, 40–42, 47–48, 59,
 62, 68, 70–72, 81, 83, 162, 195n.3,
 201n.23, 214n.8, 215n.11, 229n.5,

Wittgenstein, L. (works) (cont.)
232n.10, 233n.12, 234n.24,
237nn.36,38; Culture and Value
(CV), 28; Wittgenstein's Lectures:
Cambridge 1930–1932 (LC), 20, 30,
33, 55, 66, 196nn.4,6,8, 202n.27,
207n.13, 208n.15, 209n.16, 213n.7,
234n.24; Lectures and Conversations on Aesthetics, Psychology,
and Religious Belief (LCAPRB),
167, 232n.5; Wittgenstein's Lectures
on the Foundations of Mathematics, Cambridge 1939 (LFM), 19,
42, 51, 56–57, 85–86, 89, 92–93,
110–11, 116–17, 124, 207n.11,
210n.26, 216n.11, 221n.3,
224nn.9,11, 226n.19, 227n.21;
"The Language of Sense Data
and Private Experience" (LSD),
171, 178, 219n.10; Last Writings on
the Philosophy of Psychology
(LWPP1/2), 28, 72, 144, 157, 161–
63; Notebooks 1914–1916 (N), 58,
209n.20; "Notes for Lectures on
'Private Experience' and 'Sense
Data'" (NFL), 178; "Notes for
the 'Philosophical Lecture'"
(NPL), 185; On Certainty (OC), 1,
10–11, 21–24, 31, 35, 37–39, 43, 48,
63, 67–68, 71–72, 76, 79–80, 138,
158, 160, 163, 165–66, 184, 191,
196n.8, 199n.12, 203n.32, 211n.28,
217n.1, 232n.5, 236n.29, 238n.40;
"Philosophy" (P), 203n.28; Philosophical Grammar (PG), 1–2, 7–
11, 18–19, 21, 23, 31, 33, 35, 37, 40,
47–48, 59, 62, 67, 70, 72, 82, 116,
129–30, 132, 134, 137–38, 141, 144–
49, 185–86, 191, 195n.7, 210n.25,
215n.9, 229n.6, 231n.16, 235n.28;
Philosophical Investigations (PI), 1,
9–11, 18–19, 21–22, 25, 28, 32, 34,
37, 40–41, 47, 50–51, 55, 59, 66–
69, 71–74, 81–85, 87–88, 97–98,
109, 112, 114–15, 123–24, 131–33,

135–36, 141–42, 148, 158, 161, 164,
166, 174–75, 177–79, 189–91,
193n.3, 195nn.7,3, 198nn.8–9,
199n.12, 200n.18, 202n.27,
203nn.30,32, 205n.5, 206n.6,
210n.25, 212n.28, 213n.8, 215n.9,
216n.11, 219n.10, 222n.3, 227n.22,
228n.3, 229n.6, 235n.28, 237n.36;
Philosophical Remarks (PR), 33,
175–76, 234n.24, 235n.28; Remarks
on Color (RC), 157, 173; "Remarks on Frazer's Golden Bough"
(RFGB), 30, 130; Remarks on the
Foundations of Mathematics
(RFM), 1, 7–8, 10–11, 16, 21–22,
32, 34–35, 39, 42, 44–46, 48, 50,
52, 55–57, 62–64, 66–68, 72–79,
86, 89, 94, 108–12, 114–17, 126–
27, 135–36, 138–39, 143, 157–59,
165, 178, 191, 195n.1, 196n.7,
200n.18, 201n.22, 206n.5, 207n.14,
210nn.22–23,25–26, 211n.28,
215n.9, 216n.12, 217n.2, 219n.10,
220n.18, 224n.11, 227n.21,
228nn.1–2, 229n.7, 238nn.38–40;
Remarks on the Philosophy of Psychology (RPP1/2), 22, 26–27, 50,
72–73, 116, 177, 198n.8; "Some
Remarks on Logical Form"
(SRLF), 233n.12; Tractatus Logico-
Philosophicus (T), 24, 44, 57, 108,
124, 194n.5, 197n.8, 200n.18,
204n.3, 209nn.15,21, 213n.7,
230n.12, 233n.12; "Wittgenstein's
Lectures in 1930–1933" (WL),
19–20, 66, 162, 165, 201n.23,
203n.31, 214n.8, 234n.24; Wittgenstein's Lectures: Cambridge 1932–
1935 (WLC), 11, 19, 23, 31, 48–49,
55–57, 68, 83, 123, 128, 138, 145,
196nn.5,7, 214n.8, 228n.25,
235n.28, 237n.33; Wittgenstein's
Lectures on Philosophical Psychology 1946–1947 (WLPP), 16, 23,
40, 118, 161, 163, 168, 172, 174,

179–80, 213n.3, 233n.13; *Wittgenstein und der Wiener Kreis*
(WWK), 207n.13, 233n.12,
234nn.21–22,24, 235n.28, 236n.30;
Zettel (Z.), 1–2, 11, 15,

21–23, 34, 39–40, 42, 47, 59, 62,
66, 80–81, 134–35, 137–38, 145,
147, 161, 213n.8, 230n.14, 234n.18
wood-sellers, 22, 110f., 155f., 159
Wright, C., 210n.27, 220n.11